JIHAD

T0096608

About the Author

Andrew Hyde co-wrote the three-volume work *The Blitz: Then and Now* and is the author of *First Blitz*. He contributed to the BBC *Timewatch* programme of the same name and to a recent Channel 5 TV documentary on the Windsors.

JIHAD

THE OTTOMANS
AND THE ALLIES
1914–1922

ANDREW P. HYDE

AMBERLEY

For Tayjah, Clöe and Deandre

First published 2017
This edition published 2021

Amberley Publishing
The Hill, Stroud
Gloucestershire, GL5 4EP

www.amberley-books.com

Copyright © Andrew P. Hyde, 2017, 2021

The right of Andrew P. Hyde to be identified
as the Author of this work has been asserted in
accordance with the Copyrights, Designs and
Patents Act 1988.

ISBN 978 1 3981 0332 0 (paperback)
ISBN 978 1 4456 6616 7 (ebook)

All rights reserved. No part of this book may
be reprinted or reproduced or utilised in any
form or by any electronic, mechanical or other
means, now known or hereafter invented,
including photocopying and recording, or in any
information storage or retrieval system, without
the permission in writing from the Publishers.

British Library Cataloguing in Publication Data.
A catalogue record for this book is available
from the British Library.

Typesetting and Origination by Amberley
Publishing.
Printed in the UK.

CONTENTS

Acknowledgements   vii

Introduction   1

1 The rest of Europe do me as much harm as they can   5
2 I am not ordering you to attack; I am ordering you to die   19
3 In the event of a total or partial partition of Turkey   46
4 Let us march, friends!   66
5 The Greeks were nice chaps too   90
6 You will get no cooperation from us   124
7 All talk was of war   145
8 In a good cause, we are prepared to venture our all   171
9 Stop this new war   186
10 None of us can pretend that the treaty is a
   glorious instrument   200
11 We cannot alone act as policeman of the world   220

Notes   234
Appendices   249
Bibliography and Sources   268
Index   274

ACKNOWLEDGEMENTS

The story of *Jihad* has required much research and preparation. Consequently, I would like to take this opportunity to acknowledge those individuals and sources that have been particularly instrumental in assisting me in finishing this project. As well as consulting published works and original documents I have been fortunate in unearthing several gems from sources which can only be said to have appeared solely as the result of providence and serendipity.

A prime example of this is George Horton's *The Blight of Asia*, which provides an incomparable study of the doomed city port of Smyrna/Izmir both before and after its destruction. Horton's first-class account is, if not impartial, extremely lucid and brings home the true human tragedy of the Greco-Turkish War. I should also like to take this opportunity to thank Sotirios Georgiadis, Rear Admiral of the Hellenic Navy (retd), who kindly granted me permission to quote extensively from this work.

In addition, I have been privileged in having been granted access to such valuable sources of primary material as the National Archives of Australia. These records provide a first-hand account of the angry exchange between the Australian Prime Minister of the time, William Hughes, and the British Government when the conflict in Turkey threatened to drag Britain's unwilling imperial partners into the fighting. I am therefore immensely grateful to Helen Wade, Senior Reference Librarian, Information Services Section of the National

Library of Australia, as well as Beth Rogers of the National Archives of Australia, for their assistance and guidance.

At the other end of the world is the Imperial War Museum. Here, at the Department of Printed Documents, I found several eyewitness accounts in the form of simple diaries or unpublished autobiographies written by servicemen stationed in Turkey at the time of the crisis. In particular, their heartrending accounts of the Smyrna/Izmir massacre and subsequent fire make for harrowing reading. Unfortunately, the museum has lost contact with the copyright holders of the Private Papers of C. Petherick, OBE, MC, Major General C. N. Wood, CB, CBE, DSO, MC, MA, and T. W. Bunter. Every effort has been made to locate the copyright holders but unfortunately we have been unsuccessful. Efforts have also been made to request permission from the copyright holders of the Private Papers of Lieutenant M. M. Carus Wilson, but these efforts have also been to no avail. Nevertheless, I should like to record my sincere thanks to the Trustees of the Imperial War Museum for allowing access to the collections.

The Guildhall Library in the City of London also provided a wealth of information. It contains the Official Reports of the House of Commons Debates of the period, and these helped to explain the political storm that accompanied Lloyd George's stubborn and insistent support of the Greeks. It also contains essential but difficult-to-source printed books covering the period, such as *The Chanak Affair* by David Walder, which have provided priceless additional material in the form of contemporary critiques of British Government policy, as well as giving another dimension to many of the characters involved in the period. To this end I am especially thankful to King's College London Archives and Corporate Records Services for granting me access to General Charles 'Tim' Harington's autobiography, *Harington Looks Back*, which provides further intriguing insights into the period of the crisis from the point of view of a man on the spot.

The priceless knowledge resident in the National Archives at Kew needs no explanation. Here can be found the original documents that provide the researcher with copious data, and the essential primary sources that are vital to balanced historical analysis, such as Cabinet Papers and official cables, minutes and notes from some of the key participants in the unfolding tragedy that befell the players in this fascinating drama.

The British Library Newspaper Library in Colindale, a vast repository of newspapers from around the world, furnished me with microfilm copies of *The Times* and *Daily Mail* from the period, adding more colour and context to the dramatic events of 1922 and 1923 in particular, especially the latter's vitriolic condemnation of Lloyd George and his stand against Mustapha Kemal.

Files and papers are only good insofar as they can be identified, catalogued and made available to the reader, so I am equally indebted to Dorian Hayes of the Canada House Library, who not only made available to me every relevant book held by the library on Mackenzie King, the Canadian Government and their exchanges with the British Government, but also allowed me unlimited access to those records.

I am pleased, too, to record my thanks to the *Daily Mail* newspaper, for permitting me to quote from its issues of the time, and to the Random House Group, publishers of Ernest Hemingway's *The Snows of Kilimanjaro*, for allowing me to quote extracts from his work.

On one point of style, the reader will see that I switch from using the name Smyrna to Izmir, and swap the two frequently. This is due to the fact that I use the name employed by the Greeks when writing about the city in connection with the Greeks, and I use the Turkish name when referring to the city relative to the Turks. I do this because neither the Greeks nor Turks would countenance using the other's name for the city, much in the way that the Argentines insist upon calling the Falkland Islands the Malvinas.

Whilst researching and writing this work I have had several sparks of inspiration which came purely as the consequence of comments passed here and there, or by noting down snippets of information, the origins of which I failed at the time to record properly. I hope that in doing so I have not offended anyone who recognises their work as a point's genesis, and that they will be content if I take this opportunity to thank them for their contribution.

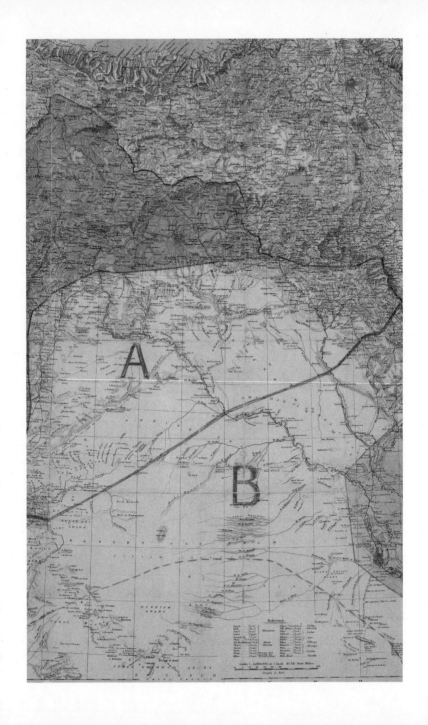

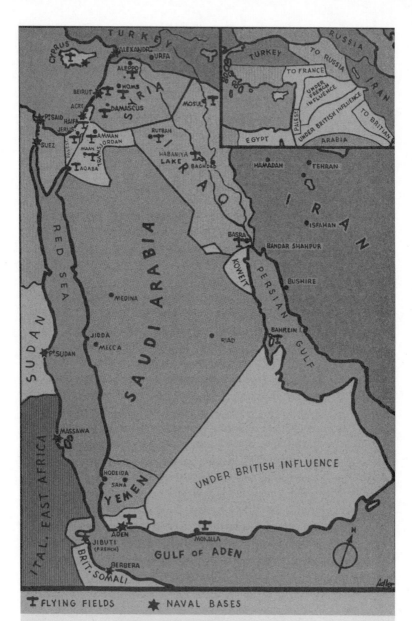

1919: How England Kept Her Word
The Sykes-Picot Plan (Top, right)

Map verso

When ISIS posted pictures of a bulldozer crashing through the earth barrier that forms part of the frontier between Syria and Iraq in May 2016, they announced they were destroying the Sykes–Picot border. 'Allah facilitated that it [ISIS] step over the Sykes–Picot borders in its jihad.' The secret Sykes–Picot agreement designated each power's areas of future control in the event of victory by the Triple Entente. Britain (A) has the coastal strip between the Mediterranean and the river Jordan, southern Iraq and Transjordan and the ports of Haifa and Acre. France (B) was given south-eastern Turkey, northern Iraq, all of Syria and Lebanon. Russia would get the Dardanelles, Constantinople and the Armenian districts then held by the Ottoman Empire. 'By Allah's permission, the coming days will witness more events that result in removing borders of Sykes–Picot and its like, that the world might be re-divided, but based on creed, The Islamic State and the World after Sykes–Picot and not race, nation or tribe. At that time, each person will choose for himself what he seeks, whether the camp of faith, wherein there is no hypocrisy, or the camp of disbelief, wherein there is no faith.' (ISIS)

Map recto

Much the same outrage over Sykes–Picot was expressed in *The War in Maps 1939/40*, published in New York in 1941 by The German Library of Information. Under the heading 'Arabs duped by England', the authors explain, 'The map shows the grotesque contrast between the original promise [the McMahon letters] and its later "fulfilment."' (Courtesy Perry-Castaneda Library Map Collection, University of Texas)

INTRODUCTION

In 2003, Britain was completely absorbed by events in the Middle East when the United States went to war against Iraq. She had as her staunchest ally the British Prime Minister Tony Blair, who stood by US President George Bush in spite of vehement opposition from the British public and much of the media, as well as a hostile international community. Blair also found himself alienating whole sections of the Muslim community in Britain and across the world, in addition to compromising friendly relations with countries once counted upon as friends and allies. Even his own Cabinet was far from united behind his decision to go into what would inevitably be labelled 'Blair's War'. He was at turns condemned as reckless, foolhardy and unprincipled, or castigated for slavishly following on the coat tails of the world's only superpower, itself led by an egotist with an agenda of his own.

As I continued to watch the nightly bulletins, read the detailed newspaper accounts and listen to the pundits, it all began to sound alarmingly familiar. The rhetoric, the condemnation, the charge and counter-charge and the odium all had strange parallels in a crisis that took place a little over eighty years before.

At the end of the First World War, the then Prime Minister of the United Kingdom, David Lloyd George, had tendered his support to the Greek Prime Minister, Eleutherios Venizelos, who was embarking upon a bitter war against Turkey, a Muslim country that was at that time at the very heart of the Islamic faith, and which had found its origins in that global conflagration which had only recently ended. Lloyd George was to face increasingly severe opposition from Parliament and from many of Britain's Indian Muslims, as well as across the wider Islamic world. Furthermore, his actions served to sow divisions with two of the United Kingdom's closest friends and partners, Canada and Australia, and to accelerate increasing estrangement with others.

Whilst the events of 2003 are of course still fresh in our minds, those of 1919–22 are remote to many. However, they show that history can – and does – repeat itself.

The jihad we will discuss actually began in 1914, when the Ottoman Empire threw in her lot with the Central Powers against Britain, France and Russia. It did not end in 1918, however, when Turkey officially surrendered. A peace settlement had been imposed at Sevres, dictated by the Entente Powers and meekly accepted by the de jure Ottoman government of the Sultan in Turkey. Turkey's defeat had coincided with the expansionist dreams of her neighbour and long-time adversary Greece, and she was determined to impose Sevres at all costs and realise her own revisionist aspirations. However, an almost unknown Turkish general decided to act in defiance of the imposed peace: Mustapha Kemal, who like his modern-day counterparts in the region, such as Saddam Hussein in Iraq and more latterly President Assad of Syria, was seen as an evil influence who had to be removed in the interests of international peace and stability. Subsequently, the Turkish general found himself vilified, condemned as a threat to the peace of the region and consequently the subject of attempted regime change. In 2003, President George Bush, like Venizelos before him, saw himself as the standard bearer of freedom and justice, entrusted by fate to lead a liberating *crusade* against his tyrannical nemesis. Mustapha had to be overthrown in order that the Treaty of Sevres could be successfully imposed upon the Turkish people, whilst in 2003 the United States saw her national interests served by removing the regime sitting in Baghdad and imposing a new order based upon dubious principles of democracy and justice.

In attempting to overthrow the Nationalist Turkish government, Britain and Greece were seeking to refashion the region to accommodate their own strategic and geopolitical national interests. Instead, Lloyd George fell from power as a result of his support for the Greeks and debate raged over the rights and wrongs of his actions and those of his Greek ally, whose Turkish adventure was to have tragic consequences. Indeed, the fate of innocent civilians and national minorities has been a key feature of both conflicts. Whether it is the tragic multitudes killed across Armenia in 1915/16, in Smyrna/Izmir in 1922, or the Iraqi families slaughtered in Baghdad and Basra from 2003 until the present day, Greek, Turkish, American, British and Iraqi combatants cannot help but find the unwary and undeserving crossing their sights. In the heat and fury of battle no soldier can be expected to tell Greek peasant from Greek soldier, Turkish brigand from Turkish farmer, or Iraqi fedayeen from a hijab-clad Muslim mother. Tragically, when Christian Armenian, Coptic Greek or Turkish civilians fell victim to deliberate murder during this first jihad, they served simply as a precursor to the internecine slaughter now witnessed in Iraq, Afghanistan, Syria and elsewhere in the Middle East today.

In considering these two conflicts, it is easy to see nothing but similarities. However, there were differences. Whilst Saddam Hussein's military machine effectively dissolved in the face of overwhelming Coalition firepower, the Nationalist Turks under Mustapha resisted, then countered and finally ejected the invader from their soil.

Anarchy followed the Coalition occupation in Iraq, whilst in Turkey a united country swiftly established a stable and orderly secular state. In 2003 the Coalition succeeded in their overriding aim of ousting the dictatorship of Saddam Hussein, whereas Mustapha not only retained but increased his hold on power, serving as a positive role model to fellow Muslims around the world and proving that Western economic and strategic interests could be challenged if sufficient courage, determination and fortitude were displayed.

Finally, one other very fundamental difference between the two dramas stands out. In the Turkish denouement almost a century ago the British were very much the senior partner, although the Greeks provided most of the manpower and did all the fighting. In 2003 the reverse was very much the case. President Bush called the shots, and Tony Blair played only a supporting role, although the courage and professionalism of all arms of the British armed forces made a huge contribution towards overthrowing the Iraqi regime.

That set of coincidences aside, this is not intended to be a book about Blair's war or indeed the current tragedy unfolding across the Middle East today. The references to the modern jihad being waged against the West serve simply as a convenient but nonetheless highly relevant link. The parallel demonstrates that the maxim 'that those who forget the past are condemned to repeat it' remains as cogent as ever. It proves that when politicians and the vested interests they represent embark upon ill-conceived adventures they invariably drag those who follow them into the disastrous consequences. This is so whether it is Lloyd George in Turkey in 1922, Anthony Eden at Suez in 1956 or Tony Blair in the Iraq of today.

I

THE REST OF EUROPE
DO ME AS MUCH HARM
AS THEY CAN

The sprawling Ottoman Empire was at its nadir by November 1914, when she declared a jihad – holy war – against the Allied Powers and threw in her lot with Germany, a disastrous decision that set in motion a series of cataclysmic events that culminated in the demise of an ancient regime and the emergence of a modern, secular republic. The first jihad in the Arab world since the Crusades was to continue long after the official armistice of 1918, however, as a prostrate and defeated empire faced a resurgent Greece – supported only by Britain – that sought to re-establish hegemony over Anatolia in a holy war that caused outrage throughout the Muslim world and threatened British paramountcy in India, damaging diplomatic relations with close allies and the political unity of her empire. Confronted with the indefatigable resistance of one man, Kemal Ataturk, Greek dreams ended in ashes, whilst British Prime Minister David Lloyd George's stubborn support of Greece resulted in his own political extinction. It is a warning from history, unheeded today, with tales of ethnic cleansing, pogroms, regime change, political hubris and national survival. It is the story of steely determination against expediency, and of dogged bravery in the face of brazen territorial expansionism. It is littered with many parallels to the dangers facing the Middle East of today, but with one distinct difference: this first jihad heralded relative peace and stability, whilst the present jihad shows no sign of abating but instead of spreading and escalating into an unending conflict between East and West. This, then, is a history of that jihad.

The story begins over 1,000 years before, with a tribe of Seljuk Turks serving the Ghaznavid Persians as a dissolute band of hired hitmen. Before very long these men chose to branch out on their own, turning against their erstwhile masters in 1038 and extending their sphere of operations until by around 1071 they had almost reached the court of the Byzantines in Baghdad. In an effort to put an end to this terrifying phenomenon, Byzantine emperor Romanus IV led 40,000 men into battle against 70,000 Turks at Manzikert, and at the end of a day of no-holds-barred hand-to-hand fighting the Byzantines were swept from the field. Soon the Seljuks had captured Antioch, Damascus and Jerusalem, and Romanus' successor Alexius I was panicked into appealing to the Pope for help. This plea led to the Crusades, and heralded the coming of Osman, the man credited with founding the great dynasty that followed.

He was succeeded by Orhan, who consolidated his power, irresistibly leading his army northwards to carve out the European portion of his empire. His earliest gain was made in 1354, when he crossed the Dardanelles Strait, capturing Gallipoli, just 45 miles across the water from a town which would one day become a place of international notoriety: Canakkale, or Chanak. Orhan's successor, Murad I, moved northwards through Thrace until his army reached Adrianople in around 1365, which he captured and made his capital the following year. The victorious Ottomans were now well placed to dominate the trade route through the straits and the vital maritime corridor linking the Black Sea and the warm waters of the Mediterranean. There was still much work to be done, but henceforth it was evident that this natural barrier between Europe and Asia had assumed a key strategic role. It would continue to be a magnet for ambitious and powerful men for the next 500 years.

The Turks' progress was so breathtaking that within a few years they were on the threshold of the Balkans. A confrontation was inevitable, and in September 1371 Serbia met the Ottomans in battle on the Maritsa River in Thrace, where Murad's' will prevailed. He capitalised on his decisive victory to lead his army on a long and arduous march through the very heart of modern Bulgaria, capturing Sofia in 1385. Christian Europe, meanwhile, was once again growing fearful of the Muslims, prompting the Pontiff, Pope Boniface IX, to issue a Papal Edict for the expulsion of the invaders. A force of 50,000 marched against the encroaching Turks, meeting them in September 1393 at Nicopolis in northern Bulgaria, but again they emerged victorious.

A new Sultan, Murad II, sought the same laurels as his predecessors. He captured Salonika (Thessalonica) in March 1430, and in doing so rekindled Christian fears. A truce was negotiated, but the nervous Europeans tried to stage a disastrous pre-emptive strike that resulted in humiliation at Varna on Bulgaria's Black Sea coast in 1444.

Tensions in Serbia were rising as well, and in October 1448 a 24,000-strong army of Hungarians clashed with Murad at Kosovo. Predictably the Turks left the field as victors once more, the Christians as humiliated vassals. A new Sultan, Mehmet II (the Conqueror), now eyed the ancient city of Constantinople, which lay astride the Bosphorus and commanded the entrance to the Black Sea. It had preoccupied the Ottomans for generations, so in an all-out effort to claim this elusive prize he laid siege to the city in May 1453. Its capture was followed by a three-day orgy of pillage, rapine and massacre but established the Ottoman Turks as the guardians of this crucial transit point. With both Constantinople and Gallipoli in their hands, they were almost unassailable.

In 1470 the Venetian colony of Negroponte came under Mehmet's avaricious gaze, and he set about constructing a large fleet designed to capture the prosperous maritime city. If he could control this prize he could dominate all the region's trade, turning the Eastern Mediterranean into an Ottoman lake.

A period of relative calm followed for the Christian Europeans, with the Ottomans choosing to consolidate their hold on their existing conquests and to suppress resistance within their borders. Even then movement eastwards was hard to resist and in 1514 the new Sultan, Selim I, looked towards Persia, seizing large tracts of her empire up to and including Azerbaijan on the Caspian Sea, and Kurdistan. When two years later Egypt went to Persia's aid, the Turks soundly punished her at Mari-Dabik, near Aleppo in Syria. Syria and Damascus fell under Selim's control and he then crossed the Nile into Egypt itself. In 1517 the Turks captured Cairo. Turning again to the Balkans, Belgrade was the objective and in 1521 it finally fell. A year later the Christian outpost of Rhodes went the same way.

The capture of Belgrade in particular was a terrible blow, as it left Christian Europe seriously exposed to further Turkish aggression. In 1526, Suleiman I marched an army of some 100,000 men into modern-day Hungary, where he met and destroyed an army of 20,000, marching on to and capturing Budapest.

In 1529 Vienna, almost at the very heart of European Christendom, came in for Suleiman's attention, but the Christians, no doubt aware of the consequences of defeat, resisted valiantly for three weeks. They repulsed one furious assault after another until the Turkish army, having exhausted itself against the city walls, admitted failure and withdrew. This would prove to be the high-water mark of the Ottoman Empire in western Europe, and 150 years would pass before the Turks got another opportunity to extend their frontiers in this direction.

Despite this setback the Ottoman Empire was still a regional superpower, and whilst Suleiman had been busy in Europe, trouble flared again in the East. The challenge was stamped out, adding Mesopotamia to the empire in 1534.

Suleiman now turned his attentions to maritime expansion, employing the services of the mercenary Barbary pirate Hayreddin Barbarossa to extend his empire along the Mediterranean littoral. Tunis fell in 1534, and in response to this new threat, the Holy Roman Emperor Charles V despatched a formidable Christian fleet of 600 vessels, which dealt Suleiman a rare blow, and severely if only temporarily curtailed Turkish maritime aspirations in the region.

This reverse did little to thwart the Turk's ambitions, and maritime competition continued until, in 1538, the interests of the Holy Roman Empire and Venice combined against the Turkish menace. The protagonists clashed at Preveza on the Ionian coast of Greece, where the Turkish, Holy Roman and Venetian fleets engaged in a bloody duel from which the Turks finally emerged victorious. Fired by this spectacular success, the Turks continued to seek hegemony over their neighbours, but met their nemesis when they tried unsuccessfully to wrest the tiny island of Malta from the Knights Templar of St John in 1565, the invading army sent reeling in the face of steadfast resistance.

Suleiman's successor, Suleiman II, attempted an ambitious invasion of Russia in 1569, but soon discovered that he had bitten off more than he could chew; withdrawing to safety, he turned his attention to Venetian-held Cyprus. In July 1570 he mounted an invasion of the island with 50,000 men, but her defenders were eventually subdued after a cruel and merciless campaign that lasted longer than a year.

An alarmed King Philip II of Spain and Pope Pius V formed a Holy League to try and liberate the island. An armada of over 300 ships set out to give battle with a Turkish fleet of some 250 vessels, meeting in October 1571 at Lepanto in the Greek Gulf of Corinth. A long-drawn-out and bloody battle saw the Turkish fleet badly mauled, but she negotiated a treaty with Venice which later ceded her the island anyway.

In 1593 the thirteen-year 'Long War' opened between Turkey and Austria. At its conclusion in 1606, with Turkey unable to force a decision, Austria emerged powerful enough to persuade her Ottoman adversary that she commanded respect.

In 1646 Turkey embarked upon the conquest of Crete. However, complete victory would elude her for another twenty-three years as her troops fought a sporadic but desperate campaign to suppress the island. Meanwhile, another Ottoman army under Sultan Mehmet IV retraced its steps into Hungary, here meeting a coalition at Saint Gotthard in August 1664. The Turks were again unable to achieve a breakthrough. Instead, they had to sign a second peace treaty.

Another assault against Vienna in 1683 proved a failure. The city's defenders succeeded in lifting the siege and then proceeded to mount assaults on several fronts from Hungary to Greece, pushing the Ottomans back. The rout was so humiliating, the subsequent collapse in morale so complete, that it would lead to the deposing of Mehmet. The Ottomans had now reached the peak of their power and influence in Europe; all would be downhill from here.

Further reverses followed. At Harkany in 1687 and Belgrade in 1688 the Turks experienced defeat, and they faced a new threat from

Louis William I of Baden-Baden, who routed them at Slankamen, north-west of Belgrade, in August 1691. Russia's Peter the Great was also casting a covetous eye on Ottoman territory, and in 1695 he launched an attack on Azov, which commanded the entrance to the Black Sea, and a year later incorporated the territory into his own expanding Czarist empire. In 1697 Turkey was forced to cede territory to Austria, Venice and Poland after another disastrous defeat outside Belgrade. Turkey faced a coalition of Russia, Prussia and Austria. The Russians sent a fleet into the Mediterranean, where they met a Turkish force at Cesme, west of Smyrna. The Turks were completely routed, and the conflict ended in 1774 with the Turks divested of swathes of territory in south-east Europe. Between 1774 and 1783 the Crimea fell to Russia, followed by Odessa in 1791. Now, however, the once-feared Turk faced internal as well as external pressures.

Serbia proved to be one of the earliest hotbeds of resistance to Ottoman rule. A serious revolt raged from 1804 until 1813 and ended with self-government reluctantly being ceded to the rebels, whilst external pressures returned with the Russian occupation of Eastern Moldavia between 1806 and 1812. It seemed that rents were appearing in the patchwork of Ottoman territories.

A vassal of Turkey since the middle of the fifteenth century, Greece had long festered under hated Turkish rule, and in 1822 she finally rose in revolt. In 1827, Britain, France and Turkey's ever-prowling neighbour Russia joined forces to help free the feisty Greeks. Naval humiliation at the Battle of Navarino in 1827 secured the freedom of significant tracts of the country – mostly Morea – which in 1830 formed the genesis of a new nation. It would take until the end of the century before all the Hellenic lands united as one country, but it was a promising start. It was the origin of the nation that, ninety years later, would cross the Aegean and attempt to turn the tables on its erstwhile master.

In 1828 a Russian army crossed the Danube. The following year it moved into the Balkans and seized Adrianople while another column crossed the Caucasus. These moves forced the Divine Porte to make further concessions to the Russian interlopers, surrendering all the lands as far as the southern mouth of the Danube in return for peaceful coexistence. This peace was not to be enjoyed for very long.

In 1832 Egypt rose against Turkey, invading Syria and inflicting a series of defeats over the course of the next eight years. European concern over the possible destabilising effect of the fighting and the possibility of a power vacuum resulted in British intervention, and in 1840 Egypt became a self-governing province of the Ottoman Empire, recognising the sovereignty of the Sultan but very little else.

Mid-nineteenth-century European power politics heralded the next crisis to embroil Turkey, with Russia becoming increasingly vociferous over her right to protect Slavic minorities within the empire. The ongoing tension between the two powers came to a head in 1853 when Russia marched into Wallachia and Moldavia; though self-governing, these territories still recognised Ottoman sovereignty.

The resulting Crimean War is remembered more for Florence Nightingale and the Charge of the Light Brigade, but to the Ottomans it meant yet another chapter in their slow decline. In order to retain control of their domains they had to call upon the help of Britain and France, and although Turkey emerged from the war ostensibly a victor alongside her allies, it was clear she was no longer a regional power, rather a fragile state reliant upon the 'Great Powers' for her survival.

Key among Russia's long-held aspirations was control of the sea route between the Black Sea and the Mediterranean, a role Turkey had jealously guarded ever since Osman staked his claim there in 1354. It was the prospect of Russia dominating this vital route that had terrified both Britain and France for decades and motivated their increasingly frequent efforts to prop up the ailing Ottoman Empire. This long-running saga evolved into what was to become known as the Straits Question.

In 1833, a secret clause to the Treaty of Unkiar Skelessi had been signed between Russia and Turkey during a brief period of friendly diplomatic relations. It was an eight-year mutual assistance pact by which Turkey would close the Straits to foreign warships in wartime whilst allowing free passage to Russian vessels. When it expired Britain masterminded its replacement, the Straits Convention of

July 1841, which closed the seaway to all foreign warships while Turkey was at peace. The Treaty of Paris, which ended the Crimean War in 1856, reaffirmed this. The issue continued to torment Europe's statesmen, and Turkey's new reputation as the 'Sick Man of Europe' cast doubt on her reliability as guarantor of the Straits' integrity. The solution to the Straits Question would be a bone of contention right up to the outbreak of war in 1914.

As well as the threat to the Straits and the external pressures that were increasingly brought to bear on the empire, the sheer cost of fighting wars and maintaining garrisons across such far-flung territory had become prohibitive. This burden compounded the empire's growing financial problems, especially when levying revenues locally to pay for garrisons was all but impossible and tributes for the Sultan were frequently ignored. In an attempt to rationalise the mishmash of territories and hopefully make them partly self-sufficient, the union of Moldavia and Wallachia into Rumania was permitted between 1858 and 1861. Serbia soon followed this lead. Self-governing since 1817 after the uprising in 1804, Serbia was abandoned by her Turkish garrison in 1867 and her independence was finally recognised in 1878. As the expensive garrisons withdrew, the Balkans increasingly degenerated into 'bandit country' where it was impossible for the Turks to maintain order. The 1870s were a particularly dire decade for the fortunes of the empire.

In 1875–76, rebellions broke out in Herzegovina and Bulgaria. They were met with brutal repression and massacres as the Turks desperately tried to hold their fractious empire together, provoking international outcry and again catching the watchful eye of Russia. Keen as ever to be seen as guardian of the Slavs, Russia moved into the Balkans and inflicted a bloody nose on the Turks. The subsequent peace resulted in the Ottomans ceding further large tracts of the Caucasus to Russia and having to agree to pay an indemnity they could ill afford. Britain also took advantage of Turkey's plight to extract the right to administer Cyprus on behalf of the Sultan, and Greece continued to extend her borders at the expense of the old enemy until almost all the territory from Thessaly up to Macedonia had been liberated. Turkey was also forced to recognise the Austro-Hungarian occupation of Bosnia in 1878, whilst Tunisia and Algeria fell into the French orbit. This left just Tripolitania and Cyrenaica, marooned between French- and British-dominated Africa.

Turkey's growing political woes cast an increasingly long shadow over the country's status and the prestige of her national institutions. This growing sense of unease had spawned a new breed of reactionary young men who felt themselves estranged from the Sultanate, and this emerged in the so-called 'Young Turk' movement. Expatriates and political exiles living in Europe made common cause with defiant officers in the army and resolved to challenge the status quo. The movement was to draw to its colours men like Enver Pasha and Mustapha Kemal, two champions of Turkish nationalism whose influence would have profound consequences for their country.

Enver was born to a wealthy Constantinople family in 1881, and demonstrated academic qualities in his youth. He subsequently joined the army, where he showed promise as a young officer, and graduated from military school in 1902, embarking upon a career in which he hoped to make a name for himself. He went on a fateful trip to Germany, where he observed the power and strength of her army. His experiences here imbued him with the ethos and martial discipline that he had observed, and convinced him of the necessity to reform the Turkish armed forces along similar lines if they were to stand any chance of defeating the various enemies now arrayed against them.

Mustapha was born in Salonika, Greek Thessaloniki, in 1881, the son of a customs official. His father secured him a place at a progressive and secular school, at which point he may have been lost to history, but when his father died he was taken to live with his uncle instead. As a result of this turn in the family fortunes he went on to distinguish himself at a military academy, performing so well in his studies that he was awarded the rare epithet of 'Kemal', or perfect. It remained with him throughout his life.

Young Mustapha continued to excel in his lessons, so much so that in 1895 he was transferred to the more advanced military academy at Monastir, where he further cultivated his political convictions by reading the works of the classical French scholar and philosopher Jean-Jacques Rousseau, and the writings of French revolutionaries.

Having qualified from the academy with flying colours in 1899, he was appointed to the War College in Constantinople, from which he was commissioned as a second lieutenant. His unique qualities of leadership soon marked him out for further promotion, and he was recommended for staff officer training. By 1905, when he graduated as a captain, his star was clearly in the ascendant. His meteoric rise was all the more surprising given that he had been making little secret of his radical political views. As early as 1899 he had read the 'subversive' literature of Namik Kemal,[1] which had been banned by the Sultan, and when he proceeded to the Staff College in 1902 he and some of his fellow students founded a secret society and began a newspaper attacking the corruption and inefficiency of the Ottoman bureaucracy. However, it was not very long before he and his fellow 'conspirators' were reported to the secret police, who ordered the director of the college to suppress their activities and close down the newspaper. Fortunately for this ramshackle cabal, the director proved sympathetic to their aims, turning a blind eye to their intrigues and covering up for them as best he could. Nevertheless, it was only a matter of time before Mustapha was arrested, and following interrogation and a period of imprisonment he found himself posted to Syria.

In Damascus Mustapha witnessed further examples of venality and malpractice, which inspired him to join the *Vatan ve Hurriyet* ('Fatherland and Freedom') movement. Under the cover of his military duties, Mustapha proceeded to establish similar organisations in Beirut, Jaffa and Jerusalem, and took an unapproved leave of absence to establish a similar cell in Macedonia. By 1908 the empire was experiencing further convulsions, with mutinies breaking out in the army and navy in response to the dictatorial rule of Sultan Abdulhamid. Finally, on 24 July, a new political party led by Enver called the Committee of Union and Progress (CUP) staged a coup. They demanded the restoration of constitutional rule based on arrangements originally approved in 1878 but never fully implemented. The Sultan, faced with a *fait accompli*, had no choice but to accede to their demands.

Despite his acquiescence, the Sultan's days were numbered. He was forced to abdicate in favour of his sixty-four-year-old brother

Mehmet V, who, following thirty years under what was virtually house arrest, was even less qualified to fulfil the role of Sultan than his brother. However, behind this thin veil of royal legitimacy Enver could increase his own hold on power and the CUP could govern and hopefully retain what remained of the ailing empire. Stability could not come too soon, as further threats to the integrity of the state were shortly to appear.

Italy, having missed out on the 'Scramble for Africa' that had seen most of the continent go to Britain and France, saw that her chance of territorial aggrandisement lay at the expense of Turkey's colonies in North Africa. In September 1911 an invasion force crossed the Mediterranean and soon overwhelmed a Turkish garrison, much of which was being transferred to reinforce the Balkans, where fighting had again broken out. Too weak to fight a war on two fronts, the Ottomans ceded to Italy both Cyrenaica and Tripolitania, as well as officially recognising the Italian occupation of the Dodecanese Islands in the Aegean. Despite sacrificing her North African territories to face the threat in the Balkans, the war went predictably badly for Turkey, and in January 1913, fearful that the Sultan was planning to approve a humiliating peace treaty, Enver led another coup with himself at its head, which established the Young Turks as the de facto government of the empire, a position they would retain until 1918.

Nevertheless, the game in Europe was up; in the subsequent peace negotiations the Ottoman Empire in Europe had been brought to a virtual end. Crete, Western Thrace, Albania, Thessaly, Epirus, Kosovo and Macedonia were finally lost, and all that she now retained was a tiny rump of land in Eastern Thrace. Eighty per cent of Turkey's European territory was gone, much of it the most rich and developed, along with 4.2 million people. She was practically back where she had started 500 years before, her lands now mostly limited to a vast territory stretching south to the Red Sea and eastwards to the Arabian Gulf. Greece, on the other hand, had almost doubled her territory and added another 2 million to her population.

The generations-old legacy of bitterness between Greece and Turkey had now been rekindled, and it was Turkey who looked with a vengeful eye at the Balkan revanchement that had been achieved by her neighbours and erstwhile subjects. In the meantime, she satisfied her animosity by expelling 30,000 Greeks from Thrace and Anatolia, serving as a tragic portent of the population exchanges – or ethnic cleansing – that was to follow.

The loss of territory in the Balkans would also have massive demographic and ethnographic consequences for the political dynamics of the empire. In point of fact, the majority of the ruling elite of the empire originated in the Balkans.[2] Such men as party leader Talaat Pasha, Governor of Izmir Evranoszade Rahmi and the aforementioned Mustapha Kemal all originated in the Balkans. As a direct consequence of the loss of the Balkan provinces, the Ottoman Government began, perhaps for the first time, to look upon Anatolia as the natural homeland of the Ottoman Empire, and considered the need to commence the Turkification of what they perceived as 'their' land, as had been embodied in the philosophy of pan-Turanism, Pan-Turkism and Pan-Islamism. Pan-Turanism maintained that Turkey must be transformed into a Euro-Asiatic super-state, whilst Pan-Turkism harboured slightly more modest aspirations, envisaging the unification of Turkish-speaking peoples from both east and west. Most significantly for the events which were to follow in the next few years, perhaps, one school of Pan-Islamism ordained that it was Turkey's fate to govern the Islamic Khilifat (Caliphate) as well as Turanic- and Turkish-speaking lands.[3] There was little room to accommodate the interests of other ethnic or religious communities, an ethos that Enver, in his dream of creating a truly Turkish homeland, would adhere to vehemently even if it meant expelling thousands of ethnic Greeks whose commercial acumen had proved so valuable to the empire.

Economics, however, were not a new factor in the decline of the Ottoman state. Decades of expenditure which outstripped revenues meant that other European powers provided millions in financial aid and investment on condition that the Ottoman Government grant special privileges which became known as 'Capitulations'. In 1863, the Ottoman Bank had been founded with British and French capital, and foreigners also took on ownership of the national debt, of which France alone would own 60 per cent by 1914. French interests even extended to the right to impose taxes and manage certain government departments with revenue-raising powers whilst enjoying immunity from Turkey's own laws. By the time of the First World War, the French would effectively control the harbour works on the European shore of the Bosphorus at Haydarpasa, as well as other commercial interests at Smyrna, Salonika and Beirut. The British munitions firm Vickers, under the cumbersome title Imperiale Ottomane Co-Interessee de Docks, Arsenaux et Constructions Navale, had been granted a thirty-year lease on the arsenal on the Golden Horn. By 1910–11, the new dockyard, grain mill, brewery, shoe factory and cement factory were owned and operated not by Turks but by Frenchmen. In addition, the newly arrived electricity for the city was run by a company named the Societe Anonyme Ottoman d'Electricite, and the city's telephone network was operated by the Societe Anonyme Ottoman des Telephones.

Foreign capital thus facilitated major investment projects but removed control over vital areas of industry and commerce from the Ottoman Government. Consequently, successive Sultans became less and less masters in their own house, but still it was not enough, and in the search for more foreign investment to finance wars and pay for modernisation projects, Turkey made what was to be her most disastrous decision yet.

Turkey's pact with destiny was made as early as 1889, when the German Kaiser, Wilhelm II, moored his yacht off the Dolmabahche Palace and embarked upon a state visit designed to woo the Sultan and open the door to German business and investment. In 1903, the Germans were granted the right to construct a 1,280-mile railway line from Konya to Basra, as well as the rights to explore for oil 15 miles either side of the length of the line. Turkey's imports from Germany would rise from 6 per cent of the total in 1897 to 21 per cent in 1910, with imports of military hardware and steel for the railways constituting the majority of the goods. Germany also received a 'concession' on the Anatolian shore of the Bosphorus at Haydarpasa, where more German money was invested.

As we have seen, Enver also greatly admired Germany's military prowess and was convinced that the fortunes of the Ottoman Empire could be reversed only with a massive overhaul of its armed forces. His senior position in the government now made it possible for him to put his theories into practice, and he invited the Germans to send advisers who could assist him in his plans. A delegation of sixty headed by General Liman von Sanders arrived in Turkey in 1913, but many of these officers appeared arrogant and aloof, showing scant regard for the sensitivities or customs of their hosts. Resentment understandably ran deep among Turks who returned from a morning being drilled by German officers and travelled to their posts on German-built railways. However, as Sultan Abdulhamid himself once revealingly lamented, 'The Germans do me as much good as they are permitted to do, whereas the rest of Europe do me as much harm as they can.'[4] This fateful sentiment emphasised the diplomatic and economic dynamics that would lead to the empire's ultimate destruction.

2

I AM NOT ORDERING YOU TO ATTACK; I AM ORDERING YOU TO DIE

Relations between the great powers were slowly deteriorating in the years leading up to 1914, culminating in the assassination of the heir to the Austro-Hungarian throne, Archduke Franz Ferdinand, in the Bosnian capital of Sarajevo on 28 June. As Europe's complex system of alliances fell into place and the great powers jockeyed for position, the Turkish government began to weigh up its own options.

By 1914, the political machinations in Constantinople had seen Enver elevated to the powerful post of Minister of War, much to the Sultan's dismay – especially as he purged the ministry of officers whose loyalty towards him was considered suspect. Ever mindful that Turkey needed friends and allies in these increasingly uncertain times, and aware that public opinion was erring towards greater friendship with the British,[1] he sent out tentative feelers to both Britain and France to gauge the extent to which they might reciprocate any desire for closer ties. So far, however, there had been no success.

It was during a stint as Turkey's military attaché to Berlin between 1909 and 1911 that Enver crossed paths with Winston Churchill for the first time. He tactfully sounded the British out, but the response was not favourable. The prospect of binding agreements did not sit well with the general foreign policy of Downing Street, and although Churchill was slightly more sympathetic towards the prospect of a formal arrangement with Turkey than the Foreign Secretary,[2] the Ottomans were firmly, though politely, kept at arm's length.

In the middle of 1914, Enver despatched Djemal Pasha, Minister of the Navy, to Paris. Here he raised the possibility of French support in securing the return of the Dodecanese Islands from Italy, but again received a somewhat lukewarm response. In the event of war both Britain and France would find more comfort in a friendly Italy than a friendly Turkey, and this rebuff served to persuade waverers that they had little to gain from pursuing closer ties with either country.[3] It also served to reaffirm Enver's determination to seek an alliance with the only other logical contender: Germany.

In July, Enver told Baron von Waggenheim, the German ambassador in Constantinople, that his government favoured such an arrangement; the Germans in turn concluded that having an alliance with a country capable of blocking off military aid to Russia in the event of war was not an opportunity to be turned down lightly.[4] Consequently, on 2 August 1914, Germany and Turkey agreed and signed a secret treaty which committed Germany to come to Turkey's aid in the event of war between Turkey and Russia. However, in return for German protection, Clause 3 of the document handed over to the Germans 'effective influence on the general conduct of the [Turkish] army' in the event of the two nations going to war against a third party. On the following day, armed with this guarantee of German support, the Turkish government announced the mobilisation of its armed forces and the cancellation of interest payments on its foreign debt. There was by no means unanimity in this grave step, so to stifle internal dissent parliament was also prorogued. However, even at this juncture Enver had not decided which horse to back. He insisted that Turkey was to remain neutral and her actions should be interpreted as no more than prudent precautions while she monitored developments. The treaty with Germany was to remain a well-kept secret so that the empire's relations with the British were not compromised. For their part, the British, who in the event of war would at the very least need to maintain communications through the Dardanelles in order to support Russia, would have been wise to adopt the same strategy. Unfortunately, events were to demonstrate that they did not quite see things that way.

Britain was just completing the construction of two new warships for the Ottoman Government – the *Sultan Osman* and the *Reshadieh* – at a cost of almost £7 million. The funds for this enormous project had been raised partly by public subscription, and many women had even allegedly parted with their jewels in a programme many believed represented the nations' resurgence as a major European power.[5] The *Osman* would be the biggest battleship afloat, and therefore the project was a source of considerable national pride among the Turkish people, who waited in anticipation for their two new warships to be delivered. Turkish sailors had already been sent to Britain in order to take possession of the vessels.

Suddenly, with the prospect of war looming on the horizon, the two warships took on a singular significance and placed the British Government in something of a quandary. If Turkey were sincere in their assurances of neutrality, then it would have been circumspect not to endanger her status by holding on to the vessels, as much as they might prove useful to the Royal Navy. In theory, at least, a neutral Turkey meant that the Dardanelles Straits could still be available to the Allies in order to keep their Russian ally supplied. However, if Turkey was only playing for time, and her friendship with Germany was well known, then it would have been a criminal act of folly to make two of the most modern warships under construction available to a potential enemy.

It fell to the First Lord of the Admiralty, Winston Churchill, to weigh these imponderables. In order to buy time to decide what action to take, he gave orders for the completion of the vessels to be delayed as long as possible while he consulted the Cabinet.[6] The pros and cons were discussed at length until finally it was agreed that Britain needed the ships more than a potential enemy. Despite the fact that Turkish crews were actually on the quayside waiting to take possession of the vessels, the Admiralty announced that they were to be appropriated without compensation for the duration of the war. As Foreign Secretary Sir Edward Grey so glibly phrased it, they were required for Britain's 'own needs in this crisis',[7] although a vague promise was given that the Turkish Government would not lose its investment. Learning of this British act of perfidy, the Turkish crews attempted to take the vessels by force. Although there were no serious injuries, the vessels remained firmly in British hands.

Despite strong Turkish protests, the British Government was adamant and in this one act placed a priceless propaganda coup into the hands of the Germans. In exchange for the two 'stolen' warships, the Germans magnanimously offered the Turkish Government two of their own. These, the *Goeben* and the *Breslau*, were gratefully accepted by Enver Pasha's Government and renamed respectively the *Jawuz Sultan Selim* and the *Midilli*. They were both formidable men-o-war; the *Goeben* was a battle cruiser and alone was capable of 26 knots and could boast 11-inch guns. In this one act Germany had not only obtained control of the Turkish army, but was on the verge of dominating her navy as well.

The two German warships had already achieved incredible propaganda value when they raced the entire length of the Mediterranean, chased by and completely outfoxing pursuing ships from the Royal Navy. Commanded by the timid Admiral de Robeck, the British failed to prosecute the pursuit with sufficient energy and the Germans were able to elude them with consummate ease. Finally, the two German warships reached the entrance of the Dardanelles, but here they faced a quandary. They could not enter the Straits legally without Turkish consent, but by giving permission to pass, the Turks would be in breach of long-standing international conventions. After much soul-searching, Enver overruled his cabinet colleagues and decided to let them through;[8] it was made equally clear that any attempt at pursuit by the Royal Navy would be resisted, if necessary by force.

The situation was deteriorating rapidly, and once the two German warships had slipped through the Dardanelles the Royal Navy imposed a blockade. It was clear how much damage they could do if they were let loose in the Black Sea, and through this time-honoured means of coercion the Allies hoped to be able to bring about a decision. However, in order to avert an irrevocable break with Turkey, Churchill sent a personal telegram to Enver on 15 August warning of the disaster that war with the Allies would bring his country. Grey added a paragraph assuring Enver that the integrity of the Ottoman

Empire would be respected if they remained neutral, but that any neutrality must involve the removal of German personnel from her territory, a demand that was to be echoed by the Russian Government as well.[9] These dire warnings were discussed in Constantinople, but Enver had boxed himself into a corner. Rear Admiral Arthur Limpus, the British Naval Adviser to the Turkish Government, also urged them to seriously consider the implications should they abandon neutrality and go to war with the British Empire. The permanent loss of the ships without compensation, the fomenting of anti-Turkish movements in Arabia, Greek involvement in the war, and the seizure of the Dardanelles were just some of the unpalatable consequences that might result. British suspicions were vindicated by reports from her military attaché in Constantinople, Frederick Cunliff-Owen, who warned that not only was there no sign of the German crews leaving but that the Turkish fleet was indeed almost completely under German control. These suspicions were confirmed on 9 September when Limpus and his naval mission was unceremoniously expelled, leaving the Germans to complete their domination of the Turkish military. One wit remarked that so entrenched was Germany in Turkish society that her naval ratings could now be heard singing '*Deutschland uber Allah*'.[10]

Still indecisive, afraid to take that final, irrevocable step, Enver initially responded encouragingly to Churchill's telegram. He wanted to know what the British Government proposed to do with the two warships, and whether the Turkish Government could expect some compensation for their seizure. The Foreign Office and the Admiralty discussed the options, and Churchill proposed that the ships would be returned to Turkey at the end of the war, or replaced if they were lost. In either event the British would pay Turkey £1,000 in compensation for every day they remained in the service of the Royal Navy. However, the time for a diplomatic resolution was fast running out.

As the politicians debated, British warships intercepted a Turkish torpedo boat on 27 September and the Turkish Government retaliated by closing the Straits. Constantinople was now becoming gripped by hostility and fear, as the very real prospect of conflict loomed. The United States ambassador to the Divine Porte, Henry Morgenthau was among those in Constantinople who realised that time was running out and requested an audience with the Grand Vizier. He did not encounter a confident politician in full possession of his faculties at such a time of crisis, but rather a man who 'presented a picture of abject helplessness and fear',[11] terrified by the prospect of war but resigned to its inevitability.

The diplomatic tension increased for another teeth grinding month. Then the Straits were mined, and on 29 October the German officer in command of the Turkish Navy, Admiral Souchon, sailed his fleet into the Black Sea. He steamed around the coast and proceeded to bombard the Russian ports of Sebastopol, Odessa and Nikolaev and sink a couple of Russian warships. When reports of this startling escalation were received in Constantinople they sparked off a political crisis. A number of ministers, completely hostile to Enver's tactics, threatened to resign if the ships were not returned to port.[12] Enver, however, having disingenuously denied all prior knowledge of the German plan, had nevertheless provoked the Russian Government into a declaration of war.

Matters were now taking on a momentum of their own, and the few remaining diplomatic options were quickly being closed off. On 1 November a Turkish yacht anchored in Smyrna harbour was suspected of carrying mines but was scuttled to avoid being boarded. On 2 November, HMS *Minerva* demanded the surrender of the garrison at Aqaba, a town on the Sinai Peninsula close to the Suez Canal. The demand was refused and the town was shelled. On 3 November, British and French warships bombarded some of the forts on the Dardanelles in a brief ten-minute barrage. The seventeenth-century fort at Seddulbahir was destroyed when a lucky shot exploded in its magazine, destroying all ten of its guns and killing eighty-six soldiers. On 7 November, British forces landed at Basra with the intention of securing the Persian oilfields at Ahwaz.

In the face of this undeclared war, diplomacy was doomed and finally Britain and France made it official on 5 November. In response, Turkey declared jihad against the Allies six days later on 11 November. The Sheikh-ul-Islam called upon loyal Muslims to wage a holy war against the infidels, invoking the age-old totems of loyalty to the Ottoman Empire and fealty to its Sultan-Caliph:

> All the Muslims in all countries, whether young or old ... [were called upon] to resort to jihad with all their properties and lives ... to declare war against Russia, Britain and France and their helpers and supporters, who are enemies of the Islamic Caliphate ... in this way when success depends on all Muslims to resort to jihad ... the Muslims living under the sovereignty of Britain, France, Russia, Serbia, Montenegro and their supporters deserve severe suffering if they fight against Germany and Austria, who are helping the Ottoman government because it would be harmful for the Caliphate of Islam ...

Turkey was therefore not only calling upon its own Muslim subjects to rise up against the infidels but, as Caliph and head of the Muslim world, the huge Muslim population of the British Empire as well. In India alone, millions of the Caliph's loyal adherents were being instructed to turn upon their British rulers and sweep them from their shores. Secret agents had been sent to India, Afghanistan, Persia, the Caucasus, Arabia, Egypt and Libya to act as *agents provocateurs* and stir up revolt and civil disorder. As a German General Staff memo of 5 August confirms:

> Revolution in India and Egypt, and also the Caucasus is of the highest importance. The Treaty with Turkey will make it possible for the [German] Foreign Office to realise the idea and to awaken the fanaticism of Islam... [13]

Nevertheless, the declaration failed to have the galvanising effect that Enver had hoped for, either at home or abroad. There were no huge crowds to welcome the war in Constantinople or the other cities, more a sullen and reluctant resignation to the inevitable. A despondent Sultan Mehmet V himself exclaimed, 'I did not want this war, Allah be my witness. I am sure that my people did not want it,' berating the fact that 'we have sacrificed ourselves for two boats.'[14] Officers such as Mustapha Kemal, too, were far from convinced that they had taken the right decision. He saw the German achievements in the West offset by the need to support the Austro-Hungarians against the Russians in the East. He did not, he confided to a close friend, 'feel certain about the outcome of this war'.[15]

The call to jihad would nevertheless be answered in some unexpected quarters. Despite Turkey having ceded their Libyan territories to Italy in 1912, the native Senussi tribesmen responded wholeheartedly to the Caliphate's call to arms, committing its 10,000 strong militia, trained secretly by Turkish officers since the Italian occupation, to the cause. When Italy joined the Allies in 1915, the Senussi uprising became part of the wider war and Turkey felt suitably buoyed by their success to announce the re-occupation of the territory in October of that year. The campaign in North Africa brought the added benefit of diverting both British and Italian troops to North Africa, and away from the critical Suez Canal area. Nevertheless, the Italian forces here performed poorly, and found themselves virtual prisoners in coastal garrisons from which they were unable to break out while the Turkish-led Senussi were able to stage a vigorous offensive which penetrated into Egypt, reaching as far as Sollum and Sidi Barrani, driving the British as far as Marsa Matruh. Libya would inevitably become a backwater, however, as the war developed on more crucial fronts where they could decide the very future of the Ottoman dynasty. Nevertheless, the episode graphically illustrated the potential consequences of a general Muslim uprising in favour of the Caliphate if it spread further into the Muslim world.

Recognising that his services were needed, Mustapha asked Enver to recall him from his post in Sofia, where he had been assigned as military attaché, so that he could take up an active command. Despite grave misgivings (Enver saw Mustapha as a potential rival), Enver eventually assigned him to the command of the 19th Division early in 1915. He would not have to wait long to see action.

Predictably, it was not long before the Russians started pleading for Allied help as the huge but ill-equipped Russian army threw itself against the Germans. The need to bolster the Russians was clear from the start. Mobilising prematurely in order to assist the French in the very earliest stages of the conflict, her army was unprepared to meet the mammoth demands of waging a successful modern war on an industrial scale. Corruption was rife and complacency among an idle officer caste widespread. The one asset the Russian army had was its sheer size, frequently referred to as 'the Steamroller', but even numerical superiority was of little avail. Trounced by the Germans from the very outset, it was now meeting equally stiff opposition from Turkish forces in the Caucasus where Czarist forces faced a Turkish army over 100,000 strong.

The urgency of the situation was underscored in January 1915 when Russian Grand Duke Nicholas appealed directly to the Allies, requesting any military action which would serve to lure the Turks from their front. When in February Ottoman units crossed the Sinai and threatened the Suez Canal, it provoked distinct unease in Whitehall. The decidedly precarious situation in the Caucasus, combined with the tangible threat posed by Turkey along the crucial canal, convinced the British that despite its long-held 'sick man' image, the Ottoman Empire posed a threat that it dismissed at its peril.

Thoughts quickly returned to the Gallipoli peninsula, that arid, featureless, waterless and blistered strip of barren wilderness 60 miles long and between 4 and 13 miles wide. Between it and the equally daunting Asiatic shore lies the Dardanelles Strait, a 40-mile-long waterway that flows from the Sea of Marmara to the Aegean, varying in width from 1,400 yards to 4 miles. This tantalising and alluring target was to prove one of the worst places on earth in which to fight a campaign, and indeed a pre-war commission of enquiry concluded that an assault on the peninsula was doomed to failure. Initially enthusiastic Greek undertakings to participate in the operation, drawn by the prospect of humiliating an ancient foe, came to nothing. King Constantine of Greece, largely suspected of pro-German sympathies, backtracked by stating that his country would only go to war if attacked by Turkey first.[16] It became apparent that if an attempt to take the peninsula were to proceed, then it would have to be undertaken by Britain and France alone.

The task would have been perilous enough if the Allies had launched the assault as soon as possible after hostilities broke out, taking the Turkish defenders by surprise; in fact, the British compounded the felony by prevarication. Nevertheless, common sense was not to be allowed to get in the way of a bad idea, especially with the cries of Grand Duke Nicholas ringing in Whitehall's ears and the prospect of a Turkish offensive aimed at the capture of the Suez Canal looming. The Dardanelles plan was revived as the best way to divert Turkish forces away from such exposed fronts.

Churchill initially believed that the straits could be forced by naval action alone, and heralded the commencement of the campaign by ordering a preliminary bombardment of its forts to begin on 25/26 February 1915. These successfully destroyed the outer redoubts, and the arrival of HMS *Queen Elizabeth* on 5 March threw the defenders into some confusion when three forts at Kilid Bahr were damaged. However, the British failed to appreciate their stroke of luck, and despite intensive further bombardments the Turkish and German garrison began to reassert itself as the shells fired from the Royal Navy ships failed to achieve decisive results. Poor weather conditions and counter-barrages from the Turkish mobile howitzers exacerbated issues for the British. In fact, the defenders' morale had recovered remarkably quickly and the ramparts of the beleaguered forts now began to echo resoundingly to the mantra of 'Allah is great, there is but one God, and Mohammed is his Prophet!',[17] while the gun crews responded to the Allies' futile assaults.

Incredibly, even as shells and curses were being exchanged, elements within the British establishment had been involved in secret discussions with the Sublime Porte as they still hoped to bribe them into abandoning the war altogether. Unknown to the British government, Director of Naval Intelligence Sir Reginald Hall had asked three local businessmen to act as intermediaries and offer the Turkish Government £3 million if they agreed to pull out of their alliance with Germany and declare their neutrality. Then, as negotiations continued, the British learnt through an intercepted telegram that the Turkish forts in the Straits were running low on ammunition and confidence was restored. Perhaps force might win the day after all. With the British now drawn by the prospect of imminent military success, this tantalising opportunity to change the course of history was allowed to slip through their fingers.

Constantinople, however, rife with rumours about a possible Allied landing, remained on high alert. Terrified by the prospect of British and French warships steaming through the Sea of Marmara and shelling the city, the government had already moved its gold reserves and the state archives out of harm's way. Plans were now in train for the city itself to be dynamited before being abandoned completely.

In the meantime, Enver was taking decisive steps to prepare for an all-out Allied assault on the Straits. Advised as usual by Germany, he abandoned the idea of using the forward forts to defend the Straits. Instead they continued to lay mines and to use the forts to defend the minefields. No force could land successfully without first clearing the mines, but the forts would be in position to frustrate and hamper such efforts. The naval operation was also proving highly costly for the Allies. On 18 March a full-scale naval bombardment began that was designed to break through the lines of minefields and clear the way to Constantinople. The results were not encouraging. The French battleship *Bouvet* hit a mine, exploded and sank within three minutes, taking her crew of 639 to the bottom with her; the Royal Navy also suffered, HMS *Irresistible*, HMS *Inflexible* and HMS *Ocean* all hitting mines. In total the Allies lost some 700 men killed that day.

On 24 March, Enver directed Liman von Sanders to take command.[18] He hurried to Gallipoli to organise the defences and soon he had developed a sound plan, albeit with only 60,000 men at his disposal at this stage. With the naval bombardment failing to force the issue, Allied planning was now to hinge upon the landing of infantry. The intention was to execute 'a progressive military operation carried out in force in order to make good a passage for the navy'.[19] In this succinct sentence was sanctioned one of the blackest episodes in British military history, and arguably one of the most glorious for Turkey.

In the face of fierce opposition, landings were made on 25 April 1915 at Cape Helles, the westernmost tip of the peninsula, while 12 miles further north troops of the Australian and New Zealand Army Corps – the ANZACs – landed, at a place known as Anzac Cove. Poor planning and equally lamentable co-ordination led to piecemeal results and most successes were local and achieved by pure luck and individual acts of gallantry. Laxity, lethargy and incompetence at the highest levels condemned the Allies to be slaughtered by defenders who were now recovering and were receiving reinforcements of crack troops. Mustapha's appointment to the command of the 19th Division saw him transferred to the Dardanelles, and at the time of the Allied attempt to force the narrows on 18 March he was assigned the task of defending the eastern shore of the Gallipoli peninsula.

When the first landings took place on 25 April, Mustapha was a few miles from Anzac Cove. When the neighbouring 9th Division started to falter under the weight of repeated Allied attacks, he was asked to provide some support. Nevertheless, some of his men showed signs of breaking too. His gift of leadership and strength of character came to the fore when he is said to have steeled his faltering troops. With the rallying cry, 'I am not ordering you to attack; I am ordering you to die,'[20] he summoned every ounce of his resolve to hold his men, and instil in them the courage to resist and then repulse one assault after the other. The British were left exhausted, and no-man's-land littered with corpses. His own command was left almost entirely wiped out in the action, but he had saved the day.

The fighting at the Dardanelles brought Mustapha into conflict not only with the enemy, but also with his fellow commanders, including Liman von Sanders himself. He even wrote a report to Enver expressing his lack of confidence in the German general's decisions. Enver visited the battlefront to see for himself, but instead of sympathising with his officer's evaluation he decided in favour of the German general, much to Mustapha's disgust. It would not do, after all, for Enver's decision to appoint von Sanders to be challenged – let alone for that challenge to be upheld on the say-so of a relatively junior commander.

Mustapha nevertheless continued to fight with courage, and he was rewarded with promotion on 1 June. When the Allies landed at Suvla Bay on 6 August, it was to him that Liman von Sanders turned. In the bitter fighting that followed, Mustapha again led from the front, avoiding a serious injury when a shard of shrapnel struck him in the chest and was deflected by his watch.

However, it was not the enemy shrapnel which rankled most with Mustapha but the dubious decisions of von Sanders. Finally, frustrated by the German's domination of the decision-making process and his apparent insistence upon promoting German officers over Turkish commanders, he tendered his resignation. Even a surprisingly conciliatory telegram from Enver could not sway him, but as no other post became available he had to remain in Gallipoli anyway, where he continued to resist von Sanders' directives, openly defying him and criticising his decisions. Finally, he departed for Constantinople in December on medical grounds. With the war widening on all fronts, Mustapha would have little shortage of postings from which to choose. Eventually he would find himself serving on one of the most brutal war fronts of all, the Caucasus – that vast area straddling northern Turkey, Russia and Persia to the east. Here, the Turkish and Russian armies were fighting a bitter war in the most cruel and unforgiving of environments, and where his gift of leadership would be put to the most challenging of tests. First, however, Turkey's armed forces would have to endure the consequences of a far less talented commander.

Within a month of declaring war, the Turks had launched an audacious offensive. It was here that Enver Pasha dreamt of reconquering the lands lost to Russia in the 1870s, and uniting all the Turkic peoples of Russian Central Asia. Impulsively placing himself in personal command of the 3rd Army, which numbered between 100,000 and 190,000 men, he faced a Russian army of 60,000 under General Yudenich, who studiously withdrew his force back towards the city of Kars in the face of the Turkish advance. At Sarikamis, just inside the Russian border, and commanding the vital railway line north to Tiflis, the Russians decided to make a stand. Here they held the advancing Turkish forces, and following intense fighting from 29 December 1914 to 4 January 1915 inflicted a stunning and humiliating defeat on self-styled military supremo Enver Pasha.

This rout compelled the Turkish forces to mount a terrible retreat through the freezing mountains in temperatures of -26°, where many more of the tens of thousands of Turkish casualties suffered[21] until

Turkish losses exceeded 80 per cent. Enver emerged from this calamity chastened by his bruising experience. Although he had to relinquish his field command, hubris compelled him to resist the ignominy of exposure as precisely what Mustapha suspected him to be: an inept leader and strategist.

Fortunately for him, the region provided a ready-made scapegoat: the empire's 200,000-strong Christian minority in Armenia, long subject to abuse, prejudice and periodic pogroms. Thus, the entire population was accused of actively colluding against their Turkish masters by forming a fifth column that had given support to the invaders and contributed to the Turkish failure. These hapless souls were therefore accused of being 'the cause of trouble' that had contributed to, if not caused, the devastating defeat at Sarikamis.[22] The subsequent tragic fate of the Armenians, which is shrouded in controversy and denial to this day, arrived whilst the jihad continued elsewhere.

In an effort to extend their influence with their allies, Turkey took jihad beyond the immediate confines of her own borders. Enver in particular was anxious to demonstrate his nation's power and martial prowess, so in 1916 he agreed to provide men to fight in Galicia, Romania and Macedonia. It was a serious gamble, compromising the resources he could allocate to his other fronts, particularly those which threatened Turkey itself.

In Galicia, the newly formed XV Army Corps supported Austro-Hungarian forces against the Russians in September 1916 but were forced to withdraw in the face of determined attacks during which they sustained some 7,000 casualties. The front was stabilised until October, when further Russian assaults were repulsed, and then quietened down for the remainder of the year. Reinforcements arrived from Turkey at the beginning of 1917, ready to repulse further Russian attacks through January and February, followed by a major Russian onslaught on 29 June. After three days of heavy fighting this attack was repulsed as well, and the Russians began to fall back. In August the Turkish forces commenced their pursuit of the Russians, but before they could prove their worth they were ordered to stop.

When Romania joined the Allies in August 1916 and launched an attack across the Austro-Hungarian border, Turkish forces were again mobilised to come to the aid of their allies. They were to participate in a joint campaign with the Germans, but while preparations were underway the Romanians launched a further offensive against the town of Dobrija, and it fell to the Turks to hold them back. The Turkish defenders fought well, holding their ground against successive Romanian attacks until finally the defenders gave up and broke off. The Turks then responded with their own offensive on 19 October, and by 27 October they had penetrated deep into Romania, this time operating in conjunction with the Bulgarians. Romania then sought help from their Russian allies, who launched an attack against Turkish positions on the Danube. Again, the Turks not only held their ground but in December counter-attacked and drove the Russians back 40 miles. The German commander Mackensen received further Turkish forces to enable him to execute operations on other fronts, and a renewed offensive was mounted on 1 December which sent the Romanians into a headlong retreat. In January 1918 Turkish forces left Romania for assignments elsewhere, being desperately needed in other, more volatile and exposed theatres such as Palestine and Mesopotamia.

On 3 October 1915, an Anglo-French Expeditionary Force had landed in Salonika in Greece; the nation was still technically neutral, but its government-in-exile had worked in concert with the British and French. They were to support Serbian forces that were being mauled in a combined onslaught by the Germans, Austro-Hungarians and Bulgarians. By September 1916 the Allied force had grown to such a size that the Germans again asked the Turks for support, and almost immediately the 50th Infantry Division received orders to deploy to the Balkans. On 31 October the British launched a major assault from both sides of Lake Tahinos, which was repulsed. The front then fell relatively quiet during the winter of 1916/17, but elsewhere the Russians had again threatened the Caucasus and the British were marching on Jerusalem. This prompted the Turks to reassign their forces in Macedonia elsewhere, and in March 1917 the 50th Division was sent to Aleppo, where the British were now threatening Baghdad. This left only a very small force in Macedonia, the so-called Rumeli Field Detachment.

When the French launched an offensive on 13 March between Lakes Ohrid and Prepa, they threatened the Bulgarian 1st and German 11th Armies, prompting the assignment of the Rumeli Field Detachment to the Lakes. Despite French superiority in numbers, the smaller Turkish and German forces repulsed their attacks and then launched their own offensive. However, they encountered stiffer opposition this time and were thrown back. Fighting slowed down as the weather deteriorated, the exhausted Turkish troops getting bogged down in trench warfare. The Turkish commander was compelled to resign after his calls for rest and supply were ignored by the Germans, but his replacement had little more success in securing much-needed respite for his men. There were now accusations of favouritism cast upon the Germans and Bulgarians, and eventually the animosity engendered reached General Ludendorff. He finally agreed to the transfer of the detachment to a quieter zone, and its replacement by a Bulgarian unit. Fighting along this sector was petering out in any case, and in May 1918, the Rumeli Field Detachment was ordered back home, Turkey's wartime exploits in Europe having come to a not undistinguished finale.

Following his victory at Sarikamis, General Yudenich was promoted to the command of all Russian forces in the Caucasus, and early in 1915 launched an offensive in the direction of Van. The Turks staged a counterattack and inflicted a severe setback on the Russians at Malazgirt, but August brought a further Russian victory at Kara Killesse, forcing the Turks to retreat with the loss of considerable numbers of men and much-needed materiel. Apart from the ongoing slaughter of the Armenians, militarily at least the front was quiet for the remainder of 1915.

In January 1916 General Yudenich planned a renewed offensive against Erzurum, where Turkish forces were badly mauled at the Battle of Koprokoy. Meanwhile, another Russian offensive met and despatched a Turkish force on 14 February at the town of Tafta, and two days later the Russians entered Erzurum itself. General Yudenich then split his army in two, with one marching north to capture Trebizond, Turkey's key Black Sea port, while the other was despatched to capture Mush and Bitlis.

The situation was looking bleak for the Ottomans, and under a new commander, Vehip Pasha, orders were issued for the recapture of Trebizond. However, faced with a further Russian assault towards Erzingian, he was forced to delay his attack whilst he stabilised his front lines. Here, Mustapha Kemal, commanding two divisions and demonstrating the kind of leadership skills and military prowess he exercised so emphatically at Gallipoli, managed to recapture both Mush and Bitlis in August, and was rewarded with the Medal of the Golden Sword. This was a serious blow to the Russian plans, and even though they later retook the towns, the front around Van was now generally reduced to one of inconclusive thrust and counter-thrust. Russia began building up for a renewed push in 1917, planning to inflict a decisive blow against the Ottoman army. But the Russian Revolution arrived, throwing General Yudenich's plans into chaos. This disorder gave the Turks priceless time to regroup and reorganise, and to plan their renewed offensive. They were also now under considerable pressure from the British in Palestine and Mesopotamia, and the near dissolution of the Russians in the Caucasus allowed them to release badly needed men to the south. Indeed, the virtual disappearance of the once vast Russian army in the region had changed the military dynamics completely.

In January 1918, Turkish forces mounted an offensive that, albeit against negligible opposition, swiftly took Trebizond, Erzurum, Kars, Van and Balami. When the new Russian government signed the Treaty of Brest-Litovsk on 3 March, they ceded all the territory that had been captured, and delivered a crowning achievement to Enver's government. Nevertheless, this was not enough for the vainglorious Pasha and he pushed to extend the jihad even further. He formed an 'Army of Islam', consisting of somewhere between 14,000 and 25,000 men, and with this force swept into Armenia in May 1918. Bitter fighting ensued in which the Armenians inflicted severe damage on the invader, but the Ottomans eventually emerged victorious. Enver then turned his attention to Azerbaijan, reaching Baku in September and ejecting the small British garrison they encountered there. These were to prove pyrrhic victories for the Ottoman general, however, as the ever-strengthening Allies prepared to strike the killer blow that would serve to undo all of the Ottoman gains.

The jihad, as we have seen, started in Turkey's southerly possessions in Mesopotamia and Palestine, and it was here that its ultimately disastrous endgame would take place. When the British decided that they needed to guarantee the integrity of the enormous and strategically vital oil refinery at Abadan in Iran, they determined to act, and on 6 November 1914 the Turkish fort at Fao was seized, followed by Basra a fortnight later. The next obvious step was to capture the city of Baghdad itself.

In April 1915 the commander of the British force, General Townsend, made swift progress, advancing northwards and despatching what little weak Turkish opposition he encountered, prompting Enver to send German General von der Goltz, a seventy-three-year-old veteran of the Franco-Prussian War, to take command. Townsend met von der Goltz at Ctesiphon, 25 miles south of Baghdad, but the ensuing battle was inconclusive. Townsend found his encounter with the German general a disconcerting experience, though; perhaps sensing tougher resistance was building up, he concluded that a withdrawal to the dusty town of Kut was tactically justified. It was to prove a fateful decision. The town was fortified and his defenders awaited the arrival of the Turkish army, which surrounded them with siege works and proceeded to wait it out as its hapless garrison slowly starved.

The chances of resupply for the isolated post were slender, and three attempts to break out between 7 December 1915 and 29 April 1916 failed. Thrown back inside the disease-ridden town, the British and Indian troops inevitably succumbed to hunger, thirst and disease. Approximately 23,000 would perish in what was to become one of the most humiliating military disasters in British history. Townsend finally surrendered with what remained of his command and put his army at the mercy of the Turks. While his men were sent on a death march from which few survived, he chose to accept a comfortable imprisonment as an honoured guest of his Turkish hosts. Baulking at the experience at Kut, the British appointed a new commander, General Maude, with renewed orders to plan for the capture of Baghdad and deal the Turkish armies in the field an irreversible blow, thus atoning, at least in part, for the disaster suffered at Kut.

The offensive began in December 1916, advancing up both banks of the Tigris, pushing aside Turkish resistance and recapturing Kut in February 1917. The outskirts of Baghdad were reached in early March, and after decisively trouncing the defenders British troops entered the city on the 11th. There were further attacks to the north and east of the city, but operations were suspended with the onset of winter.

In the meantime Enver, ever mindful of the need to preserve his own status and of the need to pursue his own expansionist credo, concocted convoluted plans for Baghdad's recapture. His foolhardy approach was vehemently opposed by Mustapha. He believed the appalling state of Baghdad's communications made it as impossible to recapture as they had made it to defend in the first place, and bitterly criticised his new German commander, von Falkenhayn. He had hardly shone in his command of operations on the Western Front, and Mustapha now suspected him of wantonly sacrificing Turks in the pursuit of Germany's own strategic interests. For once Mustapha managed to make his point, and the plan for the offensive was dropped.

Mustapha, however, saw that the writing was on the wall for Turkey. On 20 September 1917, he wrote a strongly worded memorandum to Enver in which he expressed in no small terms what he felt. He claimed that the people were exhausted by war and on the verge of collapse, and that the government was not only riddled with corruption but was in disarray and close to disintegration. Furthermore, the Turkish army itself was in a parlous state with grossly understrength divisions of nearly starving men struggling against impossible odds. He insisted that what remained of the army ought now to be deployed for purely defensives operations, and not allowed to be sacrificed by the Germans for their own ends. With this damning indictment of the war situation, Mustapha resigned his command on 4 October, and made plans to return to Constantinople.

The British, however, indifferent to the machinations and internecine wranglings behind the enemy lines, were determined to proceed with their own offensive preparations. Late February 1918 saw a resumption of operations, with the capture of Kifri and Hit, before transferring temporarily to support offensives in Iran. October witnessed a resumption of activity in which the Turks were routed at the Battle of Sharqut that left the way open for the occupation of Mosul on 14 November 1918. Elsewhere, other battlefronts were facing similar fates.

For a year after the abortive Turkish attack on the Suez Canal, things were relatively quiet in this sector until in July 1916 another attempt was made on the vital waterway. This too was repulsed following heavy fighting, but now the British, persuaded by the efficacy of extending the defensive perimeter, decided to launch an offensive of their own. In December 1916, British forces captured Maghdaba, close to the border with Palestine. The capitulation of the garrison meant that the way into Palestine itself was now wide open, and a renewed offensive commenced in March 1917.

Turkish forces initially put up a robust defence, repelling a British assault on Gaza in late March, which was followed by an equally unconvincing attempt a month later. This prompted the British commander, General Allenby, to call for reinforcements, and by October he felt the time was ripe for a renewed offensive. This time he decided upon a feint, intended to persuade the Turks that Gaza was again the objective, while the real target was in fact Beersheba. By the simple expedient of sending a British officer out into the desert, where he expeditiously 'lost' his haversack complete with misleading and erroneous plans, the enemy took the bait and made the wrong preparations. The deception worked and the Turks were taken completely off-guard. The city fell on 31 October, and offensive operations resumed the following month. This brought about the Third Battle of Gaza, which resulted in the capture of the city, while the retreating Turkish army was now pursued relentlessly until on 9 December 1917 Jerusalem itself was captured.

Britain was confident that the Turks were now close to collapse, and planned a final push early in 1918. However, the German Spring Offensive on the Western Front put all such plans on the backburner, and Allenby's offensive had to wait until 19 September. Using clever techniques of deception similar to those that had worked so well to confound the enemy at Beersheba, he completely outwitted the enemy. The British were also ably supported by the legendary T. E. Lawrence, whose Arab tribesmen harassed and harried the now exhausted and demoralised remnants of the Turkish forces, further denuded by the transfer of many of their best men to other fronts and deployment in

Enver's so-called Army of Islam. With the Turkish army now all but non-existent the British forces ploughed on, entering Damascus on 1 October 1918, ending the war in Palestine and bringing disaster to yet another parched corner of the Ottoman Empire.

Events were now developing at an ever-increasing rate, and on the Macedonian front the huge Allied army, which included 250,000 Greek troops, compelled Bulgaria to seek an armistice on 29 September. This was particularly disastrous for Turkey as it meant that there were no longer any forces to protect the capital, and the Grand Vizier Talaat was forced to admit finally, 'We've had it.'[23]

With the situation deteriorating on nearly every front, Turkey badly needed all the good officers it could get. After his return to Constantinople, Mustapha was appointed aide-de-camp to Crown Prince Vaheddin, later to become Mehmet VI, in which capacity he accompanied the heir to the throne on a state visit to Germany. This distasteful experience, and the depressing effect that the prince had made upon him, soon had him hankering for active command again. To his great relief, Mustapha was posted to Syria to command the 7th Army, but his arrival only coincided with the last desperate death throes of the Turkish forces in the region. What he encountered upon his arrival filled him with despair. It was clear the war was lost, and the army's task was now simply one of preventing the complete territorial collapse of Turkey in the face of the victorious allies. Mustapha realised that unless Turkey could keep something like the nucleus of an effective army, the Allies would overrun not only their imperial possessions but the very homeland itself. He would do his utmost to prevent this, playing a pivotal role in keeping the remaining forces intact. His intervention would come not a moment too soon.

On 2 October even Enver, that die-hard nationalist, passionate advocate of the empire's destiny and the man who plunged his country into this catastrophe, was forced to concede that the game was up. The government in Constantinople was now in complete disarray, riven by squabbling and with no further options open to them but to capitulate. On 24 October the Sublime Porte made overtures to the British and conceded that it was now prepared to negotiate an armistice. The British acquiesced to the request, appointing Admiral Calthorpe, commander of the British Mediterranean Fleet, to head the British delegation. There followed a great deal of undignified wrangling as to who should form the delegation that would negotiate with the Allies. To nearly everyone's consternation, Mehmet wanted the task given to an almost unknown member of the royal family, his brother-in-law Damad Ferid, convinced that his best interests could be properly served only if a member of his own family represented the Ottoman Government. However, his cabinet was appalled, aware that such a sensitive task required the skills of an experienced politician and negotiator. After considerable argument and much resistance from the Sultan, the job was given to the Navy minister Hussein Rauf.

On the morning of 26 October the Turkish plenipotentiaries arrived at Mudros, a small port on the island of Lemnos in the Aegean Sea, hopeful that they could invoke both President Wilson's Fourteen Points and Lloyd George's War Aims to secure a peace that would not leave the once-mighty Ottoman Empire completely devastated and prostrate. They were encouraged by the high-minded Wilson, who envisioned a world rid of war and open to free trade, with freedom of the seas and the right of self-determination for all people. This, Point Twelve of the aforementioned Fourteen, contained a compromise that the defeated Ottoman Government felt they could live with. As President Wilson explained to the US Congress on 8 January 1918:

The Turkish portion of the present Ottoman Empire should be assured a secure sovereignty, but the other nationalities which are now under Turkish rule should be assured an undoubted security of life and absolutely unmolested opportunity of autonomous development ...[24]

British Prime Minister David Lloyd George had intimated something similar three days previously when he said that '[while] we do not challenge the maintenance of the Turkish Empire in the homelands of the Turkish race with its capital at Constantinople',[25] the Allies reserved the right to dispose of the rest of the empire as they saw fit. Thus resigned to the loss of their empire, but persuaded that Turkey proper within Anatolia would be preserved, the Turkish government were confident that the British and French, anxious to expedite a Turkish surrender and reopen the Straits, would be fair, if not exactly lenient.[26] Indeed, so keen were they to appease the Allies and distance themselves from the Central Powers that rumours began to circulate that they were prepared 'to massacre all the Germans and open the Dardanelles'.[27]

Unfortunately, matters did not proceed quite so smoothly. Admiral Calthorpe was to prove a stolid negotiator, and had been thoroughly briefed by the government beforehand. He had a list of twenty conditions with which the Turks must comply if the armistice was to come into force. Above all else, there were four crucial undertakings that the Turks had to make:

1. Opening of the Dardanelles and Bosphorus, and secure access to the Black Sea. Allied occupation of the Dardanelles forts and Bosphorus forts;
2. Position of minefields, torpedo tubes and other obstructions in Turkish waters to be indicated, and assistance given to sweep or remove them as may be required;
3. All available information as to mines in the Black Sea to be communicated;
4. All allied prisoners-of-war and Armenian interned persons and prisoners to be collected in Constantinople and handed over unconditionally to the Allies.

Negotiations stalled almost immediately on clause one. The prospect of the Greeks being among the forces occupying the forts was one that the Turks could not contemplate. They were their most implacable enemy, former subjects of the Sultan and a despised adversary whom they had been fighting on and off for centuries. Turkey had already suffered one humiliation after another at their hands and to see Greek troops in occupation of the Straits as part of a gloating Allied army of occupation was more than any self-respecting Turk could stomach. They had to be assured that no Greek soldier would be allowed to set foot on Turkish soil. Rauf told the British quite clearly that 'if the Greeks or Italians [occupy the straits] ... I tell you plainly that we had better see ourselves killed properly than allow it'.[28] Calthorpe countered that such a refusal could stall the negotiations before they had even started. Hostilities would resume and Turkey's suffering would continue, but they were adamant, and he reluctantly agreed to send a wire to London asking if he could make such an undertaking. Fortunately London was ambivalent towards the prospect of Greek troops occupying Turkish forts if it meant bringing the fighting to a swift conclusion, and advised Calthorpe that:

> The first four conditions are of such paramount importance to us and if completely carried out will so inevitably make us master of the situation, that we do not wish to jeopardise obtaining them, and obtaining them quickly, by insisting unduly on any of the rest, or indeed by raising any particular one of the remaining twenty if you think it might endanger your success in getting the vital four at once … [29]

This one point was further considered by the British, who eventually concluded that it was foolish to compromise everything for it, so the Turks were given the assurance they needed that neither the Greeks, nor for that matter the Italians, would be permitted to set foot on Turkish soil. This removed a crucial obstacle and negotiations could now proceed – up to a point.

Another potential bombshell was dropped when the French insisted that they ought be represented at the conference as equal members of the Allied delegation. They even despatched a naval officer for this purpose, arguing that they had fought the Turks as Allies and ought to negotiate peace terms on the same basis. As Lloyd George recorded in his war memoirs, 'the Turkish Armistice led to the only real unpleasantness I ever had with [President] Clemenceau',[30] and this falling-out would have bitter consequences. Calthorpe deliberately sidelined the French officer, whom he considered to have no authority there, and by embarking on discussions without French involvement provoked a sense of resentment among the French that would have serious repercussions later. Lloyd George was attending an inter-Allied conference in Paris when he was cornered by Clemenceau and the French Foreign Minister, Pichon, who raised heated objections to Calthorpe's behaviour. Lloyd George had anticipated something like this would happen, however, and had his response prepared:

Except for Great Britain no one had contributed anything more than a handful of black troops to the expedition in Palestine. ... The British had now some 500,000 men on Turkish soil. The British had captured three or four Turkish Armies and had incurred hundreds of thousands of casualties in the war with Turkey. The other governments had only put in a few nigger policemen to see that we did not steal the Holy Sepulchre! When however, it came to signing an armistice, all this fuss was made.[31]

It was certainly the case that the French had negotiated their own armistice with Bulgaria without British involvement, even though the Bulgarians too had made their initial approaches to the British, so Lloyd George had a point. The French calmed down, but this uneasy truce was not to last. There was a long way to go before a formal peace treaty could be negotiated with Turkey, and the French were determined to make sure that they took every step necessary to protect their national interests. Lloyd George would have been wise to see this little spat as an indication of things to come.

Despite the falling-out between Allies, the armistice was finally signed on 30 October. Under its terms, the Turks agreed to an Allied occupation of the Dardanelles and Bosphorus forts, of the railway tunnels constructed by the Germans in the Taurus Mountains, and of 'any strategic points in the event of a situation arising which threatens the security of the allies' (Article 7). Furthermore, the Turks were to surrender all the Turkish garrisons remaining in the Arab provinces including Mesopotamia, Syria and Hejaz, and their evacuation of Cilicia and Transcaucasia (Articles 16 and 17). For their part, the British undertook not to seize Constantinople itself, nor to interfere in Turkey's internal affairs unless the government indicated that they were unable to maintain order. In their expediency to conclude the armistice, however, little enough care was taken in the wording of the text, which in British diplomat Harold Nicolson's opinion was 'breezy, haphazard and optmistic'.[32] It was to prove a huge problem for those who followed and attempted to interpret and invoke its clauses. This issue would be further exacerbated when other nations became involved in the wider discussions to decide the long-term fate of Turkey.

The Allies first had to establish their credentials before the new order could be imposed, and on 10 November *Daily Mail* correspondent G. Ward Price recorded the momentous occasion of the Allied armada's entry into Constantinople as conquerors:

> We rounded the point of the old Seraglio and entered the Golden Horn ... there was no demonstration of any kind ... but as we drew near to the quay one saw that the houses and windows were thronged with people ...
>
> A German officer stood on the quay close to where the destroyer gradually came alongside ... [he] affected indifference and yawned with care from time to time. A little group of German soldiers and sailors gradually formed behind him as if for mutual support ... For years they had been the self-ordained military gods of this place, but now their altars are overthrown and they see Turkish naval officers of high rank hurrying past them to pay respects to the representative of the nation they once thought they could despise ...[33]

Whatever posture the Germans and their Austrian allies sought to convey, they saw that the game was up and decided to hasten their departure, leaving for Haydarpasa, a suburb of Constantinople on the Asiatic shore, there to await repatriation. Their four-year residence was ended, and in its wake had come occupiers cut from a different cloth.

Similar scenes were repeated elsewhere as the Allies set about occupying strategic points throughout the country. On 9 November, British war correspondent H. Collinson Owen recorded the British occupation of the Gallipoli peninsula. This barren place which had defied countless Allied efforts to capture it, and was paid for with the blood of thousands of British, ANZAC and French troops, was now theirs for the taking without a shot being fired:

> We went ashore at Chanak and walked to Hamidich battery ... which is the strongest on the strait. At Chanak were Turks aplenty, both soldiers and otherwise ... The population appeared pleased to see a group of British officers walking about, glad that the war for them was over.[34]

Before very long there would be some 40,000 British troops alone around Constantinople and the Straits costing – much to Winston Churchill's dismay – some £50,000 a day. Whilst such scenes of occupation took place throughout his homeland, Mustapha was in Syria, secretly removing into the Anatolian interior as many men, stores and supplies as he could. The news of the armistice made very disturbing reading for the general, who very much shared Harold Nicolson's appraisal, advising Izzet Pasha on 8 November:

> The armistice, in the final form in which it has been concluded, does not secure the well-being and integrity of the Ottoman Empire ... Eventually they will seek the right to control our army, and even to choose the ministers of our Cabinet ... it is necessary for the state to decide the exact limit of the sacrifice that it is prepared to make.[35]

Mustapha had already had altercations with the British over the use of Alexandretta, or Iskenderun, on the Syrian littoral, where there was disagreement over rights of access and other serious issues. As he indicated in his note to Enver, these issues were made no easier to resolve by the vagueness of the armistice. He sensed that worse was to come if they did not put up a stand, but the Ottoman government, keen not to upset the Allies so early on, overruled him. Angry at what he rightly sensed was the almost complete capitulation of the government to the will of the Allies, he made his way back to Constantinople in disgust.

He arrived in the city on 13 November to find the flags and ensigns of over fifty Allied warships at anchor in the harbour. Looking out across the anchorage at this testament to the final prostration of his country, he is reported to have commented quietly, but with prophetic determination, 'As they have come, so shall they go.'[36] As far as he was concerned, the jihad was far from over.

For the time being, however, the Allies were there, and it looked like they were there to stay as they sat down to divide the spoils.

3

IN THE EVENT OF A TOTAL OR PARTIAL PARTITION OF TURKEY

As we have seen, when the first peace feelers went out to the Allies, the Ottoman government hoped that an honourable and lasting peace could be achieved within the tenets of President Woodrow Wilson's Fourteen Points and Lloyd George's War Aims. On the face of it, it ought not to have been difficult for the aspirations of the Turkish government to fit neatly with the assurances of both Wilson and Lloyd George, but it was not to be as straightforward as that.

So many contradictory offers and promises had been made to so many interested parties, either to bring them into the war against the Central Powers or to keep them acquiescent in its prosecution, and these were to clash with any notions that the Turks might have for their future. Most critical were the conflicting promises the Allies had made to one another, the disparate tribes of Arabia and to Italy and Greece, which as Arthur Balfour the Foreign Secretary lamented in March 1919 were 'not consistent with each other ... [as] each can be quoted by Frenchmen, Englishmen, Americans and Arabs when it happens to suit their purpose',[1] which is precisely what emerged.

Furthermore, Turkey was seen not as a problem in itself that required a resolution, but instead as the instrument through which other issues arising from the German settlement might be resolved through territorial incentives.[2] Little thought had been given to the possibility that the Turks themselves might resist being exploited in this manner, and the consequences of this oversight would prove disastrous for the Allies.

The first of these inducements was the Treaty of London, signed on 26 April 1915. Essentially a bribe of cosmic proportions designed to bring Italy into the war on the Allied side, it made what in retrospect were ridiculous assurances. It was also so 'unscientifically worded'[3] that it was to prove to be the root cause of many of the problems outlined by Balfour. In addition to a loan of £50 million, it confirmed Italian occupation of the Dodecanese Islands, and also promised Trieste, Dalmatia, Istria and parts of the Tyrol, and, most generously of all, Article 9 undertook that 'in the event of the total or partial partition of Turkey in Asia, she [Italy] ought to obtain a just share of the Mediterranean region adjacent to the province of Adalia', a vast swathe of hinterland intruding north into southern Anatolia. Nor did Allied largesse end there. Article 13 promised that 'in the event of France and Great Britain increasing their colonial territories in Africa at the expense of Germany, those two Powers agree in principle that Italy may claim some equitable compensation',[4] which would be specified 'at the proper time'.[5]

Anxious to make that proper time sooner rather than later, the Italian Foreign Minister Sidney Sonnino cajoled the Allies into convening another meeting at the small village of St Jean de Maurienne, on the Italian–French border in April 1917. Here the terms of the Treaty of London were reaffirmed, and Italy was also promised 70,000 square miles around Smyrna[6] and Konya in Western Anatolia in addition to the area around Adalia that had already been promised. The same month Balfour had written to the Italian ambassador extolling the benefits to be had from Italian acquisition of this prime real estate. The vast lands of south-west Anatolia, he enthused, would be the perfect place to settle her 'surplus population', where they would find 'a soil and a climate admirably suited to its needs'. 'I should rejoice,' he continued, 'that a united Italy should bear a great share in restoring to civilisation the neighbouring lands which the Turk has so long laid waste.'[7] Thus, with such 'equitable compensation' at the top of their agenda, the Italian delegation to the Peace Conference in Versailles led by Prime Minister Orlando and Sonnino, was determined to have their fair share of any plunder.

The Italians were backed by a domestic agenda fuelled by the outrageous promises contained within these treaties, but there is little doubt that from her point of view Italy had a sizeable debt to call in. Italy had originally been a member of the Triple Alliance with Germany and Austria-Hungary, but got cold feet when the war broke out in 1914, at which point the government deemed it prudent to bide its time and see how the war developed. Finally deciding to enter the conflict in 1915, following the Treaty of London, her unprepared and woefully ill-equipped armed forces were to face a severe test of their martial prowess. She was to suffer casualties of some 615,000 men fighting the Central Powers for three years along the mountainous northern border in the south Tyrol and along the Isonzo River, pinning down several German and Austro-Hungarian divisions which might have otherwise achieved a decision on other fronts. Thousands of men perished trying to defend, capture or recapture jagged, ice-capped peaks, and place names like Caporetto and Vittorio Veneto were to become shrines to the heroism and sacrifice of the fighting men whose sufferings entered into national folklore. For the Italians, therefore, the position was clear. They had kept their side of the bargain, and now it was for the British and French to stick to theirs whatever the cost. But there was one more ingredient to be factored in: the almost limitless territorial claims to be demanded by another loyal ally, Greece, most of which directly clashed with those of Italy.

Their champion was her tireless Prime Minister, Eleutherios Venizelos. He would bound into the Peace Conference in Paris bearing a schoolmasterly air, with his grey goatee beard and wearing a 'square skull cap of black silk',[8] and persuade the Allies to make manifest his country's long-cherished dreamed of an Anatolian empire. As Harold Nicolson – now one of Lloyd George's advisers at the conference – put it, 'never has there been a more tragic illusion'.[9]

Born in Canea in the Turkish island province of Crete in 1864, he grew up to become a leading light in the island's independence movement. Indeed, his family's ambitions had been made clear from his youth. Young Eleutherios, or 'Liberator', was destined to assume the mantle carried so heroically by three uncles in their struggles against Turkish rule. He eagerly embraced the vision of a resurgent Greece, the 'Megale Idea', rekindling her glorious past at the expense of the hated Turk, a dream that became more and more feasible as the Ottoman Empire atrophied and shrank. He went so far as to draw out an imaginary boundary of his New Greek Empire, stretching from Albania well into the Anatolian Plain, and when he was appointed President of Crete's island assembly he seized the opportunity to make it a reality and pushed for union with Greece. His political career continued to progress until he became Prime Minister in 1910, presiding over a programme of constitutional, social and military reform.[10] He was also widely credited with being the architect of the Balkan League and playing a key role in the subsequent wars that saw his country expand to include Macedonia and Western Thrace.

His potential as a useful ally was certainly appreciated by Great Britain, carefully observing the declining fortunes of Turkey in Europe and pondering the inevitable consequences should the empire suddenly implode. In 1912, Venizelos had early meetings with senior British politicians such as Lloyd George and Winston Churchill where a number of vital topics were aired. Even then, Lloyd George courted the Greek statesman with the prospect of the Turk being expelled from Constantinople and supplanted by the Greeks in order to fill the inevitable power vacuum. Churchill was more prosaic. He mooted the idea that perhaps the Royal Navy might secure the services of a Greek port in exchange for Cyprus, and the prospect of an entente similar to that with France was also raised.[11] Churchill even ventured to discuss the future role of a Greek navy in any future conflict in the region, suggesting that the Greek government cancel its contract for the dreadnought battleship currently under construction in a German shipyard and adopt a fleet of smaller, faster vessels instead.[12] These secret discussions were the kernel of Venizelos' delusive belief in future British support for his designs in the region, but it would be another two years before the prospect of an alliance against the Turks arose again, with the outbreak of the First World War.

Encouraged by his military success in the Balkans, and flattered by British overtures in 1912, he was to play a pivotal role in pushing for Greek entry into the First World War, confident that being on the winning side promised even richer plunder. Standing in his way, however, was King Constantine, who favoured neutrality to nailing his country's colours to the Allied mast. His stance was suspect enough as far as the Allies were concerned, but his marriage to a German princess, the Kaiser's sister, also led to strong suspicions of a pro-German bias that further rankled with the British. Nevertheless, despite royal disapproval, secret discussions were held as early as 1915, in which the then British Foreign Secretary, Sir Edward Grey, offered Greece 'important territorial concessions on the coast of Asia Minor' including Smyrna and Aidin,[13] appealing to the Prime Minister but leaving the king unmoved, even when Cyprus was again offered as a further inducement. Constantine obdurately favoured neutrality, and found support among politicians who believed that at best the war would end in a stalemate and probably more likely outright German success. Furthermore, influential general Ioannis Metaxas believed that Greek participation in the war could only bring disaster[14] and questioned the practicality of attempting a colonisation of Anatolia even should the British fulfil their promise. He cited in particular Anatolia's hostile landscape, rimmed with mountains that could conceal an enemy perfectly placed to impede the progress of an invading army, employing guerrilla tactics to outflank and slowly wear it down. His evaluation was in fact to prove perfectly prescient in the face of subsequent events, but Venizelos rejected such arguments. Instead, he trenchantly assured Constantine that on the contrary, 'with the complete dissolution of the Ottoman state, our Muslim subjects will be excellent and law-abiding citizens',[15] a bold assertion that nevertheless failed to sway the king. With friendly diplomacy falling on deaf ears, the Allies resorted to more underhand and duplicitous means, gradually tightening the noose around Constantine and his supporters, whilst simultaneously cultivating its Prime Minister.

When in March 1915, the king again refused Venizelos permission for a division of troops to participate in the Gallipoli campaign, he was forced to resign in frustration. He was succeeded by Dimitrios Gounaris, who was more content to toe the royal line and continued to resist Allied overtures and pursue a neutral policy. The political situation faced a stalemate, but then Venizelos saw a chance for another change in his fortunes when elections were called.

Venizelos was returned to power in June, but his efforts to join the war remained thwarted. Then on 22 September he was presented with a *casus belli* when Bulgaria attacked Serbia and pushed her retreating army all the way to Corfu, prompting Venizelos to urge the invoking of the Greco-Serbian Treaty of 1913. He mobilised the Greek army and asked the Allies for help. Constantine objected to this but not before the Allies landed at Salonika in time to stem the Bulgarian advance. Venizelos henceforth acquiesced to further Allied encroachments, culminating in the forming of the National Defence Movement in Salonika in August 1916, in effect an entirely separate, pro-Allied administration.

His 'government-in-exile' dissociated itself from the royalist regime in Athens and proceeded to establish an Allied-backed 'Provisional Government' which was finally to bring Greece into the war. It was also to drive deep schisms between the two factions. In June, Venizelos returned to Athens and Constantine was compelled to 'resign the throne'[16] and effectively retire to Switzerland in favour of his son Alexander, chosen because he was considered easier to manage than his elder sibling George, who was next in line of succession. Venizelos then proceeded to purge the government of royalists and in doing so drove an even deeper wedge between himself and his opponents, storing up serious trouble for the future.

Meanwhile, the Greek forces proved to be useful allies. In May 1918 they fought in Macedonia and Serbia, and participated in the spectacularly successful Vardar Offensive of September 1918, which ultimately led to the collapse of Bulgaria. Greek martial prowess was particularly highlighted for praise by the French commander-in-chief, Franchet d'Esperay. Victorious Greek forces, basking in the glow of their success in the Balkans, crowned their triumph with their participation in the Allied parade through Constantinople. Her warships added insult to injury when they joined the naval flotilla that moored in the shadow of the Sultan's palace. Revelling in the plaudits of many of his countrymen and having won the respect of his Entente partners, Venizelos saw this as an auspicious time to settle his claim. He knew, too, that such were the schisms in his country, and such were the high expectations brought about by the costly war, that he had no alternative but to return laden with the 'fruits of victory'.[17] Consequently, on 3 February 1919, he set his case before the British, French and Americans. In his opening argument he condemned Turkey's track record in its governance of the region, stating:

> The Turks are good workers, honest in their relations, and a good people as subjects. But as rulers they are unsupportable and a disgrace to civilisation, as is proved by their having exterminated over a million Armenians and 300,000 Greeks during the last four years.[18]

It was time, he argued, for Greece to reclaim sovereignty over great swathes of Ottoman land, stretching from the southern region of Albania (or Northern Epirus), Thrace, and all of Asia Minor from halfway along the southern shore of the Sea of Marmara almost 400 miles down to the city of Smyrna. If this was conceded, Greece would inherit not only extensive territory, but 1,720,000 people, increasing the national population to over 6,600,000 as compared to 2,760,000 just eight years before. Venizelos was at the top of his game, and used his consummate charm and personality to persuade and sway his distinguished audience, but employed somewhat dubious statistics to back up the provenance of his claims. He argued, for example, that the total Greek population in Western Anatolia was at least 1,080,000, while in the same territory the Turkish population was only 943,000. These figures were naturally challenged by the Turks, who had their own sets of statistics based on census data from 1910, but it was not they who had the ear of the 'Big Four'; it was the diminutive and personable Greek.

His charisma was undeniable. One observer remarked how 'in asking, he always had the air of offering, and in obtaining he appeared to be conceding something'.[19] He would not have been out of place as a TV evangelist, citing time and again President Wilson's own aspirations, enshrined in the very same Fourteen Points to which the Turks were looking for their own salvation. The subsequent atmosphere he created was, as Harold Nicolson described it, 'a strange medley of charm, brigandage, *weltpolitik*, patriotism and courage'.[20] Indeed, less articulate and persuasive members of the other national delegations observed him with some antipathy if not jealousy. One in particular is reported to have remarked how 'every time Venizelos sees Wilson the map of Europe is changed'.[21]

At the very heart of Greek aspirations was the bustling city port of Smyrna, with its population of 300,000, of whom around half were of Greek descent, outnumbering the Turks by about two to one. Izmir to the Turks, this ancient city alone had very compelling historical and ethnographical Greek credentials going back millennia.

It was named by the Ionian Greeks, who invaded around 1050–955 BC in the wake of the collapse of the Mycenaean civilization. By the 700s BC an Ionian League had been formed from the twelve states that had been established along the coast of Asia Minor. Homer lived and composed in Ionia around 750 BC, and in the 500s the grandest of the Greek temples were built at Ephesus, Samos and Didyma, giving birth to the Ionic order of architecture.

The non-Greek kingdom of Lydia warred frequently with the neighbouring Ionians, and under their King Croesus finally conquered them. Then, in 546 BC, the Persians under Cyrus seized Croesus's kingdom and Ionia became a tribute-paying part of the Persian Empire. In 479 BC a force of Greeks from the mainland invaded, defeating the Persians and liberating Ionia. The Delian League was established in 478 BC, but by 413 BC many of the states had defected to Sparta, and then in 404 BC, after the defeat of Athens, Sparta handed Ionia back to the tender mercies of the Persians.

Smyrna disappeared from the scene for the next 300 years or so, until it was reconstituted in the reign of Alexander the Great in the fourth century BC. It then reclaimed its key position in the Aegean as a leading element of Rome's Asian provinces renowned for its beauty and culture and as an early centre of Christianity. When the Byzantine period arrived, Smyrna became the capital of the province of Samos. Early in the fourteenth century her fortunes changed again, when the Turks occupied the city. It became a prize to be seized in turn by the

Crusaders sponsored by Pope Clement VI and then Tamerlane, before finally being incorporated into the Ottoman Empire in 1425. It would be 500 years before a Greek could again – albeit briefly – call Smyrna his own.

In the course of all these tumultuous ups and downs, and especially during the lengthy period as a 'Turkish' city, Smyrna and its hinterland retained much of its Greek character. Indeed, along with a number of other cultural and ethnic colonisations, the Greek presence remained relatively constant over the years until, by 1918, there existed a bustling cosmopolitan and multicultural city, thriving on and enjoying its reputation as the region's centre for business, trade and commerce.

George Horton, US Consul in Smyrna, had served in this area of the world in the US Diplomatic Corps for thirty years, and he later provided a fascinating insight in his work *The Blight of Asia*, describing the city as it stood at the end of the First World War:

> The harbor of Smyrna is one of the best in the world, comparable to that of Vancouver ... in which the largest sea-going craft can anchor. Smyrna has attained great importance in late years as a commercial port. While other harbors, especially that of its' ancient rival Ephesus, have been filled by deposits brought down by the rivers, that of Smyrna has not suffered the same fate, the silt of the delta of the Hermus having tended only to narrow its mouth.
>
> The principal promenade was the quay, on which were located the American theater, the prettiest building of its kind in the Ottoman Empire, many cinemas, the best hotels, various modern and well-constructed office buildings, besides the residences of the most prosperous merchants, among whom were Greeks, Armenians and Dutch. ... The principal business thoroughfare of Smyrna was the Rue Franque, on which were situated the great department and wholesale stores of the Greeks, Armenians and Levantines. At the shopping hour in the afternoon, this street was so crowded that one moved through it with difficulty, and among the motley throng ladies in costumes of the latest

fashion, looking for that sort of merchandise that ladies shop for everywhere formed a large part.

Social life presented many attractions. Teas, dances, musical afternoons and evenings were given in the luxurious salons of the rich Armenians and Greeks. ... In no city in the world did East and West mingle physically in so spectacular a manner as at Smyrna, while spiritually they always maintained the characteristics of oil and water ...

One of the chief institutions of Smyrna about which naval men always inquire, was the 'Politakia', or orchestras of stringed instruments, guitars, mandolins and zither. The players added great zest to the performance by singing to their own accompaniment native songs and improvisations. The various companies gave nightly concerts in the principal cafes and were often called upon for entertainments in private houses ...

Horton particularly described the extensive American commercial presence in the city, which included the Standard Oil Company, the McAndrews & Forbes Liquorice Factory 'with its spacious offices and thousands of employees and laborers', plus tobacco, figs, raisins and carpet exporters. The Americans had also established a number of educational and humanitarian institutions, including orphanages, schools and religious foundations for the benefit of the local population, and American missionaries were very active in spreading the Christian Gospel. It was a prize to be valued and sought by Greek and Turk alike.

Venizelos may have been able to make his aspirations seem like simple logic, but they clashed with many other promises, assurances and undertakings. Greek designs on Albania clashed with Serbian, Montenegrin and Italian demands, aspirations towards a slice of Western Anatolia were at odds with Italian ambitions for a protectorate, and the dream of taking Constantinople not only clashed with Russian plans[22] but were mired in controversy regarding the fate of the Sultan and the Caliphate.

However, in addition to his articulate presentation skills and powers of oratory, Venizelos enjoyed another advantage over his competitors: Grey regarded him more highly 'than any other statesman in Europe',[23] as he flattered Wilson and Lloyd George with homilies such as how he perfected his English by reading copies of *The Times* whilst a partisan on Crete.[24] Some key figures in the Supreme Council, among them President Clemenceau of France, extolled the virtues and civilising qualities of Ancient Greece. These sentiments were echoed elsewhere, and many august organs such as *The Daily Telegraph* took the opportunity to explain how Greece stood as the natural inheritor to the former Ottoman Empire.[25] Venizelos was also supported in his endeavours by the sterling efforts of Greek clubs and benefactors who spread the gospel throughout Europe by raising money, sponsoring lectures and distributing maps and pamphlets which proved Greece's ethnographical rights to Turkish lands. Even Rudyard Kipling, the eminent British author and poet, was recruited, translating the Greek national anthem into English. The concept of a renascent Greece, spreading its culture and civilising influence throughout much at least of Asia Minor, seemed to enjoy a broad appeal, whilst Italy's claims by contrast could be represented as little more than a craven lust for more territory. Thus as Britain's ambassador to France, Lord Hardinge, observed, while Venizelos was able to call upon historical and ethnographic justifications for the territory he was asking for, the Italians just seemed to be 'voracious' and after anything they could get their hands on, regardless of its provenance. Eyre Crowe, Permanent Under-Secretary of State at the Foreign Office, called Smyrna in particular 'almost purely Greek, highly civilised and flourishing', whilst Harold Nicolson insisted that 'economically it [Greek occupation of Anatolia] is defensible on the grounds that the Turks have not shown any aptitude or inclination to control their own commerce'.[26] Such positive feedback prompted Venizelos to report confidently to his deputy in Greece, Emmanuel Repoulis, that 'we shall be given Smyrna ... with a corresponding hinterland ... also Cyprus and the Dodecanese'.[27]

Even so, by no means was everyone convinced by Greek motivations. As early as 1917, the then French Prime Minister, Aristide Briand, had expressed concern at just how far the Greek politician was prepared to go to achieve his ambitions:

> I fear that Venizelos may have very long teeth when peace negotiations open. He has not renounced his dream to recreate the Byzantine Empire ... Now, a large-scale expansion of Greece would be a threat to the peace of the world. I have for a long time desired the cooperation of the Greeks but not under these conditions.[28]

Briand was not alone in his reservations. British businessman Herbert Whittal, who lived in Smyrna, warned:

> Unfortunately ... they all join their idea of liberty with the idea of becoming masters where they were servants of the Turks, and proclaiming and enforcing the fact by trampling upon their former masters.[29]

Admiral Calthorpe endorsed Mr Whittal's observations, and expressed his fear that Greek occupation would only result in 'exploitation and tyranny' being heaped upon the Turkish population, while Sir Henry Wilson, Chief of the Imperial General Staff, worried that any foreign occupation, and particularly one by Greece, would inevitably provoke 'an organised attempt by the Turks to reconquer this territory' and plunge the region into years of conflict. Furthermore, by no means everyone was even convinced by Venizelos' claims of Greek ethnographic legitimacy. American statistics strongly suggested that Greeks might have a majority in Smyrna, but did not concur that their claims to Eastern Thrace were as valid. This caution led Harold Nicolson to consider Greek claims in greater detail, and in April he would submit his own solution. In it he proposed that the Turks be left in Anatolia and that the Greeks be permitted to take possession of European Turkey, while the Straits were placed under an Allied Commission, as any of the more grandiose solutions would simply store up trouble for the future.

Such newly acquired but nevertheless prudently articulated wisdom went largely unheeded. The great powers continued to wheel and deal in the heady atmosphere of the Hall of Mirrors in Versailles, and appeared to think that they could rearrange the world's frontiers like the furniture in their own drawing rooms. Venizelos, however, was not prepared to sit back and simply await the outcome of their deliberations, and in the Pontus region of Northern Anatolia and Constantinople Greek minorities were being actively encouraged to engage in guerrilla activity against the Turks. Many had already been active for over a decade,[30] and it could have done their cause little harm for the Turks to be seen as repressive and hostile to legitimate Greek desires for autonomy and self-determination. Meanwhile, Venizelos pursued his charm offensive with even greater vigour.

One man in particular who had long been beguiled by the Greek advocate was the equally charismatic and influential David Lloyd George. Born in Manchester in 1863, he trained as a barrister; his gift for oratory brought him into politics, and eventually he stood for Parliament as a Liberal in 1890. In 1908 he was appointed to the post of Chancellor of the Exchequer. He used this opportunity to promote social provision for the working classes, for whom his Liberal philosophy had given him strong sympathies. His moment came in the First World War, when he proved to be one of the most energetic and determined members of the War Cabinet, revolutionising everything from munitions production to labour relations. When he became Secretary of State for War in July 1916, and with the slaughter on the Somme still in the back of his mind, he did all in his power to move the main weight of Allied operations away from the Western front to the Balkans and the Middle East. In December 1916, the ineffective Herbert Asquith was finally ousted from the premiership and succeeded by Lloyd George. He used his authority to change the manner in which the war was prosecuted, insisting upon the adoption of the convoy system to reduce maritime losses, and pushing for a single unified command of all Allied forces on the Western Front. Nearly sixty years of age when the war ended, he emerged with his political achievements lauded and his personal popularity greatly enhanced.

His willingness to embrace the aspirations of the Greek Prime Minister was consistent with his individual style; he judged him as a man with whom he could do business. Indeed, his opinion of him had not changed since their secret collusions in 1912, and he is reported as going so far as to extol him as 'the greatest statesman Greece has thrown up since the days of Pericles'.[31] Whether he was entirely taken in by the enthralling Greek or not is debatable, for there was clearly a hidden agenda behind Lloyd George's public expressions of support. He hoped that the Straits could be held in trust by the Greeks, a pro-British surrogate, with Britain standing as absentee guarantor. A dominant Greek presence in Anatolia, the Aegean and Thrace would achieve these objectives whilst also appearing to meet the Greeks' own legitimate territorial aspirations.[32] Lloyd George's secretary Frances Stevenson summarised the appeal: 'a New Greek empire will be founded friendly to Britain, and it will help all our interests in the East. He [Lloyd George] is convinced he is right over this, and is willing to stake everything on it.'[33] It was to prove a tragically expensive gamble to make.

As we have seen, the Italians by comparison would prove woefully unequal to the challenging task of negotiating their new empire in Anatolia. In response to Venizelos' breathless round of lobbying and engaging flattery, all the Italian delegation seemed to do was irritate and alienate their audience – especially the crucial President Wilson, who found them particularly pompous and opinionated, and their ambitions were considered a menace to peace. In fact, Balfour went so far as to comment that their foreign policy 'almost suggests the idea that she thinks it better to have enemies rather than friends',[34] while Sir Horace Rumbold, Britain's High Commissioner in Constantinople, believed that they were more fit 'to sell ice cream than fight a war'.[35]

It became clear even to these obtuse delegates that they were fighting a losing battle. Even their efforts to secure a protectorate over Albania fell on stony ground when the recently created Kingdom of Serbs, Croats and Slovenes objected to sharing a border with Italy. Her endeavours were further stymied when the conference gave the tiny mountain kingdom its independence. Feeble attempts to claim the city of Fiume based on ethnographic grounds also met with a wall of indifference from the Allies, especially Wilson, who was by this time exasperated by such blatant demonstrations of territorial aggrandisement. In the end the only way the Allies could come to an arrangement was to cede Italy some of their own colonial territory; as British Colonial Secretary Lord Milner succinctly put it, 'Italy will have to be satisfied with what France and Great Britain are prepared to give up.'[36] Nor was she to see any of the vast former German territories come her way, the British having agreed to share Cameroon with France and abandon claims to Togo in return for the mandate over Tanganyika. German South-West Africa was to elude her as well: it was awarded to the Union of South Africa. Instead, she was later offered an extension of Italian Somaliland south to the Juba River, territory previously part of British East Africa (Kenya), and Libya's rather vague and chaotic borders were expanded and rationalised at the expense of Egypt and French deserts of Algeria. The 'equitable compensation' she had been promised fell far short of Italian expectations.

Their delegation was in despair. The deal on offer was a mere fraction of the lavish offers made to bring them into the war, and they stared instead at a few miserable crumbs whilst the Greeks, British and French prepared to walk away with the lion's share of the cake. They walked out of the peace conference in disgust on 24 April, and would not return until 5 May. The hiatus this created played right into Venizelos' hands and made it even easier for him to push his case. When reports that the Italians were taking matters into their own hands and landing troops at Adalia were received on 6 May, followed by news that Italian warships were steaming to Smyrna supported by columns advancing up the coast, alarm bells sounded in Paris.

Venizelos seized on this to claim that Italy was doing a secret deal with the Turks, attempting to act unilaterally and present the Allies with a fait accompli. In addition, reports were being received of civil disorder among the Turks and attacks on Greek minorities with the connivance of local Turkish officials,[37] while rumours were circulated of outrages on Rhodes and attempts by the Italian government to incite the Bulgarians to attack their neighbours. Venizelos managed to convince the British, French and particularly the suspicious

Americans that urgent steps needed to be taken to forestall the Italians. On 5 May Lloyd George proposed that the Greeks should be allowed to occupy the city because 'their compatriots are actually being massacred at the present time and there is no one to help them'.[38] They met again the following day to discuss the escalating situation, and Lloyd George summoned Venizelos to advise him that 'President Wilson, M Clemenceau and I decided today that you should occupy Smyrna'.[39]

It was a decision that horrified the military experts. Henry Wilson condemned it as 'mad and bad',[40] asking Lloyd George if he realised that the occupation would start another war. In spite of dire warnings from Metaxas, who again warned that such an adventure was wild folly that could only end in disaster, the Greek leader leapt at the offer. He immediately telegraphed the Greek High Commissioner in Constantinople and jubilantly informed him to

> kindly inform very confidentially the French High Commissioner that I was advised today by the ministers of England and France, and by the President of the United States, that they had resolved among themselves immediately to occupy Smyrna by the Greek army.[41]

Lloyd George had some stern words of caution for the Greek, however. He realised he was taking a risk that was far from universally welcomed by his colleagues. If the Greeks were to be charged with this weighty task, then they would have to do it effectively. If they succeeded, then perhaps even more laurels might come their way. When they dined on 9 May he insisted that the Greeks 'must be as powerful as possible in the military sense', adding that if the plan succeeded he could see 'Constantinople coming under Greek sovereignty in the fullness of time'.[42] Thus fortified by what he saw as an irrefutable expression of solid British backing, Venizelos proceeded with the plan. Although the Americans and French soon had second thoughts, the die was cast and 15 May was set for the city's occupation.

Greek troops departed from the port of Eleftheron on 13 May, and anchored off the island of Lesbos the following evening. Admiral

Calthorpe had earlier informed Ali Nadir Pasha, commander of the Turkish forces in Smyrna, that the fortified positions of the port were to be occupied by Allied troops in accordance with the Armistice terms, but understandably declined to advise him that these troops were to be Greek.

The small flotilla of seven ships then continued on its passage to Smyrna, escorted by British, French and Greek warships, and at 11.00 a.m. on 15 May the first contingents were disembarked. They were to be greeted by a population verging on hysteria, thousands of whom lined the port sides screaming and waving Greek flags. Finally, after hundreds of years under Turkish rule, they were to achieve Enosis with the homeland, which just a year before would have appeared a complete pipedream.

The city streets were decorated with flags flanked by cheering ethnic Greeks crying 'Long Live Venizelos' as the liberators marched as conquering heroes, dressed in the traditional Evzone garb of pleated skirt and boots with bobbles. Greek naval commander Mavroudes wasted no time in asserting the credentials of the new regime and assembled Metropolitan Chrysostomos and his clergy together with other local dignitaries while he read out a proclamation on behalf of Venizelos in which he announced:

> The time has come. Hellas was called by the Peace Conference to occupy Smyrna so as to safeguard public order. Our fellow Greeks understand that this decision was taken because the leaders of the Conference have decided the Union of Smyrna with Greece. Myself, having remained enslaved under the same yoke until the Balkan Wars, I understand well what feelings of joy overwhelm today the souls of Greeks in Asia Minor ... let the expression of joy be combined with expressions of brotherly feelings towards other [*sic*] populace. Let them understand too that we are not celebrating the abolition of one yoke, in order to substitute it with our own prevalence against others. But, that Hellenic freedom will bring to everybody, regardless of race and religion, equality and justice ... [43]

The Turks looked on in horror. George Horton likened their reaction to what 'the white citizens of Mobil [Texas]' would feel if they were 'given over to a mandate of Negro troops'. Tensions in the highly charged atmosphere quickly deteriorated. First the Turks experienced minor isolated incidents of intimidation, with men having their fezzes knocked from their heads and trampled on,[44] but this soon escalated into more sinister treatment. City businessman and long-term Smyrna resident Donald Whittal observed how 'the Turks were made to go through no end of humiliation and received a good deal of knocking about',[45] while the captain of HMS *Adventure* saw a Turkish officer hit on the head with the butt of a rifle for simply marching out of step.[46] Suddenly, perhaps inevitably considering the heightened tension, a shot was heard somewhere near or in the army barracks. No one could be sure if it was deliberate or just an accidental discharge, although the commander of a US warship in the harbour, Captain Drayton, was sure a Turk had fired it,[47] but it was enough to set off a disastrous chain of events. Turkish troops spilled out into the streets to be met by hostile crowds where they were pushed, shoved and jostled until finally there was pandemonium and the vengeful Greeks fell upon their erstwhile masters. Horton later described how, in one instance,

> The Greeks took a number of prisoners whom they marched down the quay in the sight of the Allied and American battleships, making them hold up their hands. They are said to have stabbed several of their prisoners with bayonets in sight of the people in the houses and on the ships.

Such scenes were alleged to have been repeated all over the city. The bloodshed finally ended with about 500 Turks lying dead in the streets, and with many more injured. British sailors on board warships in the harbour itself observed corpses floating past in the water,[48] while buildings had been looted and set alight. All over Smyrna and its outlying villages, Greeks seized the opportunity to avenge, as George Horton described it, the 'unforgettable insults and injuries smouldering in their hearts' in a slaughter that would be avenged with interest when the tables were turned three bloody years later. In one example he noted how 'a certain powerful Turk [who] had made free with several Christian girls' was hunted down by their male relatives and summarily hanged.

As reports of atrocities poured in from numerous outlying towns and villages to horrified politicians, demands that the Greeks stop their excesses reverberated around Versailles. In a classic understatement, one of Venizelos' lieutenants confessed that 'I could not have imagined a more unfortunate execution of the Greek occupation',[49] while the Italians protested that it demonstrated beyond doubt that the Greeks were incapable of carrying out a peaceful occupation, the disastrous outcome of which had vindicated their own actions. For the American general James G. Harbord, already fearful of the ongoing accomplished slaughter of the Armenians, the Greek outrages signalled terrible revenge to come, commenting how 'the events in Smyrna have undoubtedly cheapened every Christian life in Turkey'.[50]

A Commission of Enquiry was established, and when it reported back substantiated the rumours and reports. In addition to attacks on ethnic Turks, the Greeks were also accused of assaulting local Jews and of burning synagogues, as well as large-scale looting and extortion. No doubt apocryphal reports and exaggerations were mixed in with genuine accounts, but it left a very bitter taste in the mouths of those who sanctioned the Greek occupation, although the Greek command did try to recompense the victims and afterwards tried over fifty of the looters. Venizelos hastily summoned his close colleague Aristeidis Stergiadis to serve as High Commissioner and ensure that his promise of equal treatment before the law was honoured. However, even this trusted stalwart could do little, and found himself in despair at his powerlessness to stem the killing, while his aloof persona did little to curry favour with either the Greek or Turkish inhabitants. However, driven by public opinion at home and the need to fulfil the expectations he had raised, he knew he had no alternative but to make the best of it.

Reaction to the incidents in the port did not take long to percolate through Turkey. A young Turkish soldier is reported to have said to a British official in Smyrna, 'We may appear to be sleeping but we shall wake up ... we are not dead. There will be trouble. We may die but others may die too.'[51] His council of despair was replicated much further afield. Hundreds of protest meetings were held all over the country, and in the capital itself some 200,000 people gathered to express their disgust while outraged citizens marched through the streets carrying star-and-crescent banners and declaring the birth of a new Turkey.[52] The Sultan is reported to have almost collapsed in tears when he heard the news, his melancholy reflected in a letter of protest sent by the Sheik-ul-Islam condemning the outrages. He asserted that this occupation of Turkish soil by Greece was in clear breach of promises made at Mudros the year before, adding that 'the Council was not without responsibility, seeing that it had sent the Greeks to Izmir'.[53]

When news filtered back to the capital that bands of brigands and deserters were now running amok throughout Anatolia, the Allies feared that the Ottoman government was losing its grip. The Greek landings at Smyrna had indeed set off a powder keg of emotion and anger among a previously moribund and submissive population. Fearful of how far matters could deteriorate, and sensing that the Turkish government was unable or unwilling to act, the British threatened to occupy the country completely and move against the flashpoints if the Sultan did not take decisive action to reimpose his authority. Something clearly needed to be done quickly to remove this pretext for the Allies to completely overrun his country, and he proceeded to look around for someone with the authority to restore order.

Consequently, Mustapha found himself summoned to Mehmet's presence on 16 May, where he received orders to restore royal power. He duly took his leave and made plans to assume his new post as Inspector-General of Anatolia. His official remit was therefore clear, but what were equally apparent were his own motives. When he left the Sultan's palace to take his boat, the *Bandirma*, to Samsun on the Black Sea coast, there was only one plan crystallizing in his mind: all the resources of Turkey combining to expel the despised Greeks, remove all vestiges of foreign occupation and domination, and achieve the complete liberation of the country. Furthermore, if necessary he would do this without the sanction of his Sultan or his government, and regardless of the protestations of the Allies.

4

LET US MARCH, FRIENDS!

On 19 May 1919 Mustapha landed at Samsun. It was an inauspicious start for the man later to be feted as the father of modern Turkey. Just two officers and a few local dignitaries greeted him and his staff, and his official guard of honour was a mere handful of troops. As his headquarters he chose a former hotel, for which beds and other sundries had to be salvaged from a nearby hospital. Mustapha realised that the task that he had assumed for himself was a massive challenge. He needed to ensure that he not only commanded the loyalty and commitment of the armed forces, but also the officials and local politicians, who could easily cause him problems if they so wished. Furthermore, he must galvanise the people to his cause. He also had to keep one step ahead of the British. They had already become suspicious of his motives and were starting to ask questions of the War Ministry in Constantinople. If they apprehended him before he had time to build up a following and the momentum to carry his plans through, his work would be ruined. Certainly, the British were slowly coming round to the reasons behind the despatch of Mustapha to Anatolia. On 21 May, one Captain L. H. Hurst, the British Relief Officer at Samsun, met Mustapha at Havza. He later reported to London 'with the feeling that mischief was afoot', adding, 'I am of the opinion that a definite movement against the Greeks is being organised and will be let loose as soon as it is obvious that Smyrna is irrecoverable [by diplomatic means]'.[1] The British authorities in

Constantinople began to agitate for Mustapha's return, pressure that the Sultan found very hard to resist, and Mustapha received instructions from Constantinople that he was to return to the capital. Mustapha, however, had other ideas. He employed all his energy and the telegraph network to spread the message through Anatolia, both of resistance to the Greeks, and for the message to reach the Ottoman delegation negotiating the peace treaty in Paris that the people would accept no agreement which afforded them less than absolute sovereignty behind secure borders. To underline such determination, Defence of Rights and Anti-Annexation groups were being formed across Anatolia to give greater voice to the people.[2] His entreaties were already having the desired effect, and violence was breaking out spontaneously in scattered points all along the Aegean coast where the Greeks were attempting to establish themselves. On 28 May, Greek forces had landed at Ayvalik up the coast from Smyrna, and were met with stiff resistance from a local Turkish army unit, and elsewhere the regular army, irregulars and bandits cooperated against the common enemy.

On 6 June, Captain Hurst reiterated his earlier concerns and presciently warned his bosses in Constantinople that Mustapha was 'organising a movement which is only too likely to find an outlet for its energies in massacres'.[3] On 8 June, Admiral Calthorpe warned the Foreign Office that it was clear to him that 'various army officers have left Constantinople with a view to organising opposition to the Greeks',[4] adding that 'although the military forces in and around Constantinople at the present time may be adequate to maintain order in the capital, should troubles break out, they are certainly insufficient to cope with disorders on a large scale in the interior'.[5] At the same time, Calthorpe insisted again that the Ottoman Foreign Minister relieve Mustapha Kemal of his Post,[6] in spite of the fact that he had admitted that he had neither the men nor the resources to take such affirmative action if Mustapha continued to ignore their orders.

Meanwhile, Mustafa was heading for the town of Amasya, about 50 miles south of Samsun, careful to avoid the British troops that had been stationed there to enforce the terms of the Armistice. It was here that he planned to link up with many of his wartime brothers-in-arms and political colleagues from his early days as a member of the Young Turks. He arrived at the town around the 18 June, and he proceeded to draft a circular, subsequently known as the Amasya Proclamation, which stated that the integrity of the country and the independence of the nation were in dire jeopardy and that the government in Constantinople was incapable of defending the rights of the people and was unequal to the task for which it had assumed responsibility. As a result of this only the strength and will of the nation as a whole could save it, and that a national congress would be convened to decide upon the best way to achieve this end. The proclamation was to be sent via telegraph to every military and civil organisation, with instructions to make every effort to attend the congress. For security reasons the place and time would, for the time being, be kept secret. The seizure of the telegraph offices proved a major coup, providing the nationalists with a highly reliable conduit through which to spread their message and, in controlling the medium, cutting the Constantinople government off from its own loyal servants in the provinces and preventing them from coordinating an effective counter-movement.[7] On 22 June Mustapha made the following appeal:

> Citizens of Amasya, what are you waiting for? If the enemy tries to land in Samsun, we must pull on our peasant shoes, we must withdraw to the mountains, we must defend the country to the last rock. If it is the will of God that we be defeated, we must set fire to our homes, to all our property; we must lay the country in ruins and leave an empty desert. Citizens of Amasya, let us all together swear an oath that we shall do this ...[8]

On this day, according to Ali Fuat, a close friend at the time, 'all individual and regional efforts' were diverted into showing the whole world that the nation was 'united in the struggle against the danger to the Turkish homeland',[9] while Halibe Edib, one of the country's very few female political figures and an early disciple, willingly embraced his advocacy of self-determination. She wrote later of her reaction to the call for resistance:

I hardly opened my mouth on any subject except when it concerned the sacred struggle that was to be. Turkey was to be cleared of murderers, the so-called civilising Greek armies ...[10]

Following the Amasya proclamation, the venue for the congress was revealed as the isolated town of Erzurum, where the next steps could be decided upon relatively free from the chance of the Ottoman government interfering with them. British Relief Officer J. S. Perring, who had succeeded Captain Hurst, reported from Samsun to Admiral Calthorpe on 5 July that Mustapha was on his way from Amasya to Erzurum, urging all loyal Turks to rally to his cause. Encouraged by what must have appeared to have been a spontaneous outburst of popular support, Mustapha found his declaration backed by army commanders and other sympathisers throughout Anatolia. All that remained to be done now was to harness these disparate interests, uniting them under his leadership to create one great liberation movement and to drive the Greeks out of Izmir, Thrace and the Aegean.

Shaken by his blatant but apparently effective display of dissent, the government in Constantinople urged all those loyal to the Sultanate to turn against him and his treacherous gang of mutineers. Admiral Calthorpe assured Lord Curzon – who was standing in as Foreign Secretary for the ailing Balfour – that Mustapha Kemal had been branded an outlaw, and that he intended to keep up the pressure and 'to insist on their treating him as such'.[11] If he and his small movement could be nipped in the bud, the dismantling of Turkey could proceed as planned virtually unopposed. Meanwhile, the rebel general was making his way, albeit circuitously, to Erzurum, buoyed and encouraged by the support he had been receiving for his cause. As they trudged they hummed along to an old Swedish folk song to keep their spirits up and pass the time. Eventually it would be adopted as the Nationalist *Marseillaise*, a rough translation of which ran along the following lines:

Let us march, friends!
Let our voice be heard by the earth, by the sky,
by the water,
Let the hard ground moan from the harsh tramp of our feet ...[12]

Imbued with its sentiments, the group grew daily. On 2 July Mustapha met General Kazim Karabekir, commander of the 15,000-strong 15th Army Corps, headquartered at Erzurum itself. Karebekir was one of those officers sympathetic to the cause, and against all orders he offered his services and those of his men to Mustapha, who now possessed a hard core of regular troops.

Meanwhile, with reports filtering out of the growing success of Mustapha's recruitment campaign the Allies, not to mention the Divine Porte itself, became increasingly nervous. On 9 July, Calthorpe wrote to the Grand Vizier insisting whatever 'necessary measures be at once taken concerning this officer, who has consistently defied the laws of the Turkish Government issued on my demand'.[13] The same day, with orders for his arrest issued and his dismissal from the army imminent, Mustapha decided to telegraph the War Minister, Feret Pasha, resigning his commission and thus denying the loathsome government the satisfaction of a courts martial in absentia. Now effectively an outlaw, he faced the full wrath of both Turkish and Allied governments.

Back in London, sceptics were already starting to question who would come out on top in a power struggle between the Sultan and his 'loyal subject'. C. E. S. Palmer admitted that 'he [Mustapha] will probably laugh at the Government's threats',[14] and even Calthorpe had to concede that the chances of Mustapha returning quietly to Constantinople were negligible. Nevertheless the British continued their fruitless crusade, and pursued a strategy that would ultimately end in humiliation and failure. At Erzurum on 23 July the much-vaunted congress finally convened. One of the first steps Mustapha wanted to take, and which he had previously indicated at Amasya, was to codify the new movement, clarify its aims and objectives and, most important perhaps from his point of view, establish himself as its undisputed leader. When the government in Constantinople heard of the conference, it immediately condemned it as counter to the interests of the country and the Sultan, demanding that it be abandoned and calling yet again for the arrest of Mustapha and the other ringleaders. Mustapha then suggested that the conference respond with loyal assurances to the government and the Sultan, calling for the election of a new parliament. These developments were being closely monitored, and on 27 July Calthorpe cautioned Curzon to 'take into consideration the possibility of ... the establishment of an independent and probably intensely fanatical and anti-European Government in Asia Minor, rejecting the authority of Constantinople and the sovereignty of the Sultan'.[15] Another observer, Colonel Rawlinson, met Mustapha at Erzurum, and came away with the impression that he was 'a man of great strength of character and very definite and practical views as to the rightful position of his race in the comity of nations ... he is imbued with a deep sense of duty, which causes him to place his country's interest before all others'.[16] He felt so compelled to communicate his fears and belief in the folly of British policy that he would return to London to attempt to 'awaken the British Government to the future potentialities of the Nationalist movement'.[17]

Finally, on 7 August, after long and often protracted discussions and negotiations, Mustapha was to receive official recognition as the Head of the Erzurum Congress, and here draft what would historically become known as the National Pact, the terms of which 'echoed', in Harold Nicolson's words, 'a clarion call of national honour to the average Turk'.[18]

It created a provisional government that Mustapha proposed to endorse at a national congress in Sivas two weeks later and directly contradicted the dismemberment being negotiated by the government in Constantinople. It demanded that 'the policy is inadmissible of separating for any reasons whatever from the Ottoman motherland, or one from another, the vilayet of Trebizond with the Sandjak of Janik, those vilayets known as eastern Provinces, viz, Erzurum, Sivas, Diarbekir, Mamurat el Aziz, Van Bitlis and the independent sub divisions of provinces within this area',[19] and stating unequivocally that it would 'put in action the forces of the nation; to impose the will of the nation in order to maintain the integrity of the Ottoman motherland and the independence of our nation, and to preserve the Sultanate and Caliphate', concluding that 'the government must at once invoke the National Assembly and must submit to the control of the nation all decisions concerning the destiny of the people and the country'.[20] Sensing inevitable trouble as a consequence of such rousing oratory, Constantinople yet again ordered the arrest of Mustapha and his immediate lieutenant Refet Bey's arrest. The Grand Vizier condemned Mustapha's actions as 'unconstitutional, and against the will of the Sultan'.[21]

Venizelos, however, was becoming anxious. He was convinced that every day's delay in concluding a peace treaty with the Turkish government was seriously compromising his political position as well as that of his armed forces whilst strengthening the Nationalist hand. On 27 August he wrote to Lloyd George articulating these concerns, insisting that twelve Greek divisions were now languishing in Anatolia at great expense. He could not, he insisted, keep them there indefinitely waiting to enforce a treaty that had not yet even been negotiated.[22]

While the British prevaricated, Mustapha convened the Sivas Congress, after his party arrived in the town on 2 September. He was disappointed by the patchy attendance, with just thirty-nine delegates,[23] and some areas such as those in the key Aegean provinces most directly affected by the Greek landings had no representation at all.[24] Nevertheless, even with a disappointing quorum the conference had to set to work at once to endorse the decisions taken at the Erzurum Conference and give the movement legitimacy.

The inaugural meeting was held on 4 September in a cramped old schoolroom where debates followed over the next eight days. In his opening address, Mustapha reminded the delegates that they 'had been called together at Sivas to save the nation from the present difficult situation', accusing the Allies of reneging on the original Armistice terms, and advising them how, as a result 'the Christian nationalities, encouraged and strengthened by the Allies, have commenced action against us. In Western Anatolia the Greeks have committed terrible crimes … the Armenians are spreading towards Kizil Irmak and have commenced their policy of massacres … the districts of Adana, Marash and Konia have been occupied, and this foreign occupation has penetrated to the heart of the Turkish government and to the very palace of the Sultan', concluding that 'despite all protestations, the Government has shown itself singularly incapable of dealing with the situation' and that 'the nation therefore, has been constrained to adopt an attitude of stern resistance ... in the face of the injustice of the Entente Powers and the powerlessness of our Allies, the Turkish people has risen to defend its honour and its future by force of arms'.[25] At the conclusion of his address, the delegates made the following oath:

I swear to pursue no personal interest, but to strive for the freedom of my country and the interest of the nation; I swear that I will not work for the Committee of Union and Progress or for the political programme of any party whatsoever ...[26]

One moot point, and one that invited a great deal of discussion, was the suggestion that Turkey be taken as a mandate by the United States. This step, it was held, might protect Turkey from the more avaricious designs of France and Britain, and especially Italy and Greece, and was endorsed by a number of delegates. As unlikely as it may have sounded, Mustapha had the opportunity of discussing the prospect with an American journalist, Louis E. Browne, who travelled to Sivas for the purpose, and even Lloyd George looked positively upon the idea, encouraging President Wilson to consider it, being in the eyes of the Turks the only honest broker in the region. Nevertheless, this highly unlikely prospect fell on stony ground, as the United States had never been at war with Turkey, and in any event declined subsequently to become a member of the League of Nations, the only mechanism through which a mandate could have been facilitated. Thus, another opportunity to avert the slaughter to come, no matter how slim it may have been, was missed.

On 11 September the conference made its programme public, reaffirming the demands made at Erzurum for the integrity of the Ottoman state to be recognised within secure borders, free from foreign interference or control, and for the original terms of the armistice signed at Mudros to be honoured. On 12 September Mustapha decided that it was now time to turn the screws on the Sultan, and he instructed all civil governors and commanders to cut off communications with the government in Constantinople 'until it is succeeded by a legal government'.[27] Thousands of telegrams bombarded Constantinople accusing them of sacrificing the lives of Muslims in a 'fratricidal war', calling it a 'gang of traitors'[28] and demanding its resignation. A panicky Sultan then effected the resignation of Damad Ferid as Grand Vizier, appointing Ali Riza Pasha in his place and forming a 'Ministry of Conciliation' tasked with holding new elections.[29]

The Sultan then made approaches to the British for assistance in forming some sort of armed force with which he might be able to wrest control of Anatolia back from the Nationalists. The British, however, were now as anxious to avoid bloodshed as anyone, especially as Calthorpe had already admitted they barely had the resources to defend Constantinople, never mind embark upon offensive operations. Indeed, steps were being taken to reduce Britain's commitment inside Anatolia, and between 20 and 25 September orders were issued for British forces to withdraw from Merzifon and Samsun on the Black Sea coast and Kutahya in western Anatolia, leaving only 'a few unhappy majors ... scattered throughout Anatolia'.[30] For the time being, however, British troops were to remain in Constantinople and at Chanak. Nevertheless, this dramatic development handed the Nationalists a massive propaganda coup, and was celebrated in Sivas by a huge torchlit procession heralding the British withdrawal with cries of 'Down with the Occupation'.[31] This view was in close harmony with the deliberations of the Inter-Allied Commission of Enquiry, which had investigated the May disorder in Smyrna and effectively concluded that the only feasible solution was for the Greek occupation to be brought to an end and her claims to Anatolia rejected.

Mustapha's own status was clearly demonstrated when he met Salih Pasha, Minister of the Navy, in Amasya on 20 October. The discussions concluded with the signing of an agreement that effectively enshrined all of the demands the Nationalists had made at Sivas and Erzurum with regards to the boundaries of the new Turkish state, the rejection of an independent Kurdistan and the recognition of Cilicia as an integral part of Turkey. It also reiterated the demand that Aydin Province, Thrace (with the Maritsa River as its border), Izmir and Edirne should be recognised as integral to Turkey. Regardless of these arrangements, however, an uneasy truce would prevail between Constantinople and the Nationalists.

For the Allies, it appeared that the only possible alternative to coming to an arrangement with him would be a long, protracted war, tying down tens of thousands of British troops at crippling expense. In Paris on 7 October, the Allied Supreme Council had convened to set the limits of the Greek occupation of the Smyrna region in an attempt to prevent them launching any further offensive operations without their permission. They were instructed not to advance beyond the Milne Line – named after the commander of the British forces in Turkey – which stretched from Ayvalik in the north, where they had already met with stiff Turkish resistance, to the Menderes River in the south. It was a timely step in view of the fact that the next move would likely depend upon the Turkish Nationalists and the nature of the Greek reaction to them once the outcome of the peace negotiations finally became public.

On 20 October, General Milne submitted his evaluation of the situation to Churchill based upon the reports he had been receiving on the progress of the Nationalist movement. It made cautionary reading. Mustapha and the Nationalists had, Milne insisted, 'consolidated public opinion in Turkey and now that its supporters hold the reins of power, will do so still more'. Milne proceeded to caution Churchill that it was necessary to 'contemplate a situation in which the use of military force may become necessary', if the Nationalists responded to the terms of the treaty by launching an attack on the Allies. It would, however, he emphasised, 'vary greatly according to the nature of the terms' to be presented to the Ottoman government in Paris.[32]

The prospect of a large force being needed to counter a Nationalist offensive was all the greater because 'the three main questions on which Mustapha Kemal and his followers in their defence of the integrity of their country declare a "non-possumus" are the question of Smyrna, the question of Armenia, and the question of Thrace', the first and third of which were, of course, equally 'non-possumus', or non-negotiable, to the Greeks. If they were imposed by treaty then the Turkish reaction was to be expected. It was Milne's evaluation that 'the events in Smyrna have affected the position so greatly that it is inevitable that its evacuation and return to Turkey will be one of the foremost demands of every Turk'. He concluded that 'if the decisions of the Peace Conference are so drastic in the treatment of Turkey that the older men, who have the spirit of compromise, are unable to keep the wilder spirits in check, then it will turn out that the National Movement has very greatly prejudiced the military position of the Allies.' 'The population is armed and now united for the first time,' he went on, warning Churchill that 'it is difficult to calculate the force which might be available in the event of a national rising.' He therefore asked that should the decisions taken be likely to provoke the sort of nationalist backlash that Milne feared, 'a forecast of peace terms should be presented to the Allied Military authorities in advance, so they could consider what – if any – additional force will be required to meet the situation'. He also reiterated that 'the forces at my disposal are only sufficient to bring pressure to bear on the Government at Constantinople, who may or may not be in a position to control the country'.

Whatever Milne's reservations might be, Venizelos was not ready to throw in the towel just yet. Having achieved the occupation of Turkish lands, an achievement which could only have been dreamt of a few years before, and finding himself sitting among the top table of world powers, he was determined to fight tooth and nail to hold on to his enormous gains. On 21 October, he paid a visit to England, in the course of which he called in to see Lord Curzon at the Foreign Office. As Curzon reported afterwards,[33] 'he pleaded yet again the cause of the Greeks as against the Turks or the Bulgarians in the whole of Thrace, producing a long series of historical maps, which showed that only once in bygone centuries had the Bulgarians occupied the territories in question, and placing before me stacks of figures which demonstrated the numerical preponderance of the Greek population'. Curzon, however, was noncommittal: 'I did not venture any observations on a matter which still lay on the lap of the Peace Conference, and contented myself with admiring the formidable argumentative arsenal with which the Greek statesman had provided himself.' Venizelos then embarked upon an equally compelling monologue regarding Constantinople, 'arguing that at all costs the Turk must be removed, both as a symbol of his defeat and because his continued presence ... would be a challenge and danger for years to come'. He pooh-poohed the idea that any serious trouble could possibly come from 'the expulsion of the Turk', a particularly inept observation considering the serious trouble that was already brewing in the hinterland of Anatolia. Instead he urged that an international administration be established to restrain 'the ambitions of a resuscitated Russia'.

Furthermore, he felt that if Britain or France assumed a mandate they 'would certainly find themselves involved some day or other, in a bitter conflict with the secular aspirations of the Russian people,' whereas he believed 'an international administration would be in a position to resist Russian encroachment'. However, as the Foreign Secretary politely listened to the entreaties of the wily Greek, Curzon perceived another motive. 'I could not help thinking that, in the long argument which he developed on these lines, the Greek Prime Minister had in view, more than anything else, a hope for the expansion of his own people. British, French and Russians in Constantinople might close the door forever to the ambitions of Greece, but it might well be that, at some future date, an international administration (always a difficult thing to maintain) would be glad to hand over the reins of power to those who would be the numerical majority both in the city and its neighbourhood,' a keen interpretation that Curzon 'could not but feel sure ... lurked in his mind, even if it did not find expression on his lips.'

Intriguingly, Venizelos does not appear to have turned to the thorny subject of 'the position of the Greeks in Smyrna', and Curzon tactfully 'abstained from entering upon so troubled a field' and opening up an entirely new can of worms.

In any case, it was not his opinion that really counted. The Greek statesman was, as we have seen, partly driven by public opinion at home, partly by his belief in the unerring support of Lloyd George, and partly by self-delusion. To any doubts that may be harboured by the British government with respect to the ability of the Greek army to carry out his policy, he told the Foreign Office's George Kidston that the Greek army was still a powerful force that in the event of further hostilities would not require any assistance from her Allies.[34] Venizelos reiterated his conviction in Paris on 8 November, insisting that his army could deal with the situation in Anatolia, and that in any case the disorder in Smyrna was not due to the occupation at all, but rather to the ongoing uncertainty over the final conclusions of the peace conference. All would be well, he assured the Supreme Council, 'as soon as the Turks ... become conscious of their defeat'.[35] Others disagreed. 'The Greek occupation of Smyrna,' insisted Calthorpe, had 'stimulated a Turkish patriotism more real than any which the war was able to evoke',[36] and the consequences would soon be all too apparent.

With Lloyd George very much in the thrall of the Greeks and prepared to accept their assurances over the more cautionary counsels of politicians and especially experienced officers on the ground, Mustapha saw in the French a less dogmatic and Philhellene temperament. Their interests lay in resolving the German peace and in preserving their old titles and privileges in Asia Minor, rather than territorial aggrandisement. These interests could be secured by realising the promises enshrined in the wartime agreements Britain and France signed under the terms of the Sykes–Picot Agreement of 1916 which assigned Syria and Lebanon to France and Mesopotamia to Britain. Like all such wartime agreements, however, they were not as clear-cut as they appeared to be at the time, and would sow the seeds of discord between the two countries that Mustapha would be able to exploit to the full.

These arrangements contradicted promises which had been made to various Arab tribes, most notably to Sherif Hussein, to reward them with national homelands in recognition of the assistance they had provided to the British against the Turks – promises which had been underwritten by none other than Colonel Lawrence, under whom many Arab tribesmen had fought bravely against their hated Ottoman overlords. This arrangement was further complicated by a declaration in November 1918 in which the Allies had announced that 'the aim of France and Great Britain ... is the complete and final liberation of the peoples so long oppressed by the Turks and the establishment of governments and administrations deriving their authority from the initiative and the free choice of the native populations ... France and

Great Britain are agreed to encourage and help the establishment of native governments and administrations in Syria and Mesopotamia'. Into this melange must be added France's inherent dislike and distrust of her ally, which was not assuaged by experiences on the ground.

Still smarting from Britain's one-sided negotiation of the armistice, and jealous of her interests in Turkey, the French position in the Middle East now appeared to be challenged by the British as well. On 31 January 1919, the French Foreign Minister, Stephen Pichon, felt particularly aggrieved by the reports reaching him from the region that he was moved to complain to Arthur Balfour in the strongest terms:

> The government of the Republic deeply regrets to be obliged to draw the most serious attention of the British Government to the unfriendly attitude adopted with regard to French interests by certain officers of the British Civil Service in Syria and Mesopotamia and by a number of officials of the British Civil Service in Egypt, which attitude reveals a spirit entirely opposed to that rightly to be expected from representatives imbued with an idea of the duties imposed by the Alliance.[37]

Such assertions did not bode well, but they were not without a grain of truth. The French were keen to establish themselves in Syria, and were anxious to make their presence there felt in order to consolidate their primacy over the local population. However, to repeated requests to reinforce the small garrison there, they were met with what to them was nothing but obfuscation and delay. General Allenby, whose remit extended to Syria, refused the landing of reinforcements on the grounds that they were not required, and that in any case the Syrians and Arabs would look them upon as a 'sort of annexation'.[38]

Whatever Allenby's rationale, the French continued to complain about their treatment, prompting the British ambassador in France, the Earl of Derby Edward Stanley, to cable Lord Curzon on 24 February 1919, forwarding the French government's growing misgivings:

> French Government state that British authorities at Beyrout [*sic*] have refused to send by wireless a certain number of cipher

telegrams addressed to Ministry for Foreign Affairs by French High Commissioner in Palestine Syria. They ask that attention of HM Government may be drawn to this fresh indication of the attitude of Egyptian officials engaged in the administration of Syria and trust that instructions will be sent to competent authorities to prevent recurrence of such incidents.[39]

Despite a growing litany of complaints, little seems to have been done to remedy the worsening estrangement of the British and the French in Syria, and in addition to rows over the despatch of French troops, there were complaints over alleged repeated refusals to recognise traditional French rights in the Mosul Vilayet, and the denial of a permit to the French Consul, General M. Roux, to proceed to Mosul, affronts to French schools, the treatment of the French military attaché and accusations that speeches had been made by Lt-General Marshall, Commander-in-Chief of the Mesopotamian Expeditionary Force, and Colonel Wilson, which were 'antagonistic to France and French interests'.[40] These were all refuted, but they were clearly laying the seeds of mistrust and ill-feeling that could hardly be the basis of a harmonious working relationship over the final settlement with Turkey.

Then, in March 1919, the British submitted plans during the peace conference that flew in the face of wartime agreements over the fate of Syria. Rather than the French mandate, the British now wanted the territory to become an Arab kingdom under Emir Faisal. This would satisfy the promises made to the Arabs and get Britain off the hook without their having to sacrifice any of their claims. Clemenceau went mad. At a meeting of the Council of Four on 21 May the subject came up, and during the heated discussions which followed he went into a fury, yelling at the top of his voice in the Hall of Mirrors that 'Lloyd George is a cheat!'.[41] Again, Lloyd George used the defence that British forces had conquered the entire Middle East with only a token contribution from France, which did little to assuage the President's anger. British perfidy was writ large, and Clemenceau was being urged by public and press opinion at home to pursue their claim for Syria. Indeed, as Clemenceau argued, the French had already acquiesced to British control of Palestine, in order to fulfil the pledge contained within the Balfour declaration for a Jewish homeland, and to Mesopotamia, with its rich oil resources.[42] To back down over the Syrian question would be a step too far.

In the event both parties agreed to a commission of enquiry, which would visit Syria to gauge the opinion of the native population. The row dragged on and eventually, in September, the British agreed to withdraw its troops and leave it to the French, now advising Faisal he had best make whatever accommodation he could with his new masters. In March 1920, the Syrian National Congress met in Damascus and elected Faisal king of both Syria and Palestine. In July, acting swiftly to forestall any such act of guile, the French kicked Faisal out of the country and Syria went to France as planned. He was given the crown of Mesopotamia, later Iraq, as consolation.

Neighbouring the as yet vaguely defined northern frontier of Syria lay the Turkish vilayet of Cilicia, with its coastline stretching along the southern Anatolian littoral to the Gulf of Eskenderun. The newly installed French were now preoccupied fighting nationalist Arabs in Syria who were not predisposed to the French occupation of their country. To exacerbate the problem, Cilician bandits and guerrillas, with the encouragement of the Nationalists, were making life extremely difficult for the French. Elections held in France in November had returned a new government that was less sympathetic to the grandiose territorial designs harboured by Clemenceau, and which was prepared to make whatever compromises were required to reduce the pressure on Cilicia so they could concentrate on their Syrian mandate.

Accordingly, between 5 and 7 December the French Minister in Constantinople, Georges Picot, had taken the extraordinary step of stopping off at Sivas en route to Paris and holding discussions with Mustapha. He told him that France recognised Turkey's right to independence, and was prepared to pull its troops out of the country if the attacks on French troops were halted and her economic interests were protected. Mustapha agreed, as the very fact that the French felt compelled to approach him with compromise proposals showed the strength of his hand. Furthermore, it was inevitable that the British would discover their duplicity, and the consequence of that could only be to further deepen the schism that was already developing between them as a result of the spat over Syria.

Nevertheless, Mustapha was far from complacent. Hostile elements within Anatolia still posed a physical threat, despite the successes that had been achieved in dealing with some of the bandits and other would-be powerbrokers who had been challenging the National Pact. Furthermore it was agreed that they needed a political base sited closer to the Ottoman capital than Erzurum, which was too far to the east. After some debate it was decided to decamp to Ankara, and on 18 December 1919 Mustapha and his party set off, arriving to a rapturous welcome nine days later. Having established a firm and defensible headquarters in Anatolia, all that remained was to secure a similar political power base in Constantinople, where the long-awaited elections had returned a convincing Nationalist majority. Although a number of opposition parties who doubted the Nationalists' willingness to have a fair election had boycotted the poll, the result served to further entrench Mustapha's personal standing. He had been transformed within a few months from rebellious officer to 'the power behind the chamber' of deputies in Constantinople, a man whose cause had captured the hearts and minds of a growing proportion of the Turkish populace.[43]

The Ottoman parliament duly convened on 16 January 1920, but almost immediately the Allies challenged its legitimacy. They opposed the appointment of Cemal Pasha as War Minister and Cevat Pasha as Chief of the General Staff, suspecting them of collusion with the Nationalists in Anatolia. This attempt to manipulate the makeup of the Turkish government provoked an outcry in the chamber, and prompted Mustapha to consider retaliatory action if the Allies insisted on a veto over its members. The row failed to develop into a full-blown confrontation, however, and for the time being the Allies contented themselves with a watching brief, all the time haranguing the Sultan and bombarding him with memos and ultimatums.

While Constantinople witnessed a hiatus of sorts and the government established its newly won credentials, the uneasy truce previously agreed with George Picot in Cilicia was beginning to show signs of strain. The French were clearly the weaker and less committed of the Allies, with Greece still confident that it could realise and retain its territorial aspirations in Anatolia, encouraged by a British Prime Minister who continued to articulate his willingness to back these up by force. In the French position, however, Mustapha had recognised a weakening of such resolve even before Picot had been to meet him; now it was time to turn up the heat and see how far he could push them. He increased his efforts to stir up Arab sentiment in Cilicia, northern Syria and Mesopotamia with a view to destabilising the situation further, and urging them to combine against the 'treacherous parties'[44] allegedly arrayed against them.

The French had in fact encouraged the Armenians to return and had been raising an Armenian Legion to police the area, both measures sure to rile the Turks and provide a perfect pretext for retaliation. He therefore issued orders for his troops to cooperate with guerrillas in reoccupying the Cilician towns of Urfa and Marash, claiming that the steps were necessary to defend the local Turkish populations from French and Armenian aggression. This audacious move caused consternation and panic, with Marash being swiftly evacuated while the French decided what to do. They tried desperately to re-establish some kind of control of the deteriorating situation, but three weeks of slaughter were to ensue as the local Muslims, assisted by Turkish militia and irregulars, exacted a terrible toll on the now defenceless Christians. For some inexplicable reason, a column sent for the relief of the stricken inhabitants of Marash got almost to its very gates before being ordered to turn round again. It then began a humiliating and tragic retreat back across the mountains in sub-zero temperatures at the cost of hundreds of French casualties to frostbite alone. Thousands of hapless Armenian camp followers suffered too in a desperate experience the French would not wish to repeat. In the end they conceded to the inevitable, and by May would evacuate all of Cilicia, leaving its Armenian inhabitants to the tender mercies of the Turks, who re-established their control over the area and further endorsed the bona fides of the Nationalist movement.

These outrageous demonstrations of resistance had appalled the British, compounded by the news that the Sultan had issued a royal decree on 4 February 1920 reinstating Mustapha and returning his honours and titles. On 10 February the Allies convened in London to discuss the situation, and here they decided that Constantinople ought to be occupied as punishment for Mustapha's operations in Cilicia and to prevent the revolt in Anatolia being joined by similar disturbances in the capital itself. At a further meeting on 5 March, Lloyd George insisted that Mustapha's actions demanded 'the most energetic action possible',[45] which would continue until the Nationalists were brought to heel and the Sultan agreed terms.

Ten days later, on the night of 15/16 March 1920, the plan was put into effect. This was an almost exclusively British operation, as contingents of troops and naval personnel occupied the Ministries of Posts, Telegraphs and Telephones, Navy and War, and imposed press censorship in an effort to suppress popular opposition to the move. Random raids were made all over the city in the search for arms caches and were sometimes carried out insensitively, involving tactless spoiling of graves and acts of vandalism. In one avoidable and tragic incident, a harmless military band was almost massacred when it was mistaken for a group of soldiers. This inept and heavy-handed approach was to prove a priceless propaganda coup. Mustapha claimed that the occupation had 'struck at the principles of freedom, nationality, patriotism and conscience', and asserted that the 'forcible occupation of Constantinople today has destroyed the seven-centuries-old existence and sovereignty of the Ottoman Empire. Consequently, the Turkish nation is compelled today to defend its rights, its independence and its entire future'.[46]

There was uproar in Parliament and, summoned to the Sultan in the Yildiz Palace, some deputies respectfully warned their master that resistance to the Allies was growing and would continue to grow. As a result eighty-five of them, including many Nationalist supporters, were arrested and joined another 150 undesirables who were shipped off to Malta. This was the last straw. Others went into hiding, and bided their time before making good their escape from the city and joining the Nationalists in Ankara. Any Turk who might still harbour reservations now decided to throw in their lot with Mustapha. When parliament sat again the following day, in a final demonstration of their resistance to the British, it decided to prorogue itself until further notice. This left the National Assembly in Ankara the de facto *and* de jure representative of the Turkish state. It was to this new parliament, hundreds of miles away from any possible interference by the Allies, that Mustapha summoned the deputies to convene an entirely independent legislature and called upon every able-bodied Turkish citizen to make their way to Anatolia and throw in their lot with the Nationalists. The reaction of the authorities was similarly predictable, condemning the Nationalists and warning them that anyone harbouring these criminals was liable to be tried and put to death. This was followed by a feeble 'fatwa' issued by the Sultan that called for the rebels to face summary execution,[47] while an army of the Caliphate was to be formed of loyal troops to crush the Nationalists.

Immune from the empty threats and bombast of an impotent Sultan, the Grand National Assembly was formally opened on 23 April 1920. Mustapha wanted it left in no doubt that he and his Nationalist followers were now the true torchbearers of freedom continuing the cause of the jihad, and the delegates swore to defend not only the country and its people, but also the Sultanate and Caliphate.[48] The following day Mustapha was elected President of the Assembly with executive powers, as well as serving as Speaker.

Meanwhile, the Sultan's so-called Army of the Caliphate was being recruited in Constantinople. It appeared temporarily as if the Nationalists would be suppressed by the Turks themselves, but its ranks were swelled by criminals and the unemployed who were more motivated by the relatively high wages that were on offer than by any desire to preserve the power of the Sultan or the integrity of the state. With its poor leadership and low morale, it was therefore no match for the Nationalist forces it was called upon to 'discipline'.[49] In its first action on 14 June near the port of Izmit on the Sea of Marmara and perilously close to Constantinople, a force of some 4,000 men received a resounding mauling. Even money was little incentive to the survivors, half of whom were sent into headlong retreat while the remainder simply switched sides. It was a victory that further incensed the Allies, who anxiously opened fire on the Nationalists from behind the Milne Line in an attempt to forestall any ideas they might have to advance further. While this comic-opera charade continued, however, the Allies were finally getting down to the long-delayed business of settling their account with the Ottoman Empire.

Irrespective of the political realities on the ground, the isolation of the Sultan, the emasculation of his Government and the resurgence of a Nationalist movement in the Anatolian interior, the Allies continued to behave as if the Ottoman government was the only one with whom they needed to treat. Between 19 and 26 April the Allies attended a conference in San Remo in Italy to discuss the terms of a final peace treaty, and on 20 May 1920 they were duly presented to the Ottoman representatives at a porcelain factory in France called Sevres.

Indeed, each of its 433 articles was another nail in the coffin of the Ottoman state, and in paragraph after painstaking paragraph it specified just how complete and total a form its dissolution was to take. Turkey was to cease to exist at all in Europe, all of Eastern Thrace being ceded to Greece, apart from a small enclave for Constantinople where, under Article 36, 'the rights and title of the Turkish Government over Constantinople shall not be affected, and that the said Government and His Majesty the Sultan shall be entitled to reside there and to maintain there the capital of the Turkish state', while the Allies reserved the right to impose 'any dispositions which may be taken' in the event of the government failing to observe any of the provisions contained within the treaty.

The navigation of the Straits, including the Dardanelles, the Sea of Marmara and the Bosphorus, were to be open, both in peace and war, to 'every vessel of commerce or of war', and Turkey was to undertake never to blockade the Straits without the permission of the League of Nations. To ensure their future security, Turkey had to agree to a Commission of the Straits, with authority over 'all the waters between the Mediterranean mouth of the Dardanelles and the Black Sea mouth of the Bosphorus, and to the waters within three miles of each of these mouths'. The article added that 'this authority may be exercised on shore to such an extent as may be necessary for the execution of the provisions of this Section', which in reality would mean the creation of a Neutral Zone, stretching from the Aegean Sea, and incorporating the islands of Mudros, Imbros, Samothrace and Tenedos, through the Gallipoli peninsula and Eastern Thrace to the Black Sea on the

European Shore, and from Edremit round to Chile Gutze on the Black Sea. The depth of the territory included in the Neutral Zone would range from 5 miles or so on the Gallipoli peninsula to some 50 miles north-west from Constantinople on the European shore, nearly 60 miles from the Asiatic shore of the Dardanelles to Edremit and 50 miles or so as the zone curved round north-westwards to the Black Sea, and incorporating Izmit. A substantial chunk of territory that would, in effect, become Allied Occupied Turkey, and which alone was to provide a magnet for the resurgent designs of the Nationalists.

With regards to Kurdistan, Article 62 stipulated that a commission would be appointed to draft a 'scheme of local autonomy', whose decisions the Turkish government were compelled to accept. It went on to instruct that within a year the Kurdish people would be at liberty to make representations to the League of Nations with a view to seeking complete independence, which Turkey would also be compelled to accept. Article 65 addressed the question of Smyrna/Izmir, allocating a vast enclave around the port city to Greece that would comprise hundreds of square miles of Turkish territory. The area would 'remain under Turkish sovereignty' but would come under Greek administration for a period of five years, after which a referendum could be held to decide whether the territory reverted to Turkey or was incorporated into Greece.

Turkey was to renounce sovereignty of Imbros and Tenedos in favour of Greece, and to recognise the independence of Armenia, the future boundaries of which were to be decided upon by another Allied Commission that would also establish a demilitarised zone between the two countries. Once again, the treaty obliged Turkey to agree in advance to any decisions taken with respect to the future frontier between the two countries, effectively signing off on a document without knowing exactly what the ramifications or implications might be.

The treaty then addressed the future status of Syria, Mesopotamia and Palestine, which would 'be provisionally recognised as independent States subject to the rendering of administrative advice and assistance by a Mandatory until such time as they are able to stand alone', meaning that they were to be handed over to Britain and France as pseudo-colonies until such time as they opted to grant them full independence. Few in either the Ottoman or the Nationalist camps harboured any illusions as to the fate of these territories, and all were likewise resigned to the loss of the Hedjaz in Arabia, which Article 98 recognised as a 'free and independent state', guaranteeing free access to the Muslim Holy places of Mecca and Medina.

Turkey was now to formally renounce sovereignty over Egypt, the Sudan and Cyprus and recognise them as British protectorates. France was not to be left out of this particular tying up of loose ends either, a similar undertaking being made with regards to her protectorates over Morocco and Tunis, whilst Italy obtained the Dodecanese Islands – just about the only promise made to her by the Allies which was to be honoured. The total strength of the Turkish armed forces was to be limited to 50,000 men, 'including staffs, officers, training personnel and depot troops', and her navy limited to a handful of sloops and torpedo boats. She was forbidden to maintain 'any military or naval air forces' whatsoever, and she was obliged to surrender 'all military and naval aeronautical material', including aircraft, balloons, engines, munitions and communications equipment, leaving her with no air power at all and, the Allies clearly hoped, without the means of secretly building one up.

Furthermore, the capitulations were to stand, continuing to give the Allies power of attorney over what remained of her national finances, her revenues and her economy, binding her further into a straitjacket of dependence and subservience.

In a separate agreement to the Sevres Treaty itself, to be known as the Tripartite Agreement, Britain, France and Italy agreed that Anatolia would be divided into 'Spheres of Interest', in which each power would exercise exclusive rights of commercial exploitation and influence,[50] leaving only a dismembered rump to be ruled by the Sultan.[51] It was, in the words of one American observer, 'one of the most primitive peace arrangements and one of the most daring and deliberate divisions of war spoils in modern history'.[52] However, it could in the final analysis be a paper victory only. It was not the servile acquiescence of the Ottoman government which carried any weight, but the reaction of the Nationalist government. There was no way that they would accept it.

In dictating such a treaty the Allies had handed the Nationalists a definite cause for which to fight, and a legitimate rallying cry for every loyal Turk who wished to see its humiliating clauses ripped up and thrown back in the Allies' faces. Its clauses appalled soldiers like Henry Wilson, who scathingly commented, 'The frocks think they have done good work but we soldiers think they are all rotters ... their cynicism throughout has been perfectly disgusting.'[53] As Winston Churchill was to comment ironically, 'At last, peace with Turkey; and to ratify it, war with Turkey',[54] whilst Lawrence, who had led the Arabs against the Turks in the war, predicted gravely that 'the document is not the constitution of a new Asia, but a confession, almost an advertisement, of the greed of the conquerors. No single clause of it will stand the test of three years' practice.'[55]

Sir Horace Rumbold, only recently installed as the British High Commissioner in Constantinople, warned London that he could see no prospect of a Turkish settlement under such circumstances.[56] Rumbold was a career diplomat who had served in various capacities since joining the Diplomatic Corps, including The Hague, Cairo, Tehran, Vienna, Berlin and Tokyo before finding himself in the eye of the storm in Turkey. Events were to prove that this posting could arguably be the most demanding of his life, and would call upon his capacities like none before. He realised very early on the challenge which faced him, and that in order to tread a fine line between the various factions Britain could not hope to please anyone in the end – perhaps she could only make more enemies.

5

THE GREEKS WERE NICE
CHAPS TOO

Venizelos, delighted by the crushing terms of the Treaty of Sevres, announced the news to an ecstatic Greek public, and also to an equally appalled and outraged Turkish one. The Greeks had procured land and power beyond their wildest dreams and, fooled by this absurd illusion, they prepared to take possession of their newly awarded empire. The population of Constantinople, on the other hand, already seething at the Allied occupation, were further incensed by the terms of the treaty. Despite being censored the press took up the cause, risking serious repercussions by encouraging civil disobedience and public protests and calling for the treaty to be repudiated.

In Ankara, however, Mustapha learnt of these developments with more composure. The disorder provoked by the publication of the terms could render the jittery Allied control of the capital untenable and present him with the opportunity to take the initiative. Indeed, on 13 June Churchill warned Lloyd George that 'we have no reserves anywhere'[1] with which to suppress any serious disorder; this dire prognosis was confirmed by Henry Wilson, who noted in his diary on 16 June that General Milne had insufficient forces 'to hold Constantinople and Izmit',[2] let alone anywhere further afield, possessing just 5,469 men in the city, 2,272 between Izmit and Afyonkarahisar and just 657, roughly battalion strength, in the Dardanelles.[3] Consequently, when Mustapha decided to take a huge gamble and ordered his forces to march towards Constantinople during the night of 14/15 June he provoked near panic amongst the Allies and exasperated an already tense and volatile atmosphere within the Neutral Zone. Milne called for reinforcements, worried that he would not be able to resist the Nationalists should they be audacious enough to try to force their way through his lines, but Mustapha had achieved his aim, that of demonstrating his defiance of the Allies, and his forces were ordered to withdraw.

Venizelos, fired with misguided enthusiasm for his country's new crusading mission, believed that the Turkish threat provided the perfect justification to move his own men deeper into Anatolia. He offered two of the five divisions currently in Smyrna and another from Eastern Thrace to assist his Allies in throwing back the advancing Nationalists. The gesture met with a mixed reaction. The French warned that such an escalation could only result in a long war, a position endorsed by the Italians. Marshal Foch had warned that an army of twenty-seven divisions would be needed to enforce the treaty and suppress the Nationalists,[4] and the British General Staff also urged caution. At a meeting in London on 14 June, Lloyd George warned Venizelos that none of the Allies could risk going to war to enforce the treaty, and the foolish Greek insisted yet again that his army was perfectly able to do so alone.[5] All he required from the Allies was financial backing. Lloyd George was desperate to give his ally all the support he could, but with a divided Cabinet to convince he knew that it was going to be an uphill struggle. Only the Turkish advance on Izmit and Milne's request for reinforcements provided the pretext he needed to act further, and when the Cabinet met on 18 June the decision was taken to accept one Greek division to reinforce Constantinople.

Despite misgivings in his own ranks, Lloyd George persisted. He met the French Foreign Minister Alexander Millerand and Marshal Foch in Lympne on 20 June, and succeeded in securing approval for a Greek advance. The objective was simply to give the Nationalists, as Lloyd George put it, 'a knock',[6] and let it be known to Mustapha that he could not expect to make warlike gestures towards the Allies with impunity. To this end, the advance was to be limited to a north-eastward foray out of the Smyrna zone towards Panderma on the Sea of Marmara. It was not intended to be a full-scale invasion but merely to relieve the pressure on the troops occupying the Straits zone, keep the Nationalists at arm's length and compel them to accept the terms of the treaty. It was by no means intended to herald a full-blown war.

On 22 June 1920 the Greeks moved forward. At first, in a series of early achievements that belied the bloody disaster in which it would all end, the Greco-British position appeared to be vindicated. Crossing the Milne Line at four points, the numerically superior and (for the time being at least) better-equipped Greeks were able to advance swiftly and the Turkish forces retreated, albeit in good order, pursued by the Greeks and accompanied by thousands of desperate refugees. This was interpreted by Lloyd George as a general rout: 'They are beaten and fleeing with their forces towards Mecca,' he exulted, although Curzon correctly reminded him it was actually Ankara. Nonetheless delighted, Lloyd George conceded that 'Lord Curzon is good enough to admonish me on a triviality'.[7]

Within a month the Greeks had secured the Aegean coast north of Smyrna and the southern shores of the Sea of Marmara, and on 8 July, in an act of momentous symbolism, they captured the city of Bursa, an achievement celebrated in Athens Cathedral with a *Te Deum*. They continued their advance eastwards along an increasingly widening front and exceeded their terms of reference as they went. Nevertheless, buoyed by the apparent ease with which their offensive was proceeding, the Greek forces advanced until they reached Usak on the edge of the Anatolian plateau, 200 miles east of Smyrna. In European Turkey, Greek forces cleared Eastern Thrace of what remained of the Ottoman forces, and Edirne, the Ottoman second city, fell on 25 July. Two days later the Nationalist forces in Thrace surrendered. Apart from bandit forces behind the Greek lines, the Nationalists were now confined to the Anatolian Plateau and the Black Sea coast, prompting a euphoric Lloyd George to declare prematurely that 'Turkey is no more'.[8]

On the face of it, the Greeks were hugely successful. They were pushing all before them in a relentless and irresistible tide, apparently having built up a momentum that Mustapha and his armies, perceived as weak and unreliable, were incapable of resisting. However, Mustapha was too canny to risk his forces in a confrontation with the Greeks in circumstances not of his own choosing. Though it appeared that his troops were crumbling before the Greeks, only time would tell if this were true. Nevertheless, the Greeks allowed themselves to be 'elated by this initial victory'.[9] Only a direct order from the Supreme Council compelled the army to halt, rest its exhausted soldiers and consolidate its gains before deciding what further action to take.

On 10 August the Sultan's government, or Ministry of Marionettes, as Churchill contemptuously referred to it, formally signed the Treaty of Sevres. That it was a purely academic exercise was underlined by the fact that on 18 July the Grand National Assembly in Ankara had repeated their determination to accept nothing but complete independence within the 1918 armistice lines. The following day it had decreed that any Turk actively engaged in negotiations with the Allies was a traitor and could expect no mercy if they fell into the hands of the Nationalists.

However, rhetoric and decrees were one thing; what mattered was the wherewithal to enforce them. Against the relatively well-equipped and British-backed Greeks, the Nationalists were short of everything – arms, ammunition, heavy guns and equipment of all kinds. With no arsenals from which to produce weapons and replace wastage at the front, they urgently needed a friendly power to provide them with the materiel with which to prosecute the war. This dire situation partly contributed to Mustapha's decision to make overtures to the Russians, who had every reason to want to thwart the Greeks and British. They had particularly aroused Soviet antipathy by participating in the infamous 'Intervention' in support of the White Russians during their civil war, so there was little love lost between Moscow, London and Athens. The new Soviet regime had already eagerly revealed the various secret protocols and treaties the Allied powers had connived at with the defunct Czarist regime during the war, and this further opportunity to frustrate the Allies' designs in Anatolia proved very attractive, especially with so many hostile warships lying at anchor in the capital and uncomfortably close to the Black Sea.

On 24 August, in a development that was critical for the future of the Nationalist movement, a draft Treaty of Cooperation was agreed between Nationalist Turkey and Soviet Russia. Its crucial clauses cleared the way for massive Russian military aid to the Nationalists and relaxed tensions sufficiently to allow them to reduce their garrisons in the east in favour of reinforcing the beleaguered western front. This tremendous boost was soon followed by an extraordinary event which surprised everyone, except perhaps the Greeks themselves.

While Mustapha's reputation and authority was in the ascendant, his Greek counterpart was coming under growing pressure. The war did not by any stretch of the imagination enjoy unanimous support in Greece, where there were increasing signs of dissent, and to compound his problems he now had a huge and costly army languishing in Turkey. He warned Lloyd George in a lengthy telegram on 5 October that his position was becoming precarious, insisting that the only 'remedy would be a new campaign with the object of destroying definitely the nationalist forces'.[10] Otherwise it would soon be too late in the year to mount an offensive and he would be compelled by public pressure to begin demobilisation of the army. His concerns about the threat from his domestic opponents were compounded by mounting pressure for a general election to bring to an end the extended parliament that had governed since 1915. He had little option but to acquiesce, and the Chamber of Deputies was subsequently dissolved and an election campaign, the last thing either Venizelos or Lloyd George needed right then, was initiated.

On 14 November, Venizelos, the great architect of the 'Megali Idea', the man whose iron will and determination had transformed his country almost overnight from a quiet backwater into a European powerbroker, fell from office.[11] The Royalist Party secured 250 seats and his own just 115 in a shock result that threw the entire drama in Turkey into sharp relief and plunged Lloyd George's Anatolian strategy into chaos. Bitterly disappointed at the result and its obvious implications for his own policy, Lloyd George wrote to him soon afterwards, lamenting with no sense of irony that 'this kind of thing makes one despair of democracy'.[12]

The yawning political chasm provoked by the election was further compounded by a constitutional and dynastic crisis created after King Alexander died following, extraordinarily enough, a bite from a pet monkey (a Barbary macaque) on 25 October. The issue of who should succeed him became divisive but was resolved in a referendum on 5 December in which it was decided to invite the late King Alexander's pro-German father Constantine, who had lived in exile since the war, to return to the throne. These two decisive developments were viewed by opponents of the war as an opportunity for a change of government, and also for a serious re-evaluation of Greek policy in Turkey. France and Italy in particular took the opportunity to disavow any debt of loyalty they may owe to the Greeks, and effectively let it be known that they were on their own. The French, furthermore, wanted to thwart the return of Constantine by refusing to 'entrust important strategical positions in the Near East to an unfriendly government'[13] and British public opinion was also showing the first serious signs of disenchantment with the war. But this new realism did not percolate down to Lloyd George, and the Greeks continued to delude themselves that they continued to enjoy the implicit support of the British when in fact time was fast running out. From the moment that the outcome of the election and the imminence of Constantine's return were made known, both Britain and France took steps to revoke hundreds of millions of Drachmas in financial credits, threatening the country with economic meltdown.

Despite this sudden evaporation of Allied support, not to mention the hostility with which his return had been almost universally greeted, the new king decided to continue the war. He ostensibly did so to ensure the protection of the Christian minorities from the vengeful Turks, but more likely it was because the only alternative was a humiliating withdrawal and the abandonment of everything that had been gained in Paris.

The upheaval caused by the elections and the subsequent change in government had created additional uncertainty[14] as he purged the army of its pro-Venizelos officers and replaced them with men whom he felt he could trust. But this only resulted in the loss of experienced officers trusted by their men and their replacement with unknowns, many of whom had not seen active service for many years.[15] In the event, 1,500 army officers who had been dismissed by Venizelos were reappointed, whilst all three corps commanders, seven out of nine divisional commanders and many senior posts on the staff and in regimental commands changed hands at this critical time.

This new policy also resulted in the release from prison in Crete of Anastasios Papoulas, who was immediately promoted to lieutenant-general and appointed commander-in-chief of the Greek forces in Anatolia. He was not to prove a very inspired appointment. Despite being a relatively apolitical officer and an excellent infantry commander, Papoulas would be no match for Mustapha and his leadership qualities were unsuited to meeting the challenge represented by the Turks. These developments did not go unnoticed. Stunned by the changes which had been made in the command structure of the army, and fearful of the consequences, Venizelos now became far less robust in his belief in the capacity of the army to execute a forward offensive policy. Instead, he urged a more defensive posture, a tactic endorsed by Metaxas, but it was not a policy embraced by the military faction. Perhaps negotiation might, after all, negate the need for the army to prove itself in full-frontal conflict with the Nationalists.

As 1921 dawned, there was little encouraging news for Rumbold to report. 'The situation here is pretty black,' he wrote to Eyre Crowe, 'and I do not see any light.'[16] He followed this dire assessment with another warning to the head of the Eastern Department of the Foreign Office, Sir Lancelot Oliphant, maintaining that backing Greece could lead only to the British being forced to eat 'a certain amount of dirt ... we are bound to antagonise either the Turks or the Greeks'. The same afternoon he telegraphed Lord Curzon asserting his conviction that that the situation would be 'quite inextricable'[17] if the Treaty of Sevres were to be regarded as the basis for future policy. Furthermore, he offered his own assessment of Mustapha, warning that 'it is useless to regard Mustapha Kemal as a brigand chief', and insisting that whatever the British wished to believe, the government in Ankara had a tight grip 'on the whole of Asia Minor'.[18] It was towards this bleak horizon that the sorry saga stumbled inexorably into its next phase.

The Allied Powers, nervous about this turn of events, suggested that all the parties involved in the growing crisis attend a round table conference in London in February. Before it convened, however, the Greeks wanted to try one more throw of the dice, and hopefully enter the negotiations from a position of strength having demonstrated to the sceptics that they possessed in Anatolia an army that commanded respect and which could still achieve their aims by force of arms. Unfortunately it had quite the opposite outcome.

On 9 January the Greeks advanced towards the Turkish trenches at Eski Shehir, fanning out from Bursa. The Turks, under the redoubtable command of General Ismet, Mustapha's trusted right-hand man, decided not to stand and fight but to withdraw to better-prepared positions. Papoulas then abruptly called off the advance, and before the Turks had a chance to realise what an anti-climax it had all been, the Greeks had returned to their original starting lines. Ismet subsequently launched a counterattack which swept the Greeks back about 70 miles. Papoulas claimed afterwards that he had never in fact intended to carry out anything other than a reconnaissance in force, but whatever his intentions it was an inauspicious start. They may have been better equipped than the Nationalists, but that did little to offset the dire lack of good leadership in higher ranks, a situation hardly improved by the recent reshuffle.

Even so, poor leadership was not necessarily the worst of their problems. They had been asked to operate in pitilessly hostile terrain, with endless mountains interrupted by valleys, in bitterly cold weather where effective manoeuvre in thick mud was all but impossible. So, far from strengthening the hand of the Greeks at the London Conference, the offensive had seriously compromised their negotiating position, especially with Papoulas now demanding reinforcements. For his role in what would become known as the First Battle of Inonu, Ismet was awarded the title of Pasha and promotion to brigadier-general.

The French were now led by President Aristide Briand, whom many hoped might be more accommodating than his predecessors and who had a more conciliatory attitude towards Constantine owing to his friendship with his brother Prince George. He was not entirely predisposed to the Greeks' warlike approach, however, and urged a more conciliatory attitude. With experiences in Cilicia demonstrating the extent to which the Nationalists were inclined 'to fight savagely, and to dispute every inch of ground',[19] there was little recommending a different approach. This, of course, clashed with Lloyd George's stance, and he still harboured the dream of negotiating a peace based on Sevres. However, for this to be achieved he urged the Greek delegates 'not to surrender [their] legitimate rights'[20] and to demonstrate that whilst they would indeed discuss issues which were of legitimate concern to the Nationalists, they must be firm when it came to defending their own red-line issues.

Fortunately for Lloyd George's unrealistic position, the new Greek administration was to prove almost as hawkish and delusional as the last. Their new leader, the briefly incumbent Nikolaos Kalogeropoulos, claimed that their army was still formidable and could annihilate the Turks and sweep the whole country clear of their forces within three months. Furthermore, if the objective was still to ensure the imposition of Sevres, theirs was the only force capable to doing so. It was nevertheless still a desperate gamble, as in the face of lacklustre French and hostile Italian manoeuvrings it was going to rely upon the support of the British. Worse still, Lloyd George's tacit approval was not reflected by the opinions of a number of members of his coalition Cabinet, and should his political fortunes change then anything was possible. Lord Curzon in particular was furious at the Prime Minister's apparently resolute predilection for war and, as we shall see later, his views were far from unique among Lloyd George's political friends and foes alike. Indeed, the Italians had been articulating their growing resentment towards Greek aspirations in Anatolia for some time, especially having had their own designs in the region thwarted. The Italian ambassador to London, Marquis Imperiali, had made his government's position clear and warned the British that they intended to seek their own accommodation with the Turks. The French, in spite of President Briand's softer line, had already agreed separate undertakings to the Nationalists and were also widely suspected of providing the Nationalists with arms.

In this atmosphere of intrigue and deception, the conference dragged on inconclusively. In keeping with his policy of outwardly promoting compromise, Lloyd George proposed that Smyrna could retain Turkish sovereignty but be administered by the Greeks, and the two governments share its revenues. In the meantime a commission of enquiry would investigate Greek claims to both Smyrna and Thrace. Neither solution was acceptable to either party, especially with the Turks being egged on by the French and the Italians. They insisted that any agreement must include the restitution of their 1913 borders, the evacuation of Izmir, Turkish control of the Straits and Allied evacuation of Constantinople. The Greeks, on the other hand, were loath to concede anything at all to those Kalogeropoulos dismissed as little more than 'a rabble'.[21] He remained stubbornly convinced that they still possessed substantial forces in Anatolia, and his opinion of the Turkish Nationalists remained low despite the experience of both the French in Cilicia and Papoulas at Inonu.

By March, nothing had been achieved. Britain was anxious to ensure that when talks did finally break down, the blame would be laid squarely on the shoulders of the two key protagonists and not on the British government, or more particularly Lloyd George himself. Behind the scenes though, Mustapha's wily representative at the conference Bekir Sami was dividing his time between negotiating publicly and engaging in furtive bargaining with the French and Italians, the final outcome of which would be the complete isolation of the British and the sounding of the death knell for the Greeks.

The agreement made by the French and the Nationalists ended all French claims in Cilicia and sanctioned the evacuation of the territory they occupied north of the Syrian mandate. In exchange the Nationalists conceded privileged status for the French and an advisory role in the economic development of southern and eastern Turkey. This arrangement freed the French of the military burden of committing troops to the region but retained the economic privileges that could prove far more profitable than territory. It also handed Mustapha a precious weapon that he would use to further exploit the wedge between Britain and her reluctant French ally. Sami came to a similar arrangement with the Italians, who promised to work for Turkish rights in Thrace and Smyrna and to withdraw their forces in exchange for economic privileges in central and western Turkey. These arrangements meant that Mustapha could husband his forces against the Greeks, confident that the French and Italians no longer endangered his flanks and, as an added and much welcome bonus, both Italy and France were free to pursue their strategy of secretly aiding the Nationalists with arms and ammunition. With aid now forthcoming from three foreign powers, the trickle of supplies promised to become a flood. Indeed, on 16 March 1921 the Nationalists achieved perhaps their single greatest diplomatic coup to date. The discussions with the Soviet Union, which had been ongoing since August, were now beginning to bear fruit and the Russians promised to provide substantial amounts of military and economic assistance,[22] with promises of more to come. As an added bonus, the two countries negotiated an agreement fixing their common border,[23] which would permit even more Nationalist troops to be transferred west to reinforce the armies facing the Greeks.

Blissfully unaware of the secret protocols or the huge injection of military aid about to be sent to the Nationalists, the Greeks disingenuously claimed to have emerged from the conference with substantial gains. Back home, however, the Leader of the Opposition, Nikolaos Stratos insisted that 'the Greek Government cannot claim that it had scored a diplomatic triumph in London',[24] having failed to secure any undertaking from the Nationalists or to have had their plans endorsed either by France or Italy, leaving only Britain in the person of Lloyd George continuing to support them. So, if they had failed in the diplomatic sphere, they would have to try their only other option: military force.

The failure of the negotiations prompted a renewed offensive, with one column, the Northern Group, advancing along the same route as in January, and another, the Southern Group, pushing out from Ushak towards Afyonkarahisar. At this stage the Greeks were still better equipped, particularly with respect to machine guns and motor transport, but were at the same time disarmed by a serious underestimation of the strength and capacity of their enemy, who had used the lull in the fighting to further entrench his positions and reinforce his men with Russian artillery pieces.

Attacking on 27 March, the Greeks made considerable gains at first, including the key height of Metristepe, although it was only captured after days of heavy and intense fighting. The Nationalists then hastily transferred reinforcements which allowed the Turks to counter-attack five days later, drive their adversaries back and reoccupy the vital peak. Ismet reported proudly to Mustapha that 'the enemy had abandoned the battlefield to our arms, leaving thousands of dead behind', to which Mustapha equally proudly replied, 'It is not only the enemy you have defeated, but fate itself – the ill-starred fate of our nation.'[25]

Clearly, the huge gulf between the leadership qualities of the Greek and Nationalist generals was beginning to tell. Ernest Hemingway, reporting for the *Toronto Star*, was less than flattering about the Greek officers he encountered. He expressed serious reservations about these 'newly arrived Constantine officers, that did not know a goddamned thing' and whose lack of field craft, tactics and even basic soldiering was condemning their troops to ignominy and defeat.[26] Arnold Toynbee's evaluation of the retreating Greeks as 'an interminable procession of troops, mules, ox-carts and lorries crawling along a foundered road' did not compare favourably with the Nationalist army either.[27] Fused from disparate regular and irregular units into a more disciplined, cohesive and motivated fighting machine than had perhaps ever been put into the field,[28] Mustapha's new model army was instilled with all the zeal and commitment of that other great army that had been deployed during the English Civil War by Oliver Cromwell. Events were soon to prove beyond doubt which army was more capable of carrying the day.

Further south on 7 April there was more bad news when the Greeks were compelled to abandon Afyonkarahisar and re-establish their line at Dumlupinar, further to the west. This signal achievement prompted the Turkish commander, General Refet, to top Ismet's exultation with the announcement that his army had delivered 'the final blow against the enemy'.[29] There was no doubting that it was a terrible reverse for the Greek army. Thus ended the Second Battle of Inonu.

This news devastated Lloyd George and seriously undermined his support for the Greeks. His allies had repeatedly assured him that they would be able to sweep the Nationalists from Anatolia with ease. Twice now, the opposite had happened. He would have to try to save face as best he could but it would not be easy with an increasingly sceptical Cabinet and House of Commons to placate, and publicly he limited any reservations he might have to musing euphemistically that the Greek setbacks had put him in 'a difficult situation'.³⁰ However, in a telegram to Sir Lancelot Oliphant Rumbold he provided a starker assessment, complaining how the the Greek offensive had served only to 'upset the applecart ... and has deferred for some time to come all hope of peace'.³¹ His evaluation of the possible consequences should the Nationalists decide to continue their advance towards Constantinople was equally chilling, warning Curzon on 7 April that if they should decide to do so, 'we do not see what will stop them.'³²

The disappointment of the Greek reverse in Anatolia had serious repercussions in Athens too. Wise General Metaxas was approached and begged to help by joining Papoulas' staff and helping to plan the next effort, but he refused.³³ The war was a hopeless cause and he did not want to be implicated in such a disastrous policy. The attacks had been badly planned, ill-timed and badly executed. The Nationalists were not a rabble that would simply dissolve in the face of the enemy, but Greek thinking could go no further than to simply try again, as the new Prime Minister, Dimitrios Gounaris admitted in this despairing appraisal:

We cannot change policy, we are obliged to continue the war until the end, even if we risk catastrophe. Otherwise the English will cease to regard us as a serious nation if we do not fulfil what we promise and will abandon us and support Turkey. We must prove that we are a nation on which a Great Power can depend ...³⁴

Although faith in Papoulas and his staff had nose-dived since the debacles he had twice now presided over, the Government had to concede that there was no one to replace him, and they would have to soldier on as best they could. King Constantine, believing himself to be a gifted strategist, then set off to Anatolia to see for himself what conditions were like. Perhaps his presence might give Papoulas' command the fillip it needed, and upon his arrival in Anatolia, the King embarked upon a fact finding and morale boosting inspection tour of the front.

There was some good news he could take with him however. In response to Papoulas' call for more men, further conscription had doubled the size of the army to 200,000 men, producing, as the British military observer reported somewhat optimistically, 'a more efficient fighting machine than I had ever seen it.'[35] In reality however, the quality of the recruits was to leave a lot to be desired. Poor discipline and training was now more evident than ever before, and morale was correspondingly low. They were being failed by the lamentable quality of the leadership at the highest level, and according to Toynbee, 'the men were angry – angry at spending so much blood and labour in vain'.[36] Resources too were beginning to show the strain, as the treasury in Athens became sparse as a consequence of Allied financial constraints. In communications alone, crucial to waging an effective campaign in terrain as unforgiving as Anatolia, the Greeks were badly lacking, especially with regards to aerial reconnaissance and the wireless sets required to give that reconnaissance impact. This position, egging the Greeks on but denying them the means to do the job, appalled Winston Churchill. 'The Greeks,' he insisted, 'deserve either to be backed up ... or chilled to the bone.'[37] Instead this halfway house reflected badly on everyone concerned. Curzon tried again to broker a deal, and travelled to Paris. The compromise with regards to Smyrna was placed on the table again, but rejected by the Greeks, as they would not evacuate their troops. Even Venizelos' entreaties fell on deaf ears, and hopes continued to hang on the vain chance of achieving a positive military outcome. On 10 July Papoulas moved against the Turks once more.

The main attack was directed southwards against Kutahya in the hope of cutting the railway line between it and Afyonkarahisar. The next step would be to move north to surround the Turkish headquarters at Eskihisar. Due mainly to poor communications and uncharacteristically poor direction by Ismet, the Greeks were able to break through to Kutahya on 17 July and, as planned, move towards

Eskihisar. An elated Lloyd George received reports of their initial success with undisguised glee. On 21 July he wrote scathingly to the Secretary of State for War, Sir Laming Worthington-Evans, smugly asserting that 'the War Office's information about the respective strength and quality of the two armies turned out to be hopelessly wrong'.[38] His overconfidence however, would prove to have been even more ill-advised.

Seeing the growing danger, Mustapha rushed to meet his general the following day and they held an ad hoc field conference. The outcome was that the Nationalists were to withdraw towards the Sakarya River and reform, reorganise and counter-attack. The plan was to turn the Greek flank, scatter their forces in disarray and drive them towards Smyrna and ultimately back into the Aegean Sea itself. Resolute action was clearly needed to do this, and in Ankara Mustapha was temporarily appointed Generalissimo so that he could take the steps necessary to mobilise the entire Nationalist camp. Every available man, including some deputies, were handed a rifle and directed to the nearby railway station at Polath, from where they would be rushed to the front. Every spare wagon, mule, able-bodied man woman and child was conscripted to help transport supplies to the front; convoys of oxcarts laden with boxes of weapons and ammunition struggled to the front line in an episode destined to add to the Nationalist's growing reservoir of folklore.

On 1 August the Greeks resumed their advance towards Ankara, a move that Venizelos rightly believed would be unlikely to achieve the knockout blow that was required to defeat the Turks. So far the Greek army had achieved tactical success, capturing towns and territory, but the bulk of the Turkish army had eluded them and was drawing them further and further into hostile and alien country, where their vehicles broke down and they had to resort to horse-drawn transport. General Papoulas sent one column along the railway line to Ankara, and two more moved further south across the central Anatolian steppe to attack the Turkish left flank. The Turks had established good positions following the line of the Sakarya River along the edges of the Haymana Plateau south-east of Ankara, where a number of hills and peaks dominated the Ilica Valley in the south. The most important of all was Mount Cal.

Papoulas planned to break through the base of the right angle of the Turkish line formed by crossing the shallow Ilica stream, and then thrust north-east to Haymana whilst isolating Turkish troops on the east bank of the Sakarya. Mustapha decided that the best strategy would be to meet the invader west of Ankara with 90,000 troops against the 100,000 men fielded by Papoulas. This time however the Turks had a major advantage, with a 3:1 superiority in cavalry affording significantly improved mobility, speed and manoeuvrability. This factor was to prove decisive in the savage fighting which followed.

Battle opened on 23 August, with the Greek capture of Mount Mangal, not a very auspicious start for the Nationalists. An understandably chastened Mustapha threatened severe penalties against the commanders responsible, but then the Greeks achieved even more success when they swung northwards towards the critical positions around Mount Cal and for a time it looked as if the Greeks might carry the day. Mustapha issued strict 'stand and fight' instructions and made it perfectly clear what he expected of his troops. No retreat, no withdrawal; fight and if need be die at your posts; buy time for your comrades with your own blood, but hold on at all costs. It was Gallipoli writ large, but despite his entreaties it looked like the fibre of his men would not be enough when the Greeks took Mount Cal on 2 September.

But the invaders themselves were beginning to waver. Already close to exhaustion in the merciless heat, they had spent the last ten days clambering up the bleak, barren hillsides drenched in sweat and deprived of water, salt, rations and enduring stomach complaints, sunstroke and exhaustion.[39] They were now dangerously close to, if not at, breaking point. The dire situation was further aggravated by the Nationalist superiority in cavalry, which was cutting Greek lines of communication and depriving them of their priceless but ever dwindling supplies, being heavily dependent too upon the ships that plied between Greece and Smyrna.

On 4 September, just two days after Mount Cal fell, there was discernible movement among the Greek lines. In ones or twos at first, then in groups, figures began to melt away. Then the wholesale withdrawal of the invading army began to materialise. Learning of this, Mustapha wasted no time, immediately ordering the recapture of Mount Cal and after a period of consolidation, the Nationalist forces pushed forward. On 14 September they captured Papoulas' headquarters at Sivrihisar and the Greeks started retreating, obsessed with making good their escape all the way back to their original lines at Eskihisar and Afyonkarahisar. The pursuing Turks on their hardy mounts were barely unable to keep up with them. Before long hardly a single living Greek soldier stood east of the Sakarya. This was the turning point, the Greek Stalingrad. As Rumbold had foreseen in a letter to his stepmother, Sakarya did 'decide the fate of the campaign and of the Nationalists',[40] and although casualties were relatively low, 3,700 Turkish troops dead and 18,000 wounded, and 4,000 Greek dead and 19,000 wounded, the Greeks had also left over 15,000 men languishing at the tender mercy of their captors. This would make a total loss of nearly 40 per cent, and there were still hundreds of miles more to cover, their ranks doomed to wither further with each mile they trudged laboriously homeward. For his part, Mustapha found himself promoted to Field Marshal and appointed Ghazi, 'Destroyer of the Christians'.

The fleeing Greeks were determined to leave in their wake as much destruction and misery as they had time to mete out in their desperation to escape. As they pursued their fleeing Greek prey, the Nationalists came upon horrifying scenes of rape, murder, pillage and wholesale destruction, compounded by the decision of the Greeks to bombard Turkish coastal towns from the sea. A Commission of Enquiry was despatched by the Allies, concerned by the reports emanating from the country about Greek atrocities against Turkish nationals, and concluded:

There is a systematic plan of destruction of Turkish villages and extinction of the Muslim population. This plan is being carried out by Greek and Armenian bands, which appear to operate under Greek instructions and sometimes even with the assistance of detachments of regular troops.[41]

In doing so however, they simply provoked the most savage reprisals from the Nationalist soldiers as the helpless minority Greek population found itself stranded and unprotected. According to George Horton:

That they [the Greeks] did burn and lay waste the land may be taken for granted. The Greeks have claimed military necessity for this, and it would appear that they could plead such necessity if ever it can be pleaded. They certainly had more reason for laying bare the country between themselves and the advancing Khemalists than had our own Sherman on his 'March to the Sea'.[42]

Horton goes further in justifying the actions of the retreating Greeks when he explains:

The difficulties of the Greek retreat are well illustrated by an incident narrated to me by the Reverend Dana Getchell who came into my office [in Smyrna] from the interior a few days before the arrival of the Khemalists. He said that when he had gone to bed in the evening in his small hotel everything had been quiet, but that he had been awakened in the morning by the sound of tumult in the streets, and looking from the window, he saw the whole Christian population rushing toward the railroad station, carrying such of their belongings as they had been able to snatch. On enquiring what the trouble was he was informed that the Turks were coming. He went to the station himself and saw a long train of cars on to which a small detachment of Greek soldiers were attempting to embark the frightened people. While this operation was being conducted the Musselmen [Muslim] villagers came out from their houses, all armed, and began to fire upon the soldiers and the train. A battle ensued in which the officer commanding the detachment and several of his soldiers were killed. But the soldiers stood their ground well and succeeded finally in getting away with the larger part of the Christians.

Their nemesis came in the form of Nurettin Pasa, a coldly efficient, callous and calculating general who turned his wrath against the 380,000 Pontic Greeks who inhabited the Black Sea Coast. To him, they posed a serious threat to military operations, and he used this pretext to deport thousands to the interior where like the Armenians before them, they endured terrible hardships in the name of 'military necessity'. When Greek warships shelled Nationalist towns, the situation was made even worse for these ethnic Greeks, and men such as Nurettin were more than prepared to exercise their wide-ranging powers to exact revenge on their helpless victims. It was to prove simply a foretaste of things to come.

The Nationalist victory served another purpose. It persuaded his wavering northern neighbours that it would be wise to come to terms with him, and careful negotiation with the governments of Azerbaijan, Georgia and Armenia resulted in treaties with all three states at Kars on 13 October 1921. The French also came good with the undertakings they had made with the Nationalists during the London Conference in February and March, and finally handed over Cilicia. The result was an agreement, signed on 20 October, which effectively saw France withdraw from the mire into which the British and the Greeks continued to be dragged, happy to forgo her piece of the Anatolian pie in exchange for 'the pleasure' of seeing the British get their just deserts.[43] For their part, Rumbold reported to Curzon on 9 November, the Nationalists were 'greatly elated by the conclusion of this agreement',[44] and as Harold Nicolson commented, 'a few weeks later the Greek army would find itself shelled by the guns of Creusot and bombed by aeroplanes provided to Kemal from French sources'.[45] When the Italians concluded a similar agreement the Greeks found themselves isolated still further.

Mustapha had now topped his military triumph by securing the assistance of, or at the very least peace with, two major powers, the Soviet Union and France and a number of smaller states that could serve as compliant satellites. Greece by contrast was condemned to see her few reluctant sponsors melt away, leaving her only with the continued support of Lloyd George. He had backed the wrong horse whilst the Greek army's total incompetence had turned his Philhellene ambitions into dust.[46] Despite a number of attempts, Gounaris had been unable to secure further loans. Mindful that both domestically and militarily his country was at the end of its tether, he warned Curzon that the Greeks might have to abandon Anatolia entirely.[47] Curzon proposed another conference, to be held in Paris.

The Nationalists decided that this was now time to launch a diplomatic offensive to complement their military achievements, reinforce their power, and underline the impotence of the Ottoman Government. On 4 February 1922, Mustafa's foreign minister Yusuf Kemal travelled to Constantinople en route to Paris, to hold discussions with the various High Commissioners. Having thus successfully impressed the men on the spot, Yusuf travelled to Paris separately from the Ottoman Foreign Minister to attend the conference scheduled for 22 March. In Paris, Curzon succeeded in securing the agreement of Raymond Poincare, holding the joint portfolios of Premier and Foreign Minister, and the Italian Foreign Minister Carlo Schanzer, to a compromise plan which would involve the evacuation of Smyrna and the return of Constantinople to Turkey.[48] In exchange the Turks must agree to an immediate armistice and guarantee the safety of the Christian minorities. The Greeks agreed, grudgingly and with grave misgivings as they had little choice, having become financially bankrupt and militarily spent. The Turks however prevaricated. They were strong and gaining in strength and now demanded Eastern Thrace and the evacuation of the Greeks before an armistice could be signed. These demands were too much too soon however, and would mean everyone concerned except the Nationalists losing face. Bruised egos were one thing, outright capitulation another. So yet again a negotiated solutions failed and the talks collapsed, taking with them the one opportunity to avoid the further carnage to follow.[49]

The Nationalists however had put this lull to good use, and built up their army into one of a formidable 200,000 men, and all that remained was for the weather to improve sufficiently for them to resume their offensive. They had also been able to use their ever expanding stocks of arms and ammunition to re supply their army, while the Greeks were becoming correspondingly weaker, disorganised and desperate to flee, exacerbating their situation by discarding valuable provisions and materiel as they went. King Constantine's younger brother Prince Andrew gave his apocalyptic evaluation of the situation to Metaxas as early as January. He admitted that the offensive spirit of the army was 'exhausted ... I do not think the army will be in a state to face a serious action by the enemy ... something must be done to remove us from this nightmare ... My God when will I get away from this hell here?'[50] Many officers failed to return from leave, soldiers were avoiding the draft, and desertions were approaching epidemic proportions,[51] a situation further compounded by Communist propaganda, spread both within their ranks and distributed from Turkish aircraft which dropped defeatist leaflets urging them to throw down their arms. Many took the advice, discarded their equipment and headed westwards on their own initiative. In the meantime, the government's popularity was plummeting as it strove to raise sufficient funds to maintain the army; in the absence of foreign credit, it was forced to take extreme economic measures that lowered its domestic stock even further. Nor had these devastating developments escaped the notice of Rumbold. On 13 March he had telegraphed Curzon describing the dire situation: 'Morale of Greek troops is bad and they appear disheartened ... if Nationalists are ever in a position to press an attack home they will crumple,'[52] he warned.

On 12 May Gounaris' Government finally fell, and a little over a week later a coalition was formed from the remnants and Petro Protopapadakis became Prime Minister. Nevertheless, it was widely assumed that it would make little difference. It could not alter the naked truth that the end was in sight. On 25 May, the hard-pressed General Papoulas also resigned. His successor was General George Chatzanestes, a man of allegedly questionable personal qualities who Lloyd George referred to simply as a 'mental case'.[53] His gravitas was not improved by his decision to undertake even more changes to his staff, before setting off on a tour of the front from which he returned with a completely misguided and bizarrely over-optimistic evaluation of his army's remaining capabilities. He subsequently decided that he could afford to transfer three regiments and two battalions to Thrace, whilst the Greek government blithely announced that their war aims now included the occupation of Constantinople.

When the British heard of the Greek threat to claim Constantinople, they were astonished. Whitehall reminded them that any such step would itself be a breach of the Neutral Zone, and instructed the Royal Navy to oppose any landings that might materialise. Even the Nationalists offered 20,000 men if they were needed. Wisely, the Greeks saw that they had overstepped the mark, and withdrew. This potentially dire situation could have been the perfect moment to bring things to a peaceful conclusion and negotiate their withdrawal from Anatolia without any further loss of life. Mustapha despatched his Interior Minister, Fethi Omar, to London and Paris for this purpose, but despite his best efforts discussions proved inconclusive yet again. Still convinced that their army had at least one more offensive in it, the Greeks rejected any overtures. It seemed that they would have to be decisively beaten on the field of battle before they would finally face the realities of their hopeless situation.

On 4 August Lloyd George muddied the waters again when he spoke in the House of Commons. He accused the Turks of committing wartime atrocities and of refusing reasonable proposals,[54] in a speech that many considered to be little more than a thinly disguised invitation to the Greeks to renew their offensive,[55] which indeed it appeared to be to his Greek audience in Athens.[56] This is hardly surprising when he used such oratorical badinage as his claim that:

I do not know of any army that would have gone as far as the Greeks have gone. It was a very daring and very dangerous military experiment. They established a military superiority in every pitched battle ...[57]

Before they could rise to the bait, the Turks moved first. On 6 August, the Turkish army received orders from Ismet to open what would prove to be the final stage of their offensive. 208,000 Turkish troops faced 225,000 Greek, both sides considerably reinforced by drawing on valuable reserves, but although the latter had more machine guns and artillery, the Turks still enjoyed superiority in cavalry. The Greeks' other grave disadvantage was to be strung out along an extended front of some 400 miles, not an enviable disposition with the Nationalists able to take the initiative, choose their point of attack and gain local superiority almost at will. Only excellent communications, transport and, perhaps most importantly of all, leadership would have been of any help in redressing the balance. The Greeks possessed none of these assets.

The Greek lines now ran from Gemlik on the Sea of Marmara, to the east of Eskihisar, Kutahya and Afyonkarahisar. It then turned south to follow the Menderes Valley south-west to the Aegean Sea. The Greek 1st Corps was in the south, the 2nd in the centre and the 3rd in the north; the Turkish plan was to launch a concerted effort against the Afyon Salient, an area containing a number of formidable mountain peaks, in order to isolate and destroy the Greek forces positioned there. The Turks already held the highest, Kocatepe, which stood at 6,000 feet, and the Greeks a number of lower peaks of around 5,000 feet. Obviously these objectives would prove tough nuts to crack, involving near-suicidal frontal assaults uphill, against well entrenched positions. It was a task largely devolved upon the uncompromising General Nurettin Pasha and his 1st Army, bolstered by elements of the 2nd Army.

The assault began with an artillery barrage at dawn on 26 August against the Afyon sector, with diversionary bombardments, and fake campfires to the north in an effort to draw off the Greek forces. However, the assault itself met with surprisingly tough Greek opposition, perhaps in the knowledge that they had little alternative but to hold their ground or place themselves at the doubtful mercy of the Turk. They fought with determination, but after a while the 4th Corps of the 2nd Army penetrated the Greek lines to capture Mount Erkentepe, whilst the Turkish cavalry had found a way to the invaders' rear. The Greek 1st Corps was the first to crack, retreating in chaos as they had at Sakarya. One after another the Greek units bolted; all communications and any hope of coordinated withdrawal dissolving with them in the ensuing disorder, until the entire Greek army collapsed 'like a pack of cards'.[58] As Harold Nicolson described it so graphically, 'Within a fortnight nothing but the corpses of Greek soldiers remained in Anatolia.'[59]

Most of the Greek 1st and 2nd Corps tried to reform at Dumlupinar, 30 miles from Afyonkarahisar, where they 'dug in' up to a point, but their main aim was to use the nearby Afyon-Smyrna railway to make good their escape to the coast. On 30 August, an artillery bombardment preceded an assault that swept all before it. The two Greek Corps were all but wiped out. The few survivors fled, desperate to see the back of Anatolia; but they still faced the agonising prospect of a 250-mile forced march through savage, hostile and waterless terrain, with vengeful Turks ready to snipe at them from behind every rock and defile, picking off unwary stragglers with the slash off a knife.

Now Mustapha could sense that the end was within his grasp, and on 1 September, victory was proclaimed in an army order concluding with the exhortation, 'Armies! The Mediterranean is your immediate objective – Forward!'[60]

The following day the commander of the 1st and 2nd Corps surrendered along with 500 officers, 5,000 men, hundreds of machine guns and twelve field guns, demoralised, exhausted, threadbare and totally sick of their role as liberators of Anatolia. The commander, General Trikoupis, admitted later:

> With a heavy heart I ordered the destruction of the artillery and machine-guns … when I saw that the Turkish lancers had almost reached our lines, and that the men would be slaughtered without resistance, I agreed to the raising of the white flag.[61]

On 4 September the *Times* announced a 'Greek Appeal to the Powers', reporting that its government had advised the British that it could no longer 'be responsible for the safety of Christian minorities in Asia Minor', and asking its Allies to use their good offices to arrange an armistice. It went on to report that the Greek cabinet was on the verge of resigning en masse.[62] The *Daily Mail* reported on the same day that the Greeks had made known their intention to evacuate Smyrna 'bag and baggage', deciding that it would be cheaper to protect their 800,000 Greek, Circassian and Armenian subjects in Greece rather than continue paying for an army in Asia Minor. A conclusion that, made a couple of years earlier, would have spared themselves and the Turks much devastation and despair.

The Allies, somewhat naively, called for a swift conclusion to the abortive armistice negotiations. Mustapha replied on 5 September that there was no longer anyone with whom to negotiate, adding that he wanted the pre-1914 Thrace border reinstated and an armistice concluded there and then. He gave the Greeks until the 10th to reply to his ultimatum. It was all rather academic, the war was over and the Greeks were finished. The same day as Mustapha issued his ultimatum, *The Times* confirmed that 'there can no longer be any doubt that the Greeks have suffered disaster in Asia Minor ... The Greek army has lost heart in the face of the determined onslaught of Turkish Nationalists and the Greeks are retreating to Smyrna.' Furthermore, it spared a thought for the innocent civilians caught up in the fighting who had 'suffered far more from war than they could have done in peace',[63] while the *Daily Mail* admitted that 'the Greek army intends immediately to evacuate Asia Minor'. 'Here's a bloody mess,'[64] remarked Lloyd George as the brutal reality of the Greek collapse was finally brought home.

Until very recently life in Smyrna had been proceeding pretty much as usual in the town, strangely immune from the chaos in the interior. Slowly however, more news was filtering back and nerves were becoming frayed, although the deceptive calm was still deluding the hapless populace as to the real situation. There was however the erroneously reassuring sight of the Allied vessels in the harbour, some twenty-two warships in addition to other smaller craft. The hopes of many would hinge on the prospect of finding safety on board, but in reality the Allies were neutral and officially unable to assist the combatants. When on 6 September the first refugees embarked on board SS *Magira* and *Antioch* they were mainly Maltese and Cypriot-British subjects, for the vast majority there was only the announcement that martial law had been declared throughout the city. At last, reality was finally striking home to the doomed population.

Under the headline 'FEARS FOR SMYRNA' *The Times* confirmed that 'the plight of the Greek army appears to be most serious and in well informed British circles the early fall of Smyrna is regarded as inevitable'.[65] The latent fears of the townsfolk were now to be realised as the pathetic lines of exhausted fugitives made their first appearance in the town. George Horton recalled 'one old gray-haired woman stumbling through the streets of Smyrna with an emaciated feverish son astride her neck. He was taller than the mother, his legs almost touching the ground.' The depressing sight of refugees was bad enough, but they were to be followed by the men who were once looked up to as saviours who had liberated the port city just three short years before. But now, as Horton recorded:

> The defeated, dusty, ragged Greek soldiers began to arrive, looking straight ahead, like men walking in their sleep. Great numbers – the more fortunate – were sitting on ancient Assyrian carts ... Silently as ghosts they went, looking neither to the right nor to the left ...

Seeking solace in their faith, the Greeks and Armenians swarmed to their churches and in their desperation even sent an appeal to the Archbishop of Canterbury to intercede on their behalf.

The Times reported on 9 September that the Greek government 'is keenly concerned about the fate of several hundred thousand refugees concentrated at Smyrna' and who feared 'extermination by the Turks'.[66] A unit sent on 5 September to reinforce its defences balked at the idea and mutinied, and the Greek High Command made plans for a complete evacuation. The Urla peninsula, south-west of Smyrna was earmarked as the Greek Dunkirk. But there would be no miracle here.

Hoping to avoid a frenzied bloodbath, the Allied Powers sent a note to Mustapha, promising him the city if he agreed to spare the Christians still living there. Such appeals however were futile, as hot on the heels of the columns of retreating soldiers and refugees were the Turks, with the taste of victory sweet on their lips. Advance Nationalist units entered the city on 9 September whilst Mustapha made his own preparations for his triumphal march into Izmir, the city which had witnessed so much misery in the past and whose populace was bracing itself for even worse to come. George Horton described how:

> Now at last we heard that the Turks were moving into the town ... the supreme question was: 'how would the Turks

behave? The French and Italian delegates assured their colonies [of expatriates] that Kemal's army consisted of well-disciplined troops and that there was nothing to fear ...

Nevertheless, the anxious community was soon to be disabused of any notions of chivalry. George Horton noticed that 'not all the troops of Mustapha Khemal [sic] were provided with the smart uniforms of his picked troops' and remembered how they had on their faces an expression akin to 'that of an ecstasy of hate and savagery'. Many bore in their collective memories the reign of terror carried out by the Greeks in May 1919, the humiliations and abuses and the widespread killings. They had fought and marched hundreds of miles to avenge their fellow Turks and now there was nothing to hold them back.

Gradually worry increased to anxiety and then panic until Smyrna became a city almost paralysed by terror. Horton recalled 'frightened screams ... stepping out of the door of my office, I found that a crowd of refugees, mostly women, were rushing in terror upon the Consulate and trying to seek refuge within', as 'the panic among the Christians was now increasing to an alarming extent'. On the night of 10 September, he continued:

> The shooting could still be heard in the Christian quarters and frightened people were besieging the doors of these institutions [the YMCA and YWCA] and screaming and begging in God's name to be let in ... The Turks were now making a thorough and systematic job of killing Armenian men ... some were despatched on the spot while others were led out into the country in squads and shot, the bodies left in piles where they fell ...

Horton's evidence is substantiated by a number of Allied seamen, who from the safety of their warships watched helplessly as the carnage continued just a few yards away. An anonymous witness later recounted:

> Sudden panic [ensued] when Turkish cavalry was seen coming up the main street with swords at the 'carry'. Greek soldiers fled

in all directions. Ferry boats crowded with terrified Greeks – one passenger not understanding our neutrality and evidently disappointed at us taking no action, shouted out at us as the ferry passed, 'Thank You very much, kill us like chickens,' this was followed by the suggestive action of drawing the hand across the throat.

A Greek soldier under escort, obviously exhausted, was seen to stagger and fall – immediately one of the escorts put a sword into him. He was then seized by about a dozen Turkish civilians who dragged him by the heels along the ground and threw him into the sea, amusing themselves by throwing logs of wood at him although he was still alive. A revolver was produced and eventually the unfortunate wretch was put out of his agony. The sea was stained with blood.[67]

Medical Rating T. W. Bunter was in charge of the operating theatre aboard the US Hospital Ship *Maine* and saw

the carnage and cruelty to the Greek civilians ... We saw from where we were just off the shore the Turks bayoneting bodies, men women and children, through the windows of their homes. Hundreds of Greek civilians as well as troops hanging over the dock waterside and the Turkish soldiers coming along and deliberately severing the victims' arms, resulting in hundreds of bodies falling to their deaths in the sea. Hundreds too, were swimming towards us and eventually we received them and treated them and took them down to Malta.[68]

Lieutenant M. M. Carus Wilson of the 1/4th Dorsets described how, as he

stood on the deck of the *Iron Duke* [he] could hear the terrible wailing of the refugees who were crammed on the sea front rising above the roar of the vast circle of flames. They could also see people being cut down in the streets [but] could do nothing to prevent the butchery.[69]

Ernest Hemingway, acidly but dispassionately recalled other scenes of cruelty:

> The Greeks were nice chaps too. When they evacuated they had all their baggage animals they couldn't take off with them, so they just broke their forelegs and dumped them into the shallow water. All those mules with their forelegs broken pushed over into the shallow water. It was all a pleasant business. My word, yes a most pleasant business.[70]

As Greek civilian, soldier and donkey alike endured the fate of the vanquished, others were more fortunate. Stergiadis himself decided that it was time to make good his own safe passage out of the bloodbath, and sought refuge on board *Iron Duke*, leaving hundreds of his countrymen to their fate.[71] As he clambered aboard, the quay behind him echoed to the wails of derision and contempt from his erstwhile charges for whom a grisly fate waited. The Greek Archbishop of Chrysostomos was one of those. Nurettin Pasha, now the newly installed Governor of Smyrna had a score to settle. He believed the elderly cleric was responsible for having him ejected from the city when the Greeks arrived in 1919, and he sent a policeman to the Cathedral of St Pholeini to collect the archbishop. He was not however satisfied with returning the compliment, but instead he ordered the hapless clergyman to be hanged.[72] The terrified old man was dragged away by a baying mob, but before a rope could be found the crowd – drunk with bloodlust – turned on him. Among other violations, his beard was wrenched out by its roots and his eyes gouged out. The mutilated old man's agony was only ended when a Turk Cretan for whom he had once granted a favour put him out of his misery with a shot from his revolver.

As Mustapha entered the city on 10 September in a staff car bedecked somewhat ironically with olive branches and escorted by mounted cavalry, his dream of liberating Turkey was about to be fulfilled. There were now just a few isolated pockets of resistance to be mopped up; Bursa, the ancient seat of the Ottoman Turks was also liberated on the same day Mustapha entered Izmir, and by

16 September the last of the Greek troops, who were going to leave in one piece, had done so. Three days later north-west Anatolia was emptied of Greek forces, leaving another 13,000 killed and 35,000 wounded. Even worse was the fate that awaited the 35,000 Greek captives who fell into the hands of the Nationalists and those Greek stragglers rounded up by French troops and handed over. They may have been wiser to fight to the death and, as The *Daily Mail* reported on 11 September that 'the whole of the Greek army in Asia Minor has fallen into the hands of the Turkish Nationalists. Only a few straggling bands of Greeks remain not rounded up by Mustapha Kemal's' divisions.'[73]

G. Ward Price recounted the tragedy of the Greek Dunkirk that had started over a week before: [74]

Steaming up the Gulf of Smyrna this evening, I met abundant evidence of the headlong flight of the Greeks from Asia Minor ... shabby steamships of all sizes, which had been hastily requisitioned, Greek soldiers were clustering in them like swarms of bees. Little sailing boats laboured along laden with refugees, the coastal steamers were packed with civilians, towing more civilians in lighters ...

And still the suffering continued.

News of the capture of Smyrna was understandably met by great displays of rejoicing throughout Anatolia, so much so that they threatened to get out of hand. Particularly forceful celebrations in Constantinople degenerated according to *The Times*, 'into an outbreak of rowdism, accompanied by some hustling of Greeks and foreigners and extensive window breaking. One Greek was killed,' it confirmed, as the Turks swept forward and the final victory appeared to be within their grasp.[75]

The city, undeniably Turkish Izmir once more, was one cowering under a dark and brooding shadow of fear. Those who could sought sanctuary from streets littered with decomposing corpses and tainted by the clawing miasma of death, which clung to everyone and everything. The eerie calm, interspersed by erratic gunfire and screams, belied the fragile underlying atmosphere as Turkish soldiers looted and wandered the streets in sinister mobs, sometimes encountering Allied detachments that had been landed to protect their respective consulates and economic interests. For the most part the encounters were cordial, but despite such outward gestures suspicions were being aroused. Reports were received that Turkish troops had been seen in the Armenian quarter, carrying petrol and other paraphernalia that could have but one purpose.[76] The evidence of Miss Minnie Mills, one of Horton's contacts, was compelling:

I could plainly see the Turks carrying the tins of petroleum into the houses, from which, in each instance, fire burst forth immediately afterward. There was not an Armenian in sight, the only person visible being Turkish soldiers of the regular army ...

Another witness, Mrs King Birge, the wife of an American missionary, claimed that she 'could plainly see Turkish soldiers setting fire to houses. I could see Turks lurking in the fields, shooting at Christians. When I drove down to Smyrna from Paradise [the US Quarter] to Athens, there were dead bodies all along the road.' Horton went up on the terrace of the Consulate, from where he could observe,

Vast dark clouds of smoke arising from a wide area, for the fire had been started simultaneously in several places ... the flames consumed the Armenian quarter with such appalling rapidity as to make it certain that the Turks were augmenting them with inflammable liquids. Bluejackets [US Marines] reported that they saw Turkish soldiers throwing rags soaked in petroleum into Armenian houses.

The fire, which was being helped by a gentle breeze, made its way towards the waterfront consuming everything in its path, and here the terrified residents had only one direction in which to flee – towards the harbour waters. By midnight 2 miles of the waterfront was engulfed in flames, lapping at the heels of the fleeing civilians, who now heard rumours of Turkish soldiers lying in wait to ambush them.

The refugees stampeded even closer to the fire and, as Miss Mills told Horton,

> The flames were approaching and the soldiers were forcing these people to go into the houses. An American automobile passed and the poor wretches stretched out their hands, crying: 'save us! The Turks are going to burn us alive'. Nothing could be done of course, and the car passed on. Later two Catholic priests came up and said to the Turks: 'This is a fiendish thing you are doing', and they allowed an old woman to come out of one of the houses.

Despite such isolated examples of clemency, the general scene was one of pitiless slaughter. Horton described:

> A prominent Dutch merchant of Smyrna, who had taken refuge on his yacht during the fire, related to me [later in] Athens that all through the night of the dreadful thirteenth he heard fearful screams from the shore, ending suddenly in a queer watery gurgle. He learned the next morning that a lot of throats had been cut.

Captain Thesiger, like many other helpless servicemen listening and watching from their warships moored in the relative safety of the harbour, was on board HMS *King George V* and remembered 'the most awful scream one could ever imagine' coming out from the burning city.[77] Some utterly desperate refugees sought sanctuary on board the Allied ships. The water was now choked with men, women and children, floundering and slipping beneath the lapping blood-stained waves screaming for help, and the officially neutral crews were compelled to act. Even so, hundreds more died whilst others, frozen with fear and panic, remained onshore waiting to be consumed by the voracious flames or despatched by marauding Turks. *The Daily Mail* announced to the world, 'SMYRNA ALMOST WIPED OUT – GREAT TOWN STILL BLAZING', confirming 'the usual accounts of Turkish atrocities', and the 'frantic screaming of sheer terror [that] can be heard miles away.[78] It was taking on all the characteristics of an ancient calamity or a biblical act of godlike retribution, but this tragedy was caused by man and heaped upon his fellows – a horror which was simply bringing to a head three years of mutual slaughter. As Constantine Brown reported for the *Chicago Daily News*, the whole episode was 'a crime which will brand the Turks forever … when Turkish soldiery, after finishing pillaging, set this city on fire'.[79]

When eventually the wind had died down and the fire had in any case more or less burnt itself out, naval shore parties landed and cautiously attempted to restore some order. But it was now a city that resembled something out of Dante's *Inferno*, from which the lucky survivors emerged one by one to survey their lost world. *The Times'* correspondent in Athens confirmed that 'the damage caused by the fire up to last evening amounted to £15,000,000', and added that 'up to the outbreak of the fire about one thousand persons had been massacred'.[80] It could, however, still have been so much worse. The number of refugees to have escaped the fire varies widely, from between 50,000 to 400,000. Some of those trapped by the fire had been evacuated by the Allied warships, HMS *Iron Duke* alone finding room in its cramped quarters for 2,000 lost and desperate souls. For the battle-scarred and campaign hardened veterans of ten years or perhaps more, who had seen cruelty and carnage on a vast scale and seen hundreds of Anatolian villages laid waste, this was just another in a litany of tragic episodes. To others it had simply provided a case study in ethnic cleansing, finally expelling everything non-Turk and drawing once and for all a line under centuries of intercommunal hatred and suspicion. For the Greeks it represented the loss of their final toehold in Anatolia – within a very short time to be expunged of all but a handful of stubborn survivors. Never again could even the most dubious ethnographic statistics justify any claim on the city or its hinterland. To Consul Horton, indeed,

> Historians and archaeologists have declared that they know of but one event in the annals of the world which can equal in savagery, extent and all the elements of horror, cruelty and human suffering the destruction of Smyrna and its Christian

population by the Turks, and this was the demolition of Carthage by the Romans.

A young subaltern at the time, Lieutenant G. N. Wood, later mused:

Now only by the Greeks and Turks is that savage war remembered, ending with the fair city of Smyrna ablaze and its people perishing in the flames or in the water of the harbour ...[81]

Lord Beaverbrook, who Lloyd George sent to the region on a fact-finding mission, had little to reassure him. He warned him that these now desperate and 'embittered people' blamed Britain for their plight, accusing them of leading them to this 'adventure' and then letting them down.[82] General Harington, so often the man on the spot throughout the crisis, had his own view, and it very closely echoed that of Beaverbrook when he reflected, 'if Mr Lloyd George had not, with Mr Venizelos' help, put the Greeks into Anatolia, the tragedy of Smyrna would never have happened'.[83]

Wherever the blame for this catastrophe lay, the capture of Smyrna served as an emphatic vindication of the resurgence of Turkish nationalism. Mustapha's own growing strength and power was gaining currency and his right to be recognised as the modern Saladin was indisputable. Throughout the Muslim world this defender of the Sultan-Caliph was assuming a reputation that began to stir Mohammedans to the cause of jihad, inspire latent nationalism and threaten in its turn British interests far away from the immediate confines of Anatolia. The result was a series of repercussions for Britain's Anatolian adventure that Lloyd George could never have anticipated.

6

YOU WILL GET NO
COOPERATION FROM US

When the British Empire went to war with Turkey in 1914, there was disquiet among many of her Muslim subjects, some of whom openly articulated their concern that Muslim soldiers might be asked to wage war against the very head of the Muslim faith – the Sultan-Caliph residing in the Divine Porte. The Viceroy, Lord Hardinge, however assured these voices that whatever the outcome of the war, there was no intention of challenging the position of the Caliphate.[1] Indeed, had Britain pursued such a policy, the possible Muslim response was an unknown quantity. Had the government to call upon Indian troops to serve in Turkey for that purpose, what might their reaction be? Would there be a backlash, the likes of which had not been experienced since 1857 when Indian Sepoys turned upon the British with bloody consequences? If the government stirred up Muslim anger over Turkey, what would the long-term consequences involve for the Indian Empire itself?

Until now few of India's 60 million Muslims had expressed any political aspirations so long as the Raj guaranteed them protection from their Hindu neighbours. Even the foundation, in 1885, of the Indian National Congress had done little to stir serious nationalist sentiment. While endemic mistrust condemned the Muslim community to an existence largely on the fringes of political life, it permitted the ruling white elite to govern by employing the classic device of 'divide and rule'. Britain's position as the paramount power on the sub-continent appeared secure, and it would need a catalyst of cosmic proportions to galvanise the two communities and bring this comfortable arrangement to an end. Therefore, while most of the Hindu population demonstrated active support for the war, lured in part by promises of a greater share in government, Muslims remained at best ambivalent. Some however, such as the brothers Shaukat and Muhammed Ali, were more vocal and dismissed British assurances with protests against this 'betrayal of Islam' and were imprisoned for the duration of the war.² The majority of Indians responded positively and two infantry divisions and one cavalry division were despatched to the Western Front almost at once, where they fought gallantly and suffered terrible casualties. Indian troops were also hurriedly despatched to East Africa and Egypt, and before the end of 1914 some 300,000 Indian troops were serving in foreign theatres. As British Prime Minister Lloyd George himself conceded, 'the largest contingents of fighting troops came, of course, from India',³ and by the end of the war, over 1,300,000 had volunteered to fight for the King-Emperor, known to the sepoys as 'George Panjam'.⁴ Despite earlier unease, many also served without issue against the Caliph in the deserts of Mesopotamia, Syria and Palestine. Nowhere was any manifestation of serious dissent demonstrated by Muslim troops, and the Sultan's call to jihad was all but ignored.

However, latent concerns began to surface when Turkey found herself on the losing side, arousing amongst Muslims fears that the existence of the Caliphate was indeed in peril. It was no secret that Britain and France in particular had long coveted control of the Dardanelles, and the prospect of ejecting the Sultan-Caliph from Constantinople was now openly debated. The Foreign Office minuted that 'the Muslims of Egypt and India should realise that Turkey has been completely defeated',⁵ and one explicit way of illustrating this would be to bring Constantinople under Allied control.

Indian concerns had been communicated to the Secretary of State for India Lord Edwin Montagu, who took the earliest opportunity to confront Lloyd George on the subject. Montagu had been appointed Under Secretary of State for India 1910 and Secretary of

State in 1917, becoming something of an expert in Indian affairs. He was an ardent reformist, who had long endorsed the view that Indians had to be given an increased role in running the affairs of the Sub-Continent, and strongly adhered to the policy of separating so-called extremist elements from the more moderate Indians. Only by implementing measures that would satisfy their aspirations could the future of the Raj be assured. Implicit in this policy was the need to ensure that the more die-hard Indian Nationalists were not given any motive to provoke unrest. Such fears were made evident by Britain's policy in Turkey.

He raised the question on 3 May 1919, at a meeting of the British Empire delegation at the Hotel Majestic in Paris. Despite the Prime Ministers' assurances that no plans had been made to eject the Sultan from Constantinople, he said Indian Muslims were 'becoming increasingly apprehensive at what appeared to them the anti-Mohammedan policy of the conference'. He went on to explain that the Muslims remained loyal 'to the country in which they lived ... but they continue to pray for the Caliph'. Even in the midst of the fighting in Mesopotamia he went on, 'after an attack against the Turkish forces ... Indian Mohammedans would return to spread their prayer carpets and pray for the wellbeing of the Sultan of Turkey'. Implicit in this was Montagu's conviction that the British government had to treat Muslim sensibilities with the utmost care if they did not want to risk compromising their loyalties, and for this reason alone he continued, 'the Indian delegation were unable to understand the apparently ruthless spirit in which it was proposed to treat the Turkish Empire'. He insisted, 'If, in spite of the Prime Minister's speech about not depriving Turkey of its capital, Constantinople were to be taken from the Turk, the Mohammedans of India would feel that the British Empire, with its large Mohammedan population was embarking on a campaign which was not merely anti-Turkish but anti-Mohammedan.'

At this early stage Lloyd George declined to address what was still after all a hypothetical question, nor to give it too much of his time. He simply responded to Lord Montagu's entreaties to the effect that the 'Council of Four' had not yet discussed the question of Turkey.

When it did, the case for the Mohammedans of India 'should be presented by the Maharajah of Bikanar and Lord Sinha'.⁶

It may have been an academic exercise to the Prime Minister, preoccupied by the larger question of negotiating the peace treaty with Germany, but it was not so to the Indians. Later that month, and under growing pressure to listen to their concerns, Lloyd George agreed to one of repeated requests from the Aga Khan to bring his case to the Council of Ministers in Paris. He was the head of the Ismaili Muslims, who had urged their Indian brothers to remain loyal to Britain when the country went to war with Turkey. Having been knighted in 1898 he went on to serve as a member of the exclusive Viceroy's Council, and was therefore considered a plausible spokesman and champion of Islam, and of the need to maintain the Caliphate and preserve India's loyalty to the Raj. As such, his credentials were exemplary.

The deputation's submission was sufficiently compelling for Lloyd George to concede that, 'it is impossible to divide Turkey proper. We would run too great a risk of throwing disorder into the Mohammedan world'.⁷ However this stand was clearly inconsistent with his support for Greek designs on Anatolia, which explicitly included the division of Turkey; Greek forces were embarking on the landings in Smyrna, and both France and Italy had territorial claims to settle. In addition, there were those still advocating the ejection of the Turks from Constantinople, all aims that were completely at odds with the calls for restraint being urged by Indian Muslims and Lord Montagu. As the Afghan ambassador to Turkey explained:

Islam is a large body of which Turkey is the head, Azerbaijan the neck, Persia the chest, Afghanistan the heart, India the abdomen, Egypt and Palestine, Irak [sic] and Turkestan are the arms and legs. When you deliver rough blows at the head, how can the rest of the body not feel it? England has hit our head too hard, and we have protested...

These protests were now taking on a new dynamic with the release of the Ali brothers who were able to tap into the deep-seated passion of Muslims both for Islam itself and the Caliph in particular. The founding of the Khilifat Committee in Bombay provided a platform from which their demands could be spread. Encouraged by the promises to defend the Caliphate contained in the pronouncements made at Erzurum and Sivas, it also established contact with the Nationalists:

> Mustapha Kemal Pasha has done wonders and you have no idea how people in India adore his name. The honour of the Turkish nation has once again been vindicated ... The Musselmans of India – particularly the poor and middle classes, are doing their very best to subscribe to the Ankara fund ... may the Great Allah grant victory to the armies of Gazi Mustapha Kemal and save Turkey from her enemies and the enemies of Islam ... [8]

Those 'enemies' presumably included the British Raj as well as the Greeks, and the fund collected a handsome £125,000 towards the cause. Mustapha received reports of such movements favourably; he believed that if they could garner sympathy for Turkey then they should be exploited, and to this end sent agents as far as Afghanistan to spread dissention and stir up anti-British sentiment.

One man who was taking considerable interest in these developments was Mohandas Gandhi, one-time barrister and now a key figure in the growing Indian nationalist movement. Gandhi's ancestors had served in the courts of Muslim princes for generations, and his own grandfather owed his life to a Muslim bodyguard. He therefore held a sincere empathy for the religion and was convinced that the Koran itself was divinely inspired.[9] Born in Gujarat in north-west India in 1869, he travelled to London in 1888 to study law. He then returned to a practice in India before moving to South Africa where from 1907 to 1914 he sought to oppose the endemic racism that Indians in the colony were being subjected to, urging passive resistance in protest at their treatment. He returned to India in 1915, and from 1917 to 1918 he played a pivotal role in securing improved working conditions for peasants and industrial workers in Bihar and Gujarat. Once a firm adherent of the British Empire, his dedication to independence for India grew until in February 1919 he used his influence to have *Satyagraha*, or 'soul force', adopted by the Home Rule Leagues that had evolved during the course of the war, a philosophy that was dedicated to the cause of freedom but which was emphatic about the use of nonviolence to achieve those ends.

The conclusion of the First World War left much of India in turmoil. The war had not only seen the army increased ten-fold, but the government's revenue demands grow by 40 per cent. Food supplies became a serious problem, and inflation threatened to get out of control, putting basic commodities such as sugar, salt and fuel beyond the reach of ordinary Indians. Strikes and civil disorder were widespread, and the government was becoming uneasy. Furthermore, Indian soldiers had returned from fighting in Europe and the Middle East, where their experiences had served to shock them out of their confidence in the infallibility of the white man. The senseless slaughter had imbued in many a notion that the Raj was perhaps not the omniscient entity they had believed it to be, and the situation was compounded by the fact that the ruling elite had been confronted by a number of emergencies that it proved either ill-equipped or too inept to resolve. An influenza epidemic had killed twelve million people and demonstrated that the Raj could not solve every problem on their subjects' behalf.

The British attempted to satisfy Indian aspirations for self-government with the publication in 1919 of the Montagu–Chelmsford Reforms, which would establish limited autonomy in a number of states, with elected Indian ministers who would be responsible for key functions. Ultimate power nonetheless remained in the hands of the Viceroy, who enjoyed the right of veto over legislation. It was a major step forward, but was overshadowed by the worsening situation in the country.

March witnessed a series of demonstrations and public meetings, and on 6 April Gandhi called for a general strike that, despite his pleas, descended into violence. On 13 April 1919 the biggest blunder since the partition of Bengal was committed when Brigadier-General Reginald Dyer, British Officer Commanding in the town of Amritsar in the Punjab, ordered the fifty men under his command to open fire on a crowd of unarmed demonstrators in the Jallianwala Bagh. He believed he was nipping serious disorder in the bud, and by the time his men had discharged some 1,650 rounds at point-blank range, 400 lay dead and another 1,200 were wounded. The massacre caused outrage, and compounded Gandhi's growing sense of estrangement from the very institution he had once held in such high esteem.

By this time Shaukat and Mohammed Ali's activities had come to his attention, and he saw that by tapping into their growing movement he might be able to combine resentment over Amritsar and the campaign against the fate of the Caliphate to inspire the shared goal of *Swaraj,* or independence.[10] He was convinced that providence had delivered 'such an opportunity of uniting the two communities as would not arise in a hundred years' [11] and stressed that Hindu-Mohammedan brotherhood was 'an unalterable act of faith', urging his fellow Hindus to embrace the cause of the Khilifat Movement.[12]

Gandhi had been impressed by the effectiveness of a 'Khilifat Day', which had been held on 20 October 1919 in protest, reported the *Bombay Chronicle,* at the 'proposed dismemberment of Turkey', and Gandhi launched his association with the movement by addressing an open letter in the edition of 3 November 1919, expressing his opinion that the forthcoming peace celebrations should be boycotted by all Indians of whatever faith 'if the Khilifat question was not satisfactorily settled'. He urged strongly that 'it is hardly possible for the Hindus, Parsis, Christians, Jews and others for whom India is the land of their adoption or birth, to be taking part in the forthcoming rejoicings', whilst the Muslims could not. The Viceroy, Lord Chelmsford, counselled calm, but Gandhi insisted that 'if the Muslims sit still, all that they have done during the last four years will be proved to have been hollow. If the Muslims have no peace, Hindus can have none.'[13] He concluded by expressing his hope that the Viceroy would convey to the government in London the concerns held by the Muslims and 'recognise the necessity of securing and publishing an honourable settlement of the [Turkish] question'. Indeed, Lord Montagu had been taking note of the concerns brought to him by such loyal Indians as the Aga Khan, and concluded that a hostile policy might provoke 'grave outrage to Mohammedan sentiment throughout the world, particularly in India'.[14] In fact, such was the force of Lord Montagu's advocacy for the Caliphate cause that it would prove his own undoing.

As we shall see, he was frequently to hector his cabinet colleagues and the Prime Minister in order to influence government policy in Turkey.

The Muslims had increasingly appreciated the merits of recruiting Hindu support for their cause, and invited leading Congress members, including Gandhi, to attend a conference scheduled for 19–21 November 1919. The Muslims did their utmost to cultivate their guests, and even went so far as to suggest that they would stop slaughtering the sacred cow if it secured Hindu support for their cause.[15] The members also debated what action should be taken if the Caliphate was indeed to be abolished or exiled from Constantinople. If moral pressure did not achieve their aims then, it was argued, a complete boycott of British textiles and other manufactures should be declared, confident that an economic squeeze on the pockets of their rulers would bring them round. Discussions went on until Gandhi, it is claimed, hit upon the very phrase by which the movement to remove the British Raj would eventually be known – 'Non-Cooperation'.[16] On 24 November, the *Bombay Chronicle* ran an account of the meeting, in which the Hindus were thanked 'for cooperating with the Mohammedans on the Khilifat question', and 'urging the Mohammedans to improve cordiality with the Hindus'. The article aroused such ferment that its editor, B. G. Horniman, incurred the wrath of the government, who had him deported to England.[17]

If it were going to have the desired effect this potentially explosive new credo needed to be spread throughout the sub-continent, capture the minds of brother Indians and create a movement that the Raj would find it impossible to resist. So Gandhi and Shaukat Ali embarked upon a nationwide tour to spread the message of peaceful Non-Cooperation, travelling as widely and extensively as they could. Inevitably, these unwelcome developments were coming to the attention of many key figures in the British government. Winston Churchill had served in India as a young Subaltern, knew the country well and had developed a deep affection for its people. He was however a dedicated imperialist, saw India as the bedrock of the Empire and recognised the dire consequences for the sub-continent should men like the Ali brothers and Gandhi rouse the population against the Raj.

Furthermore, there were other serious considerations to be borne in mind. On 6 January 1920, he admitted to being convinced by

> the overwhelming evidence supplied by the Secretary of State for India, of the resentment that would be excited in India and throughout the Mohammedan world by the expulsion of the Turks from Constantinople. All our limited means of getting the Middle East to settle down quietly are comprised in the use of Indian troops. We must not do anything that will raise Indian resentment against the use of these troops or affect their own loyalty.[18]

Churchill's reservations were not without foundation. Britain was to be awarded League of Nations 'Mandates' over large areas of former Ottoman territory including Palestine, Trans Jordan and Mesopotamia. In order to exploit the oil and other mineral resources of these territories, she needed to maintain order. Churchill, as Secretary of State for Air and War, was balked at the increasing cost of maintaining order. He was now a keen advocate of policing the mandates using air power instead of thousands of troops. Garrisons were very expensive to maintain and were spread too thinly, but, more vitally Churchill conceded, many consisted of Muslim Indian soldiers. Since its occupation of Mesopotamia alone, upwards of 47,000 troops were stationed in the country, 90 per cent of whom were Indian troops, and the nationalist politicians in Delhi were far from enamoured by the prospect of using them for the purpose of suppressing native uprisings. Nevertheless, keen to save money by hastening the demobilisation of the British army, Indian troops were a vital expedient.

Others remained convinced that the Khilifat Movement was no more than a flash in the pan. Lord Curzon had served as Viceroy from 1897 to 1902, and considered himself something of an expert in the politics in the region. In January 1920 he questioned whether the British should allow their policy towards Turkey to be influenced by the sensitivities of Indian Muslims:

In order to avoid trouble in India – largely manufactured and in any case ephemeral – and to render our task in Egypt less difficult – its difficulty being in reality almost entirely independent of what we may or may not do at Constantinople – we are losing an opportunity for which Europe had waited nearly five centuries [in occupying Constantinople and controlling the route from the Black Sea to the Mediterranean].[19]

This was not the position held by the Aga Khan, who watched developments in Paris with growing concern. On 8 January he wrote to Lord Montagu from Nice, reminding him once again of the potential repercussions of ejecting the Sultan from Constantinople.[20] Writing out of 'a sense of loyalty towards His Majesty', he went to say that unless the government changed its mind 'before it is too late', it would be taking decisions 'that will have permanently evil consequences not only for India but for the peace of the world'. He went on to reiterate his conviction that any step to remove the Sultan or abolish the caliphate would 'undoubtedly once [and] for all alienate the Muslims of India, Afghanistan and Baluchistan [part of present-day Pakistan]', and prayed that 'still, at the last moment ... that justice for Islam will prevail'. After all, he warned 'if Turkish rule was to come to an end no one in India will blame the French or Italians; wrongly or rightly English Christianity and bigotry will be held responsible.' He concluded by pleading that the Allies should 'give Islam as represented by Turkey just and generous treatment', reminding Montagu that 'India sent one million soldiers to the war. It was India's help that brought Turkey to her knees.' This reason, if no other, gave Indians the right to a voice in the decision over Turkey, he claimed. These comments were passed by Montagu to his colleagues in Paris on 13 January, accompanied by a memo in which he expressed his own conviction that the 'Indians have a right to a predominant voice in this question, not only because it affects the peace and security of their country, but because they played a predominant part in the conquest of Turkey'.[21]

Curzon however, remained unmoved. After all, as he insisted in a memorandum to his colleagues in late February 1920, 'There never has been till in the last two or three years any pronounced feeling among Indian Muslims in favour of Constantinople as the seat of the Khalifate or the capital of Islam,' and therefore no serious precedent that might suggest any realistic prospect of an Indian backlash.[22] Whatever the views of old hands like Curzon, the Khilfat cause was finding willing listeners among Britain's own Muslim community. There was certainly no lack of evidence that the Khilfat cause was a profound one and gaining adherents as it garnered widespread support. In March 1920 a delegation led by Maulana Mohammed Ali arrived in the UK to put its case to the government, and paid a visit to Woking, home of the country's oldest mosque. As the *Islamic Review* of April 1920 reported:

The three members of the Indian Khilafat Delegation paid a visit to the Woking Mosque on Sunday 21 March 1920 … Mr Muhammed Ali made a strong and convincing speech to the effect that it was not fair to ignore the rights of His Majesty's Muslim subjects, whose number is greater than those of the Christians in the Empire. They were all devoted to the Caliph of Constantinople, and they all urge that the temporal power of the Caliph should not be reduced, nor should the Turkish Empire be broken into bits. Mr. Sayyid Husain, who made an eloquent and polished speech, followed Mr Muhammed Ali. He said that liberty of conscience should be granted to the people, and it should be maintained. The conscience of Indian Muslims should be respected, and the English Government should not draw a line across it.[23]

So, when the Turkish peace terms were finally made public in India on 14 May, and it appeared that such petitions had been completely ignored, Muslims were incensed. Despite the fact that the abolition of the Caliphate was not mentioned, the loss of non-Turkish territory such as Hejaz and Nejd (later Saudi Arabia) implied that the Muslim holy places in Mecca and Medina were to be taken from the Caliph. It appeared to prove that the worst fears of Khilfat supporters were coming to pass.

This bombshell coincided with the report of the Hunter Committee enquiry into the causes of the Amritsar Massacre, which concluded that Dyer ought to be absolved of wrongdoing and keep his pension. The Indian community was up in arms. Gandhi added fuel to the fire when he concluded that 'the present representatives of the Empire have no real regard for the wishes of the people of India, and they count the honour of India as of little consequence'.[24] A meeting of the Central Khilifat Committee then confirmed the strategy of nonviolent non-cooperation. This was to begin in August, and on 22 June Gandhi advised the co-author of the constitutional reforms, Lord Chelmsford:

> The peace terms and your Excellency's defence of them have given the Musselmen of India a shock from which it will be difficult for them to recover ... In my humble opinion their cause is just ... Muslim soldiers did not fight to inflict punishment on their own Khalifa or to deprive him of his territories ... Musselmen and Hindus have as a whole lost faith in British justice and honour ... I have advised my Musselman friends to withdraw their support from Your Excellencies Government, and the Hindus to join them, should the peace terms not be revised in accordance with solemn pledges of Ministers and Muslim sentiment.[25]

His damning indictment of the British also saw him assert, 'The ordinary method of agitating by way of petitions, deputations and the like is no remedy for moving to repentance a government so hopelessly indifferent to the welfare of its charges as the government of India has proved to be'; an issue of this magnitude required the galvanising of the entire country in pursuit of justice.[26] Chelmsford however replied that Gandhi's Non-Cooperation strategy could not advance his argument and, indeed, was 'the most foolish of all foolish schemes'.[27] He advised him to reconsider his tactics, still unable or unwilling to grasp the strength of Indian feeling and the groundswell of anger which Gandhi and the Ali brothers were able to mobilise.

Non-Cooperation was to commence on 1 August 1920 and would involve the return of Orders and Decorations awarded by the British, the withdrawal of children and students from British sponsored schools and colleges, and a wholesale boycott of the law courts. Instead, if Indians had grievances to air, they were to resort to arbitration and resolve their arguments independently, divorcing themselves entirely from a British judicial system which had been shown to have betrayed their interests. In July, Congress leader Lala Lajpat had returned to the Punjab and announced his intention to boycott the elections due to be held under the auspices of the Montagu-Chelmsford reforms. Gandhi endorsed this initiative and its incorporation into the policy of Non-Cooperation, commenting how

> I would not have the best attention of the country frittered away in electioneering. The issue is clear. Both the Khilifat terms and the Punjab affairs show that Indian opinion counts for little in the councils of the Empire. It is a humiliating position; we shall make nothing of reforms if we quietly swallow the humiliation.[28]

If this failed to move the government, civil servants and soldiers would be incited to leave their posts – all in all the potential ingredients of complete meltdown in the country's administration. Gandhi returned his own medals, two South African war medals and his *Kaiser-I-Hind* Gold Medal for Humanitarian work in South Africa, and proceeded to berate the Viceroy for the manner in which the British had managed the matter of the Caliphate:

> In an unscrupulous, immoral and unjust manner, going from wrong to wrong in order to defend its immorality. I can retain neither respect nor affection for such a government ... these developments have filled me with the greatest misgivings regarding the future of the Empire and have estranged me completely from the present government ... [29]

To extend this sense of estrangement among the wider Indian community, Gandhi continued to travel the country with Shaukat Ali to spread the message, again accusing the British of betraying Islam. He claimed,

Where a tyrant reigns a prison is a palace and a palace a prison ... proclaim to the Government; 'you may hang us on the gallows, you may send us to prison, but you will get no cooperation from us. You will get it in jail or on the gallows, but not in the regiments of the army. You will not get it in legislatures or in any department of government service.'[30]

He condemned 'the Satanic Empire' that had betrayed both its Muslim subjects over Turkey and its Hindu subjects over the treatment of General Dyer, further claiming,

[It] has been guilty of such terrible atrocities that, if it did not apologise for them to God and the country, it would certainly perish. I will go further and say that unless it did so apologise, it was the duty of every Indian to destroy it.[31]

However, he also knew that Non-Cooperation would require considerable sacrifice from those courageous enough to see it through when he admitted:

... I know that withdrawal of cooperation is a grave thing. It requires ability to suffer. I know that it is the right of the citizen to withdraw his cooperation from the state when that cooperation means his degradation. It is a tangible form of showing one's displeasure at the acts of one's government ... [32]

Gandhi urged all his followers to attend the Congress in Calcutta and endorse himself and the Khilifat Non-Cooperation movement. Here, on 5 September, he addressed 14,500 delegates, and after three days of debate won the motion despite opposition from other Congress leaders such as Chittaranjan Das and Ali Jinnah. Although the boycott did not prove to be the resounding success that Gandhi had hoped for, and few lawyers, teachers or administrators actually walked out of their posts, a great start had been made, and the publicity that the movement was generating was priceless in itself. Furthermore, the sense of betrayal articulated by Gandhi and the movement was bound to concentrate the minds of the politicians in Paris, and as long as they held up the prospect of serious civil disorder, both the Viceroy and the Secretary of State would be compelled to continue badgering the delegates in Paris with their concerns.

Churchill was among the more forthright. On 23 November 1920 he repeated his assertion that 'we cannot afford to go on estranging the Mohammedan world in order to hand over a greater Greece to King Constantine',[33] views that were gaining considerable currency elsewhere in government. General Charles Townsend had commanded the campaign in Mesopotamia and had been forced to suffer the humiliating surrender at Kut in April 1916. He had further undermined his position by accepting conditions of captivity far superior to those afforded to his troops, who died by the thousand from starvation and disease. He was now an MP, growing increasingly concerned at British policy towards Turkey and the effect he feared it was having on Indian Muslims. He embarked on a fact-finding mission on his own volition, and when he reported back to London, warned that unless Britain forced the Greeks to evacuate the land they occupied in Anatolia, Mustapha would unleash a 'terrible Holy War', which would consume India as well as Afghanistan, Iraq, Palestine and Egypt.

These were precisely the concerns that the Khilifat movement was designed to provoke. However, a sea change was beginning which would transform its original purpose in the face of the more extreme nationalist sentiment provoked by the Amritsar Massacre. In December 1920, a special session of the Congress Party met in Nagpur, and in the debate that followed a momentous decision was reached that would finally adopt the cause for which Gandhi had been working for years. Non-Cooperation should not only be pursued in defence of the Caliphate and in protest at events in Amritsar but, urged a young Jawaharlal Nehru, in pursuit of an independent Indian republic following its own destiny outside of the Empire.

Such developments were causing increasing anxiety. On 2 December, the Aga Khan warned Lord Montagu yet again that 'as long as Great Britain is the centre of opposition towards [the] revision that broke the heart of every sincere Muslim, I fear ... we will never have real

peace and goodwill or moral quiet in the Islamic world or in India'.[34]
On 4 December Churchill reiterated his own misgivings, warning
Lloyd George that it was 'a most injurious thing that we, the greatest
Mohammedan Empire in the world, should be the leading anti-Turk
power' and therefore the focus for anti-British sentiment throughout
the entire region.[35] There remained nevertheless no positive sign as
1920 came to a close that British policy towards Turkey was going to
be swayed one way or the other by events in India or anywhere else.

No doubt much relieved to be released from his onerous
responsibility, Lord Chelmsford stepped down as Viceroy. His
successor, Lord Reading, arrived in India with all due pomp on
2 April 1921 at a pivotal moment in the history of the sub-continent,
Indian nationalism and its British rulers.[36]

Born Rufus Isaacs in 1860, son of a Spitalfields fruit merchant in
London, he worked his way through the family business and then
went on to study law. A Liberal MP in 1903, he was appointed
Solicitor General in 1910 and in 1913 Lord Chief Justice, and served
as ambassador to the United States during the war. He was a very
close friend and confidante of Lloyd George, who helped to hold the
Welshman in check. Indeed, his appointment as Viceroy, predicted
a close friend Sir Alfred Mond, might in itself have signalled the
beginning of the end for the Prime Minister. 'Directly Reading's
calming influence is withdrawn from him,' Mond forecast, 'his power
will decline.'[37]

The new Viceroy was in no doubt of the magnitude of the task
ahead of him. Even before he left Britain to assume his new post,
Lord Reading had warned Lloyd George that he was about to enter a
political maelstrom, and he insisted that he shared the generally held
view that the terms of Sevres were one of 'the main causes of unrest
in the country'.[38]

Having passed through India Gate, he soon saw how the cooperation
between Muslim and Hindu Indian threatened to render the British
policy of divide and rule redundant, and he sought to adopt a
more conciliatory approach than his predecessor had achieved.
Non-Cooperation had produced the boycotts that were now general
all over India, where bonfires were being made from piles of clothes

woven from foreign cloth. Schools stood empty and law courts abandoned, and tax revenues were affected by a boycott of alcohol sales. He agreed almost at once to a series of meetings with Gandhi at Simla, the summer residence of the Raj in the cool mountains of northern India. These were held on 13/14 May, on which occasion Reading recorded the impact that Gandhi had made on him.[39] He appears not to have made a very good first impression, as he later noted how 'there is nothing striking about his appearance ... I should have passed him by in the street without a second look at him.'[40] Although Reading confessed to his son afterwards that he found Gandhi intriguing, he felt his views, though admirable, to be inconsistent with politics.[41] Consequently, this deep and mystical man left him none the wiser after his meetings than he had been before and, unable to rationalise Gandhi's policy of *sagayraha* to the cold realities of world politics, the discussions proved inconclusive.

Furthermore, he felt sure that the alliance between the Muslims and the Hindus would prove fragile and short-lived. He felt that the 'Hindu Muslim combination ... rests upon insecure foundations',[42] with the two races likely to divide again and the British able to exploit their differences for their own ends.

His evaluation of the fragile Hindu/Muslim truce appeared to have been accurate. As tensions grew and emotions heightened beyond the civilised confines of the Viceregal Lodge, there was always the strong possibility that extremists might hijack Gandhi's policy of peaceful non-cooperation. There were hotheaded radical elements that wanted to pursue their aims through violence, perceiving this as by far the more effective route to freedom. This was frighteningly and graphically demonstrated in August 1920, when the peasant Muslim Moplahs on the Malabar Coast staged an uprising against their Hindu landlords and in support of a Khilifat Kingdom in India. A number of Europeans, Hindu moneylenders and landlords died in the ensuing orgy of murder, rapine and looting and dealt a serious blow to intercommunal relations, increasing antagonism and stirring the authorities into action. The British decided enough was enough and proceeded on a round of mass arrests that included the Ali brothersm who were charged with trying to encourage Muslim soldiers to desert. They went to trial on 1 November and were sentenced to two years hard labour.

Mounting violence, anarchy and sedition was something that the British authorities simply could not tolerate, especially with the forthcoming visit to India of the heir to the throne, the Prince of Wales. The British authorities had anticipated possible problems with a royal visit, and the trip had been postponed many times already, but another cancellation would have been too much of a climb down in the face of such agitation; Reading insisted that to do so would 'have been a serious blunder'.[43] Instead, the government took what steps it could to remove possible troublemakers from the streets, and suspected ringleaders were arrested and thrown into gaol. The police could not arrest everybody, however, and when the visit was publicised, the Central Khilafat Committee issued strict instructions to its followers for a *hartal*, to 'Boycott the Prince's Visit'. The procession, official functions and fetes, festive illuminations, the cricket match and even the market stalls in the fair were to be boycotted. Instead, supporters were urged to attend a bonfire and public meeting dressed in homespun, hand-woven *Khadi* dress. When the Prince arrived on 17 November Khilifat supporters greeted him in silence. Clashes then took place with other 'loyal' Indians who wanted to welcome the royal visitor. Pitched battles and looting followed. The stark contrast between the controversy that greeted the Prince of Wales' visit and that of his father King George V only ten years before left a huge impression on everyone. Gandhi was dismayed by the violence, driving round Bombay and trying to stop the bloodshed. Matters had simply got too far out of hand, and despite his entreaties he was met everywhere by cries of '*Mahatma Gandhi ki jai*'. As he later recalled, 'never has the sound of these words grated so much on my ears'.[44] Reading's observation, 'that Gandhi has again called forth a spirit which he could not control', appeared to have been vindicated.[45] Gandhi went on a fast until the fighting stopped, although things did not quieten down until some fifty-eight people were dead. For his part, a somewhat deflated Prince wrote to his father, despairing, 'I'm very depressed about my work in British India as I don't feel that I'm doing a scrap of good.'[46] The King replied perceptively that 'the war and the situation in Turkey and Montagu's reforms have no doubt produced the unrest which now exists'.[47] In order to prevent trouble, the indignant prince found himself bundled furtively into some receptions to avoid demonstrators. However, the visit was by no means an unmitigated disaster. Many Indians declined to adhere to Gandhi's call for a boycott, and in Delhi over 50,000 people 'received the Prince with the greatest enthusiasm.'[48] As Reading later reported:

> The reception at Government House was attended by over 3,000 persons and the Prince shook hands with them all. It was on his own wish and caused the greatest satisfaction ...[49]

Nonetheless, the violence and the underlying tensions provoked the governments of both the United Provinces of Bengal and the Punjab into adopting the most punitive measures in an attempt to stem this apparent slide into anarchy. Both Congress and the Khilafat Committee were suspended, and hundreds of arrests followed until some 20,000 suspects were imprisoned and Gandhi decided to postpone civil disobedience. What originally had all the hallmarks of an effective movement, galvanising millions of Indians into opposition to British rule, had instead degenerated into wholesale slaughter and rape. However, there was much opposition to his decision. The far more radical Subhas Chandra Bos remarked that the chance of a lifetime had been lost. He and many others were convinced that they were turning the corner in their campaign and that all they had to do was maintain the pressure and they would win the day.

Nevertheless, the genie could not be put back into the bottle. The murder and mayhem carried out by the Moplahs the previous year and that which accompanied the Prince of Wales' visit was to culminate in an even more horrifying explosion of violence. Gandhi had decided to try a different approach. Early in 1922, he agreed to launch a tax boycott in the county of Bardoli in his home state of Gujarat.[50] It was of course intended to be completely peaceful, and his avowed intention was for no blood to be shed. Nonetheless his careful plans fell in tatters yet again when on 5 February a procession of demonstrators in the small town of Chauri Chaura in the Gorakhpur district of the United Provinces passed a police station. It is not recorded what they must have uttered to provoke the response that followed, but those in the tail end of the march were allegedly subjected to taunts and insults of some kind by the twenty-two constables watching them pass by. Within minutes the procession had turned into a violent, vengeful mob, as the exchange of insults descended into a pitched battle in which the frightened policemen opened fire. The crowd's reaction was overwhelming and the constables were driven into their station to find shelter. There was to be no haven however as the rioters set fire to the building, forcing them out into the open to escape the flames, where they were hacked to death and their corpses thrown back into the burning police station.

When Gandhi heard of the incident he was desolate and suspended the campaign. He had made it absolutely clear that under no circumstances was violence justified, and he went on a five-day fast. He refused to achieve freedom by inflicting murder and mayhem on the country. The fast did not end until the violence subsided.

Yet Gandhi's honourable stance, as colleagues such as Chandra Bos had warned, threw away the opportunity of a generation. As one commentator put it, 'Although in December 1921, at the height of the first great non-cooperation campaign against the British, the government of India found itself on the run, three months later the non-cooperation movement was in ruins, and the government's authority had emerged intact.'[51] Indeed, in May 1922 Lord Reading himself felt confident enough to inform Lloyd George that 'the internal situation has been quieter now than at any period since I have been here', and advised the India Office furthermore that the 'Non-Cooperation Movement ... remains more or less stationery'.[52]

Although he suspended the *Satyagraha*, the violence had given the British the moral high ground and Gandhi was arrested. Lord Reading instructed the authorities to award him the harshest penalty possible, and he was sentenced to six years in gaol. Muslim hostility to the treatment of the Sultan and Caliph did continue, but it never again carried the momentum enjoyed by Gandhi's participation. As Gandhi himself had predicted, the two communities failed ever again to find a common cause around which to unite against British rule, and the most effective weapon the Raj had to maintain itself in power – divide and rule – would sustain it for another twenty-five years.

Nevertheless, despite the failure of the campaign, Gandhi's role in bringing the two communities together received wide acclaim. The Law Member of the Viceroy's Council said of him in late 1921:

> To the Mohammedans he has made himself invaluable, for the simple reason that but for his personality and influence they would not have been able to command the active support and sympathy of the Hindus in their agitation on behalf of Turkey.

7

ALL TALK WAS OF WAR

The crushing and definitive defeat of the Greek army in Anatolia had drawn down the final curtain on her dreams of an imperial destiny in Asia Minor. Furthermore, the Turks' resounding victory had served to realign the prevailing dynamics within their country. The Allies, already at odds with one another over how to deal with the Nationalists, now faced a situation few of them would have envisaged a year before. Whilst increasingly few commentators anticipated a Greek victory, few foresaw such a total and resounding Turkish triumph, with the consequence that the Allies now faced a completely new and unexpected scenario. For their part, the Italians had long since abandoned any pretence of backing the Greeks and, indeed, since King Constantine's return neither the French nor for that matter the British government had offered the Greeks any material aid. However, the French were now adopting an ever more overtly pro-Turkish stance, as indicated by the new British commander at Constantinople, General Sir Charles Harington, who on 2 September reported that the French had gone so far as to openly congratulate 'the Turks on the success of their operations against the Greeks'.[1]

Even as the Greeks were descending upon Smyrna, Lloyd George convened an emergency Cabinet meeting on 7 September to discuss the escalating crisis. For their part, he insisted, regardless of the fate of the Greeks or French support for their vanquishers, they should not cede control of the 'Gallipoli Peninsula or at present abandon

Constantinople to the Turks' unless and until the Turks agreed to come to an accommodation. Churchill too was now coming round to the Prime Ministers' view. He was fearful that a Nationalist Turkish victory would throw away all the gains made in four years of bloody war. He agreed that they had to bargain from a position of strength to secure their strategic interests, even though it was now clear that the policy of using the Greeks as Britain's surrogate had long been exposed as a chimera. Lloyd George reiterated his conviction, that under 'no circumstances could we allow the Gallipoli Peninsula to be held by the Turks ... and we should fight to prevent their doing so'.[2] The First Lord of the Admiralty, Lord Lee of Fareham, added that at present only French and Italian troops occupied the peninsula and there was only a small detachment of British troops in the vicinity, stationed at Chanak. He was further worried, and not without good reason, that the French if left alone would surrender the position to the Turks. Lloyd George nevertheless assured the meeting that the Royal Navy would soon be reinforced at the Dardanelles; the Turks warned that its guns would be turned on them if they made any attempt to cross to the European shore of the Straits.[3]

On 10 September, the very day that Mustapha Kemal marched triumphantly into Turkish Izmir, Rumbold passed on to Curzon information to the effect that the Nationalists were indeed 'considering the question of [the] occupation of the Asiatic shore of the Bosphorus and also Chanak'.[4] In effect, once they had consolidated their victory over the Greeks and secured their occupation of Izmir and its environs they were expected to march on into the Neutral Zone. Any planned reinforcement could not be completed soon enough if the Allies were to have any chance of dissuading them from such a course of action. He also added rather optimistically that a united front against Mustapha would only carry any weight if France and Italy joined forces with the British at Chanak and convinced the Nationalists they were serious. The Chief of the Imperial General Staff, Lord Cavan, warned that 1,000 men now confronted a total potential force of 52,000 advancing Turks, but, as *The Times* helpfully pointed out, 'the British Government [was] determined to resist any Turkish violation of the Neutral Zone' regardless of the odds.[5]

With such overwhelming numbers there was little to stand in the Nationalists' way, except perhaps the threat by Britain of its determination to resist such a move. In order to make this threat plausible, they therefore needed to be seen to be taking measures that were compelling and convincing. The War Office decided to appoint Colonel Digby Shuttleworth, then in charge of the Ottoman War Office, to the command of the British forces at Chanak. He was to await reinforcements and in the meantime set about making the position there as defensible as possible with the limited resources at his disposal. A few days later, HMS *Ajax* weighed anchor at Chanak and the Colonel boarded a launch heading for his new command. He later described:

I [had] received orders at Constantinople to proceed to Chanak to command a force of one squadron cavalry, one Battery RFA, one section Royal Engineers and two Battalions of Infantry to be concentrated there. Verbal instructions were received that, in addition, small mixed detachments of French and Italians might be expected, and on arrival, would come under my command.

... My orders were to prevent them [the Nationalists] if possible from crossing the neutral boundary. Instructions were also received to prepare a position covering the town of Chanak which was to be defended against all attack until such time as other orders were sent. Verbally it was explained that the defensive role was to be that of a rearguard [and] that a prolonged defence of Chanak was not contemplated. Consideration was therefore to be given to the question of withdrawal under fire to Gallipoli in certain eventualities ... British troops were not to cross the neutral boundary.

... In the event of the Kemalist troops refusing to recognise the authority of the Sultan's Government and claiming the right of occupation of the territory up to the neutral line, my orders were to arrange that the Gendarmerie Battalion [local Turkish armed police] handed this area over to the Kemalist troops before withdrawing to the Neutral Zone. British supervising officers with the Battalion were not to come into contact with Kemalist troops and Ottoman Gendarmerie were in no circumstances to be employed against Kemalist troops.[6]

So Shuttleworth's orders were pretty explicit: to avoid any confrontation with the Nationalists but to prepare for the worst if Britain's game of bluff and double bluff failed to pay off. Meanwhile, as British troops filled sandbags the Turks continued to drive the Greeks back towards the Neutral Zone, prompting Lloyd George to suggest rather disingenuously that the Balkan States might be galvanised into forming an alliance against the Turks. But the chances of that were too remote to put odds on; they may well have feared a return of the Turk to Europe, but there was little sign of them making the slightest move towards raising an expeditionary force. Instead, with the Turks closing in, the respective troop dispositions available to both sides were again evaluated. They were not very encouraging, as Sir Laming Worthington-Evans explained.[7] A total of 7,600 British troops were stationed throughout the extensive Neutral Zone, including Constantinople, and although they only faced 6,000 Turks near Izmit and another 5,000 near Chanak, there were another 40,000 advancing north from Smyrna. Altogether it represented a massive superiority, which the comparatively modest British force would find it difficult if not impossible to resist, even with the considerable support of the guns of the Royal Navy to back them up. On the morning of 13 September, Shuttleworth recorded positively that 'a detachment of Italian infantry, strength some 70 rifles, 'B' Squadron, 3rd The King's Own Hussars, 92nd Battery RFA, and stores of all sorts arrived from Constantinople'. Better than nothing perhaps, but a long way short of matching the Nationalists' resources in manpower. Shuttleworth meanwhile, as instructed by London, had also been evaluating the defensibility of his command:

Chanak is overlooked at a distance of four miles by the Asmali Tepe, Bairak Tepe, Damyeri Tepe Ridge, which rises to a height of 1,000 feet above the town but which, in itself is an obstacle, making hostile deployment and the staging of an attack upon Chanak difficult. On the other hand the ridge offers excellent

1. Constantinople, at the heart of a vast empire that once straddled swathes of Europe, the Middle East and North Africa.

Above left: 2. German General Liman von Sanders, architect of the new Turkish army.

Above right: 3. British Admiral de Robeck aboard HMS *Iron Duke*. He allowed the *Goeben* and *Breslau* to slip through his fingers and precipitate war.

Below: 4. German General Falkenhayn, commander of the Turkish from 1917.

Above: 5. Turkish troops recruiting for Jihad.

Below: 6. Turkish soldiers, under German command near the Dardanelles.

Above: 7. The innocent victims of war. Armenian refugees who have managed to flee genocide in their homeland.

Below: 8. Allenby's triumphant entry through the Jaffa Gate.

9. Enver Pasha. His tragic self-delusion brought disaster to his country and the end to a centuries-old empire.

10. Mustapha Kemal Ataturk. Greece's nemesis, Turkey's liberator and founder of a modern state.

11. Mehmet VI, the last Ottoman Sultan, who ended his reign crouched in the back of a British army ambulance.

12. King Constantine of Greece. His divisive reign was to preside over military disaster for his army in Anatolia.

Left: 13. Eleutherios Venizelos, the man whose dreams of a new Greek empire heralded untold misery.

Below: 14. Marshal Foch, President Clemenceau, Lloyd George, Orlando and Sonnino.

15. French President Poincare. His country's decision to abandon the war against the Nationalists left Britain isolated.

Right: 16. David Lloyd George, victim of hubris.

Below: 17. The 'Big Four' : Lloyd George, Orlando, Clemenceau and US President Woodrow Wilson.

Above left: 18. Lord Curzon, photographed in his state robes when Viceroy of India.

Above right: 19. Horace Rumbold, British High Commissioner to Constantinople.

Below: 20. Winston Churchill, with Stanley Baldwin. Photographed in 1925.

Above: 21. Italian officers, First World War, probably on the Italian Front at Isonzo.

Below: 22. Some of the Greek troops who acquitted themselves so well in the First World War.

Above: 23. Indian lancers serving the Raj against the Sultan Caliph in the Middle East.

Below: 24. On the Western Front too, Indian soldiers fought for Britain in the First World War.

25. An Indian famine victim; one of many whose fate proved to India's nationalists that Britain had lost the right to rule the subcontinent.

26. Mahatma Gandhi. He saw in the Caliphate issue a chance to draw Indian Muslim and Hindu together in the struggle for his country's freedom.

27. Lord Chelmsford. His reforms as Viceroy failed to satisfy Indian nationalists' demands for greater autonomy.

28. Lord Reading, Chelmsford's successor as Viceroy. He came face to face with Gandhi and growing demands for independence.

Left: 29. Edward, Prince of Wales, as an officer in the First World War.

Below: 30. Australian cavalry outside Jerusalem during operations in Palestine in the First World War.

Above left: 31. General Byng, later Canadian Governor-General.

Above right: 32. Canadian Premier, William Lyon Mackenzie King.

Below: 33. Canada's sacrifice, wounded soldiers convalescing.

Above: 34. Smyrna. A once prosperous cosmopolitan city destroyed at the end of the tragic war between Greek and Turk.

Inset: 35. Smyrna in better days.

Below: 36. Greek refugees fleeing the terrible carnage in Turkey, which affected civilians in both communities.

Right: 37. Dr F. Nansen, architect of the population exchange.

Below: 38. More ordinary, innocent civilians trapped in the middle of the internecine slaughter.

Above: 39. The Nationalist Turkish delegation to the negotiations at Lausanne.

Below: 40. The removal of a French postbox at the start of the conflict.

artillery observation; but the steepness of its slopes and the difficulties of the ground make it impossible to emplace artillery except in a few positions ... Altogether, despite the great advantages the high ground offers for observation, the hills taken as a whole form a serious obstacle to hostile attack on Chanak, especially if difficulties of ammunition supply should limit the enemy's power of bombardment, and so minimise the advantage possessed by direct observation ...

It is true, that the [defence] line was too extensive for the force immediately available but risks had to be taken and the moral effect of naval support and the prospect of reinforcements influence the decision ...

Not quite as dire a position as Rorke's Drift in 1879, when 100-odd British troops faced 4,000 Zulus, but daunting enough. Colonel Shuttleworth also expressed concerns about the prospects for the hapless local Greek minority. The presence of Nationalist troops and brigands was very intimidating, and soon 'commenced to cause alarm', but despite pleas for clemency the Turkish authorities would not allow the desperate Greeks to leave and make their way to safety. Shuttleworth finally acknowledged that when 'the situation compelled the withdrawal of British supervising officers from the area beyond the Neutral Zone ... these unfortunate people [would be] left to their fate', which one can imagine would have been very unpleasant if that of the Greeks at Smyrna were anything to go by.

In London, Curzon urged caution, but Lloyd George (and to a lesser extent Churchill) was more bullish. Churchill, heretofore wary of a pro-Greek policy, was transformed into 'a fire-eating defender of British Imperial interests'.[8] He told the cabinet somewhat naively that if Britain reinforced its troops at Constantinople, France would follow suit. They, of course, had no intention of doing so, and he was equally erroneously confident that Greece, Serbia and Rumania would also 'gladly' offer to send men to defend key points, which they never of course did. Rumania especially, he insisted, had a vested interest in maintaining the 'freedom of the Dardanelles',[9] although there is no evidence that their interests would translate into positive action.

Lloyd George insisted in his now familiar bellicose fashion that under no circumstances could Britain be seen to be running away, and that if they could indeed garner an Allied army consisting of British, French, Italians, Greek, Rumanian and Serb forces, parity if not superiority of numbers would be possible. In any case, he insisted, they had to put on a show of force because the time had now come 'to do something concrete'.[10] After discussions on where more men might be obtained, it was agreed that two battalions of British troops would be despatched from Gibraltar and Malta. They would certainly take longer to get there than the speeding Turks.

Back in the heat of Chanak, Shuttleworth decided it would be a good idea, and an excellent sign of Allied solidarity, if the British and Italian flags were planted side by side to mark the demarcation line of the Neutral Zone. Unfortunately for this sterling idea, the Italians, so they claimed at any rate, had failed to bring their national flag along with them, and the idea had to be dropped. More than likely the less than enthusiastic Italians were not enamoured with such a gesture, and rather than advertise their presence, they decided to let caution be the better part of valour. Perhaps they really did steam all that way without one; either way, its outcome rather serves as symbolic of the relationship between the Allies during this period. Like their flag, the Italians would very soon become noticeable by their absence.

On 15 September, with their confidence reinforced, the Cabinet held the view that the Neutral Zone could, and indeed would, be defended by force, and decided to make a bold public statement to that effect.[11] It was in this bullish atmosphere that Churchill was instructed to draft a communiqué, simultaneously suggesting that the British Dominions might wish to support the Mother Country materially in her hour of need. At lunch on the 16th Lloyd George and Churchill worked together on the text of the fateful document, which was then issued in time for the evening papers. It made it clear that the British government was willing to fight to defend the Straits, but was just as willing to be conciliatory and hold a conference to negotiate a 'stable peace' with Turkey. They added, however, that no discussions could commence 'while there is any question of the Kemalist forces attacking the Neutral Zones' and went on to warn of the grave repercussions should the Allies have to evacuate Constantinople, as well as the likely attendant turmoil in the Balkans in the event of the 'reappearance of the victorious Turk on the European shore'. It was pretty much a catch-all document, with a distinct air of desperation, but contained some rather startling assumptions. Bad enough was the claim that Bulgaria, Rumania, Serbia and Greece had been approached and were therefore likely to render assistance, but even worse was the announcement that the Dominions had been asked to assist. Whatever the inopportune communiqué might claim, there was to be no help forthcoming from either Canada or Australia, and the Bulgarians, Rumanians and Serbs were not looking like rushing to the battlefront either. Indeed, on 16 September *The Times* reported that 'the Bulgarian Press continues to adopt a guarded and non-committal attitude ... at present the policy of the government is strongly against any sort of interference in Thracian affairs'.[12] The British were again to all intents and purposes on their own, with only the lukewarm Italians and duplicitous French by their side – and then only just. Nevertheless, *The Times* opted to put a slightly more positive spin on the situation when it reported 'ENTENTE POWERS AGREED – STRAITS TO BE DEFENDED', adding hopefully, 'Allies preparing to send reinforcements to the Neutral Zone'.[13]

Whilst the 'Frocks' in London deliberated, the military build-up at Chanak continued, and on 17 September, HMS *Marlborough* unloaded twelve machineguns and a battery of artillery, which greatly enhanced the firepower of the defenders. Naval personnel were also landed to provide crews for machineguns and artillery, and three days later the 1st Battalion Gordon Highlanders arrived from Malta. This steady trickle however was a drop in the ocean compared to the numbers that they could expect to face in open combat, although a defensive position is usually an easier proposition than an attacking one and the Turkish cavalry would be sorely tested should they have to face machineguns. However, when a detachment of Turks were confronted by a squadron of French-Moroccan Spahis near Ezirne, Shuttleworth noted with some satisfaction how these fearsome warriors 'much impressed' the Nationalists, who prudently opted to stay their hand.

When the Cabinet met again on 18 September Curzon warned that French opinion opposed fighting the Turks, and it was 'hardening' as each day passed. They had furthermore made it clear that they were going to evacuate Chanak altogether even if it meant abandoning their so-called 'allies'.[14] This was confirmed by a report in *The Times* which underlined their stance, stating that 'it is better to make it clear that the French government and the French soldiers are not willing to take up arms for the Greeks under the Constantine monarchy, and are not prepared, in pursuance of what is reputed to be British policy, to shed their blood in fighting the Turks'.[15] The Italians were now taking a similar line, according to *The Times*, which reported that 'Italy will not take part in any military action which might be provoked in the Near East'.[16] In this growing atmosphere of despondency, Leader of the Commons Austen Chamberlain asserted that if necessary, they ought be able to hold Chanak with or without French help, although Churchill cautioned that they should not commit themselves to courses of action 'for which we had not the strength'.[17] Lord Cavan then made the ludicrous claim that 20,000 men ought to be enough to hold the peninsula, which of course only left them with another 16,000 or so to find.

On the 19th the War Office telegrammed the usually cautious British General Officer Commanding in Constantinople, General 'Tim' Harington, that Chanak should be held effectively, and that it had now become a point of immense moral significance to the prestige of the Empire as well as a military necessity.[18] Harington appears to have been caught up in the optimism himself, wiring the War Office on the 20th that they were soon to be well placed to act alone if necessary, possibly encouraged by the now steady stream of reinforcements making their way to the theatre. This was all grist to the mill for the desperate Prime Minister, who was more obsessed than ever with facing off the Nationalists regardless of the cost. Rumbold however was more cautious in his appraisal of the situation. He was concerned that unless the Nationalists could be persuaded to come to the negotiating table soon, they may well attempt to march on Thrace through Constantinople or Chanak. This prospect was a chilling one for the High Commissioner, who feared that the forces available would be insufficient to hold them and 'we might have to evacuate Constantinople'.[19] This avalanche of confusing and in many cases contradictory intelligence was swiftly followed by news that the French had finally declared their intentions, and had announced they were about to abandon their positions at Chanak altogether.

An outraged, if not altogether surprised, British Cabinet sent Lord Curzon to Paris on the 20th to clear the air with the French once and for all. What subsequently transpired served more than any episode before or since to illustrate the underlying intensity of Anglo-French animosity. Curzon reported the details of the meeting to the Cabinet two days later, which he depicted as being of 'an unprecedented description'. He went on to explain how 'Poincare declared that the sole chance of peace was to make overtures to Kemal at Mudania, accusing Harington of misrepresenting the attitudes of the French and Italian Governments', which Curzon rejected. Curzon then went on to describe how 'Poincare lost all command of his temper and for a quarter of an hour raved at the top of his voice, putting words in my mouth which I had never uttered, refusing to permit the slightest interruption or correction, saying that he would make public the insult to France ... I have never seen so deplorable or undignified a scene,' he concluded.[20] In another account by Harold Nicolson, we learn further how

> Lord Curzon, in precise but cutting phrases, summarised the disloyalty of the French during the last two years, of which the betrayal of their British comrads behind the wire entanglement at Chanak was but the final culmination. In the afternoon M. Poincare responded to this attack. His voice was dry, his words were clipped, his insults were lancets of steel. Curzon's white hands upon the green baize cloth trembled violently. He could stand it no further. Rising from his seat he muttered something about an adjournment and limped hurriedly into the adjoining room ... He collapsed upon a scarlet settee. He grasped Lord Hardinge by the arm. 'Charlie', he panted, 'I can't bear that horrid little man. I can't bear him. I can't bear him.' He wept ...[21]

Poincare told the British ambassador that he would only apologise if Curzon retracted his accusation that Britain had been abandoned at Chanak. In a typical exercise in semantics, Curzon replied that he understood that there was some objection to the word 'abandon' and that he was prepared to substitute it for 'retreat' if that would satisfy French honour. After a juvenile delay and further posturing the participants in this farce agreed to try and resolve the matter at hand, namely Mustapha and the Nationalists. But it was the final straw for the British and proved a turning point. France had no further interest in this particular adventure; her problems lay much closer to home, and she had just about as much incentive to protect British interests as Britain had to defend hers. He was further warned in no uncertain terms by Poincare that 'French public opinion would not admit of a shot being fired against a Turk, and furthermore, as far as the French people were concerned, the Turks could 'cross to Europe when they pleased'.[22] Smarting from his encounter with the French, Curzon welcomed as some consolation the support that came from the King, who was not particularly well disposed to the French himself. Lord Stamfordham, his private secretary, wrote to assure him:

> [The King] naturally followed with the utmost interest your doings in Paris. You will not be surprised that the reading of your reports astounded His Majesty ... The King all the more appreciates the patience and control with which you met this violent outburst, and trusts that the arrangements which you were able to secure may happily avert the dangers of war.[23]

When Ministers met at 10 Downing Street on the evening of 20 September, Curzon confirmed that France would not give help in any possible war against the Turks. Churchill responded that in that case, British prestige could not risk 'the hurried evacuation of Chanak in the face of Turkish threats', even 'at the expense of British evacuation of Izmit and Constantinople'. Lloyd George agreed, and with the French departure it made the 'threat to Chanak ... a blow to Britain alone' and she had no choice but to confront it as one.[24]

On this basis he decided that further reinforcements should be sent from Egypt as quickly as possible, and asked Churchill to wire Harington to the effect that in the final analysis Chanak was more important than either Izmit or Constantinople and that it was to be here the final showdown would come. The general had meanwhile already come to that conclusion. As added insurance, the Cabinet looked at garrisons that might provide further reinforcements, such as that in Mesopotamia, still in the process of being pacified and occupied, and in which of thousands of men were stationed, some of whom at least could be directed to the threatened war zone. (They were also a lot closer than Gibraltar and Malta, but it was not thought necessarily the best thing if men were sent straight from Mesopotamia to Chanak, when there were first rate troops in Constantinople which could be sent instead.) As a compromise it was decided to transfer RAF ground crew to Constantinople, thus releasing Irish Guardsmen, who could then proceed to Chanak. The Royal Navy too was instructed to further beef up the maritime contingent. In order to maintain the diplomatic pressure whilst arrangements proceeded to reinforce the area, it was decided to issue a warning stating unequivocally that any crossing of the Neutral Zone would be deemed 'an act of war' and that the British would respond accordingly.

On the 22nd the Prime Minister asked Churchill to form a mini war cabinet to oversee the day-to-day running of the emergency, and at its first meeting Lord Cavan assured the committee that General Harington ought to be able 'to hold his own' for four or five weeks in the event of a nationalist assault, but added that a purely static posture could not be sustained indefinitely.[25] Thousands of men could not remain in situ on ships and in the boiling desert wastes for long, and sooner or later they would either have to take the offensive or be withdrawn. Another humiliation, such as that endured at Kut only a few years previously was a prospect viewed with a deep sense of foreboding. To help ensure that dire scenario was not realised, further reinforcements, consisting of sixteen 8-inch howitzers and the contingent of Irish Guards finally disembarked at Chanak, released by the arrival in Constantinople of the thousand airmen hastily diverted from Mesopotamia.[26] The same day Harington had cabled

Lord Curzon, expressing his growing anxiety over the situation in Constantinople. His previous optimism seems to have been coloured somewhat from reports that 'many undesirable elements have drifted to the town and it is known that some 20,000 Turks and probably an equal number of Greeks are armed', declaring that he had too few men to maintain order in 'the event of a rising'. Furthermore, precautions were being taken for the protection of British families, and 'the wives and children of British officers and men are embarking tomorrow and arrangements have been made to embark colony at very short notice'.[27] Harington's anxiety was echoed by Rumbold, who wired the British Minister in Athens, Frank Lindley, 'I do not know what is going to happen here … we may well be in for another war'.[28] Meanwhile, true to their word, news arrived from Constantinople that 'The French and Italian detachments and flags were today removed from the Neutral Zones of Izmit and the Dardanelles on order of the respective governments'.[29] Not very good news for the increasingly isolated British, both politically and militarily, with the Nationalists expected to break the deadlock and sweep into the Neutral Zone any day.

However, as is often the case in such situations, one side's evaluation of the other's intentions is not nevertheless the most accurate. Ironically, it appears that the canny Nationalist leader was pursuing an agenda completely at variance with the assumptions being made in London. As his spies relayed reports of the plans and machinations of the British, he had no intention of obliging them with an expected offensive. He confided to the Turkish journalist Falih Rifki that, far from masterminding a coordinated plan, he did not really know where his troops were. He added furthermore that 'he would not risk the life of a single gendarme by moving into Thrace before the conclusion of an armistice'.[30] His policy towards the Neutral Zone was largely the same, as he explained in a telegram to General Karabekir at his eastern headquarters on the 22nd: 'Although we are very strong, we are pursuing a very calculating and moderate policy … we are trying to isolate the British. Our troops are concentrating in the direction of Istanbul and Canakkale, but we prefer a political solution and are managing the situation accordingly.'[31] This admission more than anything reveals how the feverish activity of the British was not only causing a political and diplomatic furore both at home and internationally, with its effect on French opinion, Indian sentiment and later, as we shall see, Dominion and British domestic attitudes, but was not even really necessary. Lloyd George, Churchill and the other hawks were simply falling for his bluff.

On the ground too British interpretations of Turkish intentions were not being accurately reflected, and in some places his troops were demonstrating the same conciliatory frame of mind. In Harold Nicolson's words, the Turks 'appeared outside our wire entanglement grinning at our slender line with amicable, and by no means discourteous, expectation'.[32] Elsewhere, gifts and souvenirs were exchanged on the fringes of the Neutral Zone, while the men of both sides ensured that they carried their weapons in such a way as to pose no threat to the other side. There is one incident in which the Turks are said to have asked the British for the loan of some barbed wire so that they could appear suitably warlike for the inspection of a senior officer, and on another for the loan of some pots and pans so that they could cook a meal. Mind games were not beyond them either, interplaying the friendliness described above with hostile threats and gestures to see if they could provoke the British soldiers into making the first move and providing them with a pretext to retaliate.[33] It all appeared very carefully and cleverly orchestrated to keep the British on their toes.

There may have been overt fraternization at some points along the Neutral Zone, but on the 23rd alarm bells rang when reports were received of more Turkish cavalry crossing into the disputed territory. One Lieutenant Naylor of the 3rd Hussars had encountered a superior force of 200 Turks, who had proceeded to the village of Eren Kui, just 10 miles from the British lines, where another 800 cavalrymen joined them. When confronted by the lieutenant they refused to pull back, because, according to *The Times,* 'the Turkish commander ... "did not know it was the Neutral Zone",' so the British cautiously withdrew behind prepared positions and waited to see what the Turks planned to do next.[34] If they insisted on advancing into the zone, Naylor was on his own, and his reaction could be the final act which precipitated

Jihad

open warfare. London and Constantinople held their breaths as this Mexican standoff of classic proportions developed into a potentially explosive confrontation. Many, as *The Times* confirmed, believed that 'the Turks are trying how far they can bluff us', which, if we interpret Mustapha's telegram correctly, was precisely his strategy.[35] At this point Colonel Shuttleworth decided that the time had come to demonstrate resolution. If the Turks were bluffing, then it was essential that they were not seen to be doing so; still outnumbered and potentially outgunned, they had to demonstrate their resolve. He sent a warning to the Turkish commander advising them that unless they withdrew, 'I should be compelled reluctantly to take such measures as the situation demanded,'[36] measures that could involve requesting naval gunfire to sweep the Turks away from the boundary of the zone. After a tense period of uncertainty, news filtered back that the Turks had at last begun to pull back; if Mustapha wanted to provoke the British, then apparently this was not the time to do it. Shuttleworth could breathe a huge sigh of relief and the naval gunners in the Straits who had been on alert to open fire on the Nationalists received the order to stand down.

Despite all the expressions of confidence espoused both publicly and in Cabinet, the first chinks were beginning to appear in the collective British armour. France and Italy of course could already be discounted, but there were now signs of movement coming from the previously steadfast British. Reinforcements were arriving, but clearly they would still be greatly outnumbered by the Nationalists, and, as Churchill already admitted, they had to be realistic about what they could and could not do. However they looked at it, whatever permutations were calculated to bolster the belief that chances of success were good, all seemed to point towards the need to compromise.

In Paris on 23 September, Curzon, Poincare and the Italian ambassador to France, Count Sforza, finally agreed on a joint note in which they would view 'with favour' the Nationalist claim to European Turkey, including Adrianople, and that as soon as a peace treaty was negotiated the Allied troops and administrators would leave Constantinople.[37] They added that as long as the Turks respected the Neutral Zone, no Greek warships would be permitted to enter the Sea of Marmara.[38] This 'Paris Note' was a remarkable shift on the part of the British. The light at the end of the tunnel may have no longer been an express train coming the other way after all.

The following day, Shuttleworth was advised that, while he was not to engage the Turks, he was to continue to enforce the policy of deterrence. He did, however, report that the Nationalists retained a presence on a number of key positions around Chanak which, he warned, would give them 'command of the European shore at the entrance to the Dardanelles' if they decided to mount an attack.[39] For the first time too, it was agreed to let the British make small penetrations into the Nationalists' lines to gauge their reaction 'in order to give the Turks an opportunity of showing their hand'.[40]

But they failed to take the bait, as indeed Mustapha had already made it clear he had no intention of provoking a fight if he could help it. Shuttleworth too repeated instructions to his men that 'our patrols were not to fire unless fired upon';[41] never mind what London was plotting, no one wanted to be responsible for lighting the blue touch paper and unleashing carnage. In any case, Harington and Rumbold told Shuttleworth that 'it was believed that the Turks were bluffing', as indeed they were, and that he was to keep his cool, which he clearly was anyway. He was then advised that his demanding tenure as commander of the garrison was coming to a welcome end and that a Major-General Thomas Marden was being despatched to replace him. The more senior man was to preside over what could well be the next and most challenging phase of the standoff at Chanak.

Three days after the terms of the Paris Note were agreed, Harington came out in general agreement with the change of policy it represented, accepting that they ought to 'give Turkey Constantinople and Maritsa' as it was now time to finally 'end it all'.[42] A previously equally bullish Sir Horace Rumbold wrote to Sir Lancelot Oliphant, Assistant Secretary at the Foreign Office, admitting to the now obvious fact that, 'we think the last thing our country wants is to have another war', adding quite astutely that no one cared less at home 'whether Eastern Thrace or Constantinople belongs to the Greeks or the Turks'.[43] The same day Rumbold sent an evaluation of the situation to the King in which, despite having assured Shuttleworth he believed the Turks were bluffing, explained how 'the state of tension will continue until the Nationalists have actually accepted to come to a conference and to hold a meeting with the Allied generals at Mudania or Izmit. Until that happens,' he conceded frankly, 'we are at the mercy of incidents which might end in hostilities.'[44] The Paris Note was believed to form a firm basis for negotiation, and it was something that ought to have elicited a positive response from Mustapha. After all, he had achieved all this without even raising so much as a fist at a British soldier.

Meanwhile, it was business as usual at Chanak itself. On the 27th *Argus* reinforced the seaplane carrier *Pegasus* with six seaplanes and four fighters, by which it was hoped Mustapha would be convinced that the Paris Note did not imply weakness. In London, there was disagreement on the best way forward in the event that the Nationalists were to take the bait. Lord Cavan believed that Chanak could not now be defended and ought to be given up, whilst Austen Chamberlain insisted that they would risk losing face if they took such a pre-emptive step. Churchill agreed. He also doubted that the Nationalists would be moved by anything other than a continued show of strength, so the garrison remained in situ until the Nationalists gave a favourable response.

The 'war cabinet' met that evening at No. 10, and here Churchill finally admitted that he was uncomfortable with the state of the Chanak garrison and was musing upon the prospect of abandoning both Chanak and Constantinople and concentrating all available forces at Gallipoli. Lloyd George did not like that suggestion at all, and countered this amazing volte-face with his own evaluation of the Chanak position. A 'four miles perimeter', he contested, could be defended, and he reiterated his contention that the Royal Navy possessed sufficient firepower to hold down the Turks and make the approach roads 'unusable', as well as being capable of breaking up any attacking formations.[45] Admiral Beatty supported the Prime Minister, and said that he was confident the Royal Navy would be able to render considerable assistance by providing a substantial barrage.[46]

If the Cabinet harboured any illusions that the danger of war was now fading, they were soon dashed when that evening news was received that the Turks had rejected the demand to withdraw from the Neutral Zone. To add insult to injury, it appeared that Mustapha had also claimed British aircraft had bombed his troops. This claim, not to mention the Nationalists' intransigence, now enraged Churchill and, according to Secretary to the Cabinet Sir Maurice Hankey, he was becoming 'violently Tuko-Phobe'.[47] This played right into Lloyd George's hands and, not for the first time, a change of mood by Churchill reinforced his own unalterable stance. Indeed, at dinner later that day at Sir Philip Sassoon's house in Park Lane, London, Hankey recorded an extraordinary scene:

> All talk was of war. By violating the Neutral Zone the Turks had released us of the already hated condition re Eastern Thrace in the Paris invitation to a conference ... [48]

This was a potentially disastrous development, despite a cable from Harington to the War Office on the 28th, in which he expressed his conviction that 'I do not think Mustapha wants to attack us'.[49] Lloyd George was again convinced that his favourite scenario, that of an Anglo-Greek army turning back the mounted hordes of blood-thirsty Turks in a massive combat of medieval proportions, might yet come to pass. Such illusions were to be dashed by an evaluation of the Greek forces provided by Laming Worthington-Evans on the 30th in which he described the lamentable state of their army.[50] The Greek General Staff, he reported, admitted that the morale of the 3rd and 4th Corps had collapsed after the loss of Anatolia, and a British liaison officer reported that many troops were now 'incapable of offering organised resistance'. Further, Colonel Condilis, the 'Venizelist organiser in Constantinople', was reported to have admitted on his return from a visit to the troops that 'if the Turks reached Thrace, nothing would stop the Greeks running but the Gulf of Corinth'. Worthington-Evans proceeded to describe how the secret service had revealed that three regiments were now 'discontented and ... gradually breaking up', while other units were said to be 'unlikely to be of further use, except perhaps for supplying drafts to Thrace'. General Harington's appraisal was perhaps the most damning of all. Unequivocally he stated, 'I am afraid I have no more faith in the Greek army, and I think that to place any reliance whatsoever in it would be most unwise.' These damning indictments now meant that, in essence, not only could the French and Italians be discounted as Allies, but the Greeks who had begun this catalogue of disasters were no longer in a fit state to finish the job they had started. The British were more alone than ever.

Three more Cabinet meetings took place on the 28th, the outcome of which was to advise General Harington that he had permission to transfer forces from Constantinople to Chanak or Gallipoli if needed, and that he could enjoy their full support. Worthington-Evans, however, stated that the defensive perimeter would need to be extended to include Bairek Tepe and Sirt Tepe, thus giving command of the Narrows and a clear field of fire over Chanak, as the force now at Chanak was inadequate to stave off a prolonged attack. But the force in place by the 30th would not suffice to enable Marden to extend his position to give him possession of Bairek Tepe and Sirt Tepe. The position, he said, was 'well prepared' and wired, and 'reconnaissance has been made with a view to its extension as reinforcements arrive'.

Worthington-Evans went on to report that large movements of Turkish troops were being detected, and that the 2nd Turkish Army of 36,000 men and 112 guns 'has been concentrating northward into the area Al Hissar-Balikesri-Panderma-Endremid and this army, or part of it could attack Chanak any time after 30th September'. He added the further disconcerting news that 'it could be reinforced by the 1st Turkish Army moving north from Smyrna', and that the only thing that was likely to slow them down was the terrain itself.[51] The situation was confirmed by *The Times* when it warned its readers on the 29th that 'Turkish troops are still concentrating in the neighbourhood of, if not actually in, the Neutral Zone both near Izmit and Chanak'.[52] Thus the whole affair was still teetering on a knife edge, with the British unsure as to whether or not Mustafa was bluffing or was really prepared to fight to get what he wanted. In view of this uncertainty, the Cabinet agreed that if necessary a further two additional divisions could be found to reinforce Chanak. They also agreed a note warning Mustapha that if he did not respect the Neutral Zone, the Paris Note of 23 September, and especially the undertaking to prevent Greek warships entering the Sea of Marmara, would be rendered null and void.[53] In Constantinople both Harington and Rumbold saw the Note of the 23rd as being crucial as a basis for further negotiation. Worthington-Evans relayed Harington's contention that Constantinople ought to be able to hold out for three or four weeks if the Turks launched an attack. On the 28th Marden, concerned by reports of the Turks apparently closing in on all sides, asked Harington for permission to open fire if they attacked. Harington, conscious of the need to show strength and a willingness to negotiate, agreed.[54]

The 29th saw the government once again in a more bullish mood, especially after the Park Lane meeting, rejecting Rumbold's suggestion that the Greeks be urged to pull all their forces in Thrace behind the Maritsa River immediately and returning to the intransigent position held on the 18th. They also rejected the French High Commissioner, General Pelle's suggestion that British troops leave Chanak as an act of good faith in lieu of Harington's hoped-for meeting with the Nationalist leader. After all, it was countered, if they did evacuate and the Turks subsequently pulled out of any talks or refused to cooperate, the British would have surrendered their trump card for nothing. They also telegrammed Harington, assuring him that 'you can rely upon our wholehearted support if notwithstanding your efforts, fighting breaks out or has broken out in the Chanak zone or hostilities are forced upon you by attempts of the Kemalists to net you in'.[55] Furthermore, it was decided to raise the stakes and send an ultimatum to the Turks warning them that if they continued to menace the British forces at Chanak, then they would feel entitled to respond with 'all the forces at our disposal'.[56] The Cabinet proposed the ultimatum to Harington, but left him to decide upon a date and time for a reply to be returned. They added nonetheless that 'it should be short'.[57]

The decision to escalate the crisis at this delicate juncture is partly explained by intelligence reports that had been received suggesting that the Nationalists were making preparations for a massive all-out offensive with the encouragement and connivance of the Soviet government. The prospect of Soviet influence over the Straits was a particularly odious one for the British government, especially one with a man in it as vehemently anti-Communist as Churchill. The isolation of the British became all the more unequivocal by news received on the 27th that Greek aircraft had flown over Athens dropping leaflets declaring that the Army and People had revolted and 'overthrown the guilty government'.[58] With Greece now potentially on the verge of revolution, her army impotent, and with no other reliable allies, this was no time to show weakness and expose their precarious position.

Nonetheless, at another meeting, held at Curzon's home at 10.00 pm on the evening of the 29th, the Foreign Secretary expressed some anxiety about the ultimatum, beginning to wonder whether it ought to have been sent in the first place.[59] Lord Lee, Chamberlain and Churchill may have sympathised, but believed that it was too late for second thoughts now. In any case, they could not send Harington instructions one day only to rescind them the next without his starting to wonder if they knew what they were doing. But this episode is indicative of the fact that the British government clearly, if not admittedly, accepted that it had become embroiled in a foreign policy adventure that contained all the ingredients of a complete and utter disaster. Of all the major players, Curzon, Churchill, et al, only Lloyd George appears never to have openly articulated any doubts about the righteousness of their cause.

Nerves became further frayed when Harington failed to acknowledge the ultimatum. He did not even confirm that he had yet issued it to the Nationalists, and when he did finally get back to London, it was to say that he believed a conference was now on the cards. He therefore did not think the ultimatum could help matters, and its value was further undermined by the news that the French had dissociated themselves from it entirely. Mustapha's representative in Constantinople, Hamid Bey, had in fact assured him that the Ankara government intended to reply imminently and it therefore would have been foolhardy to provoke them unnecessarily when the crisis was possibility on the verge of being resolved.

Lloyd George was understandably furious that had Harington not only failed to reply to their telegram, but was concerning himself with the political aspects of the drama and not sufficiently attending to those which were within his remit, namely those in the military sphere. His views were shared by many of the other members at the meeting, but Curzon for one was relieved by what he felt to be qualities that confirmed him as 'expatiating on the advantages of caution and extoling the discretion of the man on the spot'.[60] Curzon himself deserves some credit for his attempts to stay the hands of Churchill and Lloyd George, whilst as events were to prove, Harington was indeed as Curzon admits, serving an invaluable role in Constantinople.

Much to everyone's relief, on 31 September Harington advised the Cabinet that he had still not issued the ultimatum because he had come to the conclusion that threatening to launch an 'avalanche of fire'[61] would put everything in jeopardy. Indeed the mere implicit threat of using violence had been sufficient so far, and General Marden had been given full powers 'to strike when he thinks fit',[62] should he feel that his position was under threat. He further advised London that General Marden had built up an effective perimeter and had established 'a defensive line of outposts ringing Chanak' but was concerned that threatening, let alone using, 'full force' might have a detrimental effect on the Christian population of Constantinople, should any of the armed Turkish bands in the city seek vengeance.[63] Moreover, he was 'horrified' at the prospect of the British troops still in the capital having to leave the civilian population virtually unprotected if they had to abandon the city.

These manifold fears appeared to be allayed when finally, at midday, a jubilant Rumbold informed London that Mustapha had finally agreed to the elusive meeting with General Harington that was to be held at Mudania. The Cabinet breathed a huge collective sigh of relief and agreed not to issue the ultimatum, 'unless he [Harington] considered the situation demanded it',[64] which now looked very unlikely. Churchill, on the other hand, still suspected that the Turks might yet spring a trap, and growled 'the safety of our troops rested with him [Harington]'.[65] Still doubtful of the Nationalists' motives, the afternoon Cabinet of 1 October instructed Harington that his sole role at Mudania would be to fix 'the line to which the Greeks were to be asked to withdraw in Eastern Thrace',[66] and accept or make no other commitments or undertakings until permitted to do so. That afternoon, Curzon telegraphed Rumbold to the effect that the meeting was not to be allowed to be hijacked by the Turks or used by them to play for time and build up their forces. Churchill's scepticism was reflected in one of his regular communications to the Dominion governments. He admitted frankly that he suspected that Mustapha was just playing for time, and believed that he was likely to launch an attack within days, no doubt while everyone was concentrating their minds on the conference. At 10.30 pm that Sunday evening, Churchill outlined the terms which Britain would deliver at Mudania. She would work towards the objective of ensuring a Greek withdrawal from Thrace, whilst in exchange the Turks would have to agree 'not to send troops either before or during a final peace conference into the Neutral Zone and not to cross Marmara or the Straits'.[67]

On Monday 2 October, a hopeful Harington boarded HMS *Iron Duke* with the ultimatum 'still in my pocket',[68] and set off on his fateful mission to Mudania. The Turkish Nationalists would be represented not by Mustapha, who chose as ever to remain enigmatically in the shadows, but by his redoubtable right hand man and hero of the Battles of Inonu, General Ismet. This canny and wily negotiator would make his first appearance on the world stage and demonstrate to the Allies what tough nuts the Turks would be to crack diplomatically, never mind, as they had already amply shown, militarily.

A still somewhat irresolute Churchill again placed great significance on the consequences should the conference break down. He furthermore cautioned gravely that, 'a rising [in Constantinople ... is almost certain when the Kemalists arrive at the waters' edge' [i.e. of the Straits].[69] His concerns were again compounded by fears of a repetition of the massacres in Smyrna and the subsequent burning of the city. 'Our fear is that Constantinople may soon afford the same spectacle on a much larger scale,'[70] he cautioned. Despite his continued reservations, the conference, which only a few days before would have seemed an impossibility, opened on Tuesday 3 October 1922.

As Harington later described, the site chosen for the negotiations was one obviously selected at random and in great haste ('we proceeded to the conference room, just a bare room on the sea ... dead Greek bodies, recently pushed off the pier by the Turks, were washed up against it'[71]) and certainly not one likely to suggest an auspicious venue for a productive meeting of minds. Nevertheless for the first three days things seemed to be going well. Ismet appeared to have agreed to abide by the Paris Note of 23 September, and at Chanak the Turkish forces were withdrawn over half a mile from the British lines. It seemed at last as if the final curtain was about to descend on the last act of a very long-winded play, one whose many subplots, twists and turns had seen it morph from a murder mystery into a bedroom farce. Then suddenly, on the 5th, and apparently at the instigation of the unwelcome French interloper and envoy to the Nationalists, Franklin-Bouillon, Ismet became intransigent, questioning and rejecting the British proposals and offering up all sorts of arguments and obstacles which had not previously been an issue. The Turks were now demanding that they should be able to occupy Eastern Thrace immediately.[72] It looked as if, once again, the British had taken three steps forward and two steps back. 'We sat every morning and afternoon for some days,' Harington recalled, 'but it all came to nothing.'[73] There were 'some 28 points on which we could not agree. At last one evening, we drafted and signed a document giving our final terms and saying we were not empowered by our governments to go further. I told General Ismet Pasha that that was the last word, and that I was returning that evening on HMS *Iron Duke* to Constantinople and would come back the next afternoon for a final reply.'[74] With that he glumly returned to Constantinople to confer with the Allied Commissioners. The Cabinet also met that night in London to discuss what to do next.

The French and Italian Commissioners, who of course were keen to see the back of the whole affair, wanted to accept the demands, but Rumbold naturally did not; the more concessions they made the more demands would be submitted. If the British side held their ground and the talks then broke down due to Nationalist intransigence, he insisted, at least the world would put it down 'to the intractability of [the] Turks' and the British could come away with clean hands.[75]

The Cabinet met again on the 6th to consider Rumbold's recommendations, whilst Lord Curzon went on another fools' errand to Paris. The outcome was that the British would seek an interim settlement on the basis of each of the three Allied nations sending men to keep the peace in Eastern Thrace for a period of one month, pending a peace conference. Venizelos in the meantime would press his government to agree to this and also to the withdrawal of their own troops. With that General Harington returned to Mudania. As far as the hapless Greeks in Thrace were concerned, it looked like the writing was on the wall. They were under no illusions that it was time to get out and, as Hemingway observed reporting for the *Toronto Star*, yet another tragic Greek migration was getting underway:

> All day long I have been passing them, dirty, tired, unshaven, wind bitten soldiers, hiking along the trails across the brown, rolling barren Thrace countryside. No bands, no relief organisations, no leave areas, nothing but lice, dirty blankets and mosquitoes at night. They are the last of the glory that was Greece. This is the end of their second siege of Troy.[76]

These tragic pawns were to join the tragic lines of refugees and homeless dependents that had been spilling out of Western Anatolia and Thrace since the tragedy began, relying on the charity and goodwill of their fellow Christians but for the most part finding themselves treated as foreign interlopers by Greeks who saw them merely as more mouths to feed.

Back in Mudania, Harington faced Ismet in 'an awful room' with 'only an oil lamp' to cast light on the proceedings whilst they continued to talk.[77] Ismet paced up and down 'saying he would not agree'. The tension mounted as both sides waited for the other to blink. 'Then quite suddenly, he said "*J'accepte*". I was never so surprised in my life,' he confessed.[78] Agreement was finally reached on the morning of 11 October and a convention was signed to come into force at noon four days later. Under its terms, Allied troops would occupy Eastern Thrace for thirty days, three Allied military commissions would take over the civil administration of the region from 16 October and the Greeks would return home. At Chanak, the Turks withdrew fifteen kilometres from the coast and agreed again not to reinforce their troops, and at Izmit they undertook to pull back behind the Neutral Zone. The Allies would remain in Constantinople, Izmit, Chanak and the Gallipoli Peninsula until a formal peace treaty was signed, and until that time the Turks would not reinforce or garrison Eastern Thrace.[79] 'I only thought,' wrote Harington later, 'that our nation did not want another war so soon ... I was glad of that word, "*J'accepte*".'[80]

One of Harington's staff wrote home to his parents, expressing his conviction that 'the chief had saved Lloyd George',[81] as indeed, on the face of it he had. After all, as he admitted himself, the success or failure of the negotiations 'rested with me alone. I was all alone at Mudania.'[82] His sentiments were shared by Rumbold, who telegraphed Curzon on the afternoon the convention was signed that the successful outcome was 'largely due to patience, tact and spirit of conciliation shewn by General Harington'.[83] Churchill too, in something of another shameless volte face, considering all his previous announcements, telegrammed the Dominion prime ministers in exultant tones, claiming that 'the Turks have signed a good agreement',[84] while Sir Horace Rumbold remained convinced that the Turks had been persuaded to come to terms 'by our display of force and their knowledge that we would use it in the last resort'.[85]

A hugely relieved government showered the General with praise. Lord Stamfordham wrote to Harington to express the King's relief at the peaceful outcome of the discussion that it was freely admitted had been largely due to his acumen and diplomacy:

His Majesty feels that you have earned the gratitude of your fellow countrymen for the wisdom, tact, patience and firmness displayed by you both in council and in the carrying out of the Government's instructions... [86]

Lord Derby wrote to say 'how much I appreciate all the tact and statesmanship that you have brought to bear in Constantinople under very trying circumstances',[87] while the Army Council too, heaped plaudits upon him, conveying their 'warmest congratulations on the brilliant manner in which you have carried to a successful conclusion the difficult and arduous task entrusted to you'.[88] Curzon too expressed his relief at the outcome, writing to Harington on 20 October that 'we should have been idiots had we not backed you up, and trusted your sound judgement and perfect command of the situation'.[89] He did concede, however, that perhaps stopping the fighting might prove easier than bringing about a lasting peace, admitting that 'the Peace Conference fills me with gloomy apprehensions'.[90] Despite this, on 17 October Maurice Hankey recalled how Churchill and Lloyd George rued the way the issue had been resolved peacefully:

> He [Churchill] quite frankly regretted that the Turks had not attacked us at Chanak ... he felt that the surrender to them of Eastern Thrace was humiliating. I don't think the Prime Minister felt very different ...[91]

Whatever the true feelings of Churchill and Lloyd George, war had been averted, lives saved and 'honour' preserved, but the fallout from the crisis was not over quite yet. The Canadian and Australian governments were still reeling from the issue of the fateful telegram that took their help for granted and, like their counterparts in the India Office and Delhi, were steeling themselves for their own confrontation with the United Kingdom.

8

IN A GOOD CAUSE,
WE ARE PREPARED
TO VENTURE OUR ALL

British policy towards Turkey had alienated millions of her Indian subjects, given rise to a nascent Indian independence movement and polarised political opinion within the government; it had created rifts between the United Kingdom and her erstwhile allies France and Italy whilst her former acolyte Greece had been abandoned by all three. In the midst of all this turmoil and upheaval, Britain might be forgiven for assuming that she could at least take for granted the continued and unquestioned loyalty of the 'White' Empire, which always gave its help in times of crisis. However, the ill-timed and ill-judged telegram that Churchill had transmitted on 15 September 1922 was to destroy this comfortable illusion forever and, as A. J. P. Taylor expressed it, 'Dominion status was openly displayed for the first time as Dominion independence.'[1]

Despite receiving various degrees of self-rule over the years, the respective governments of Canada, Australia, New Zealand and to a lesser extent the Union of South Africa and most recently the Irish Free State had been quite comfortable with their limited autonomy. Furthermore, these detached Britons had frequently demonstrated their willingness to rally to the flag whenever the Mother Country was in peril. When Britain went to war against the Boers in South Africa in 1899, the Empire's response was magnanimous – 17,000 Australians, 8,500 Canadians and 8,000 New Zealanders flocked to the Colours.

Their loyalty demonstrated to the world that when push came to shove they faced a united front if it chose to pick a fight with any one of them. An Australian confirmed that this mantra still held good in 1914 when, on the eve of the First World War, he insisted that 'when the empire is at war, so is Australia at war'.[2]

Despite some reservations, particularly among the anti-British Boers in South Africa the Dominions also heeded London's call to arms in 1914, and in the first month of the war alone some 30,000 Canadians volunteered to fight. Robert Borden, its Prime Minister since 1911, is said to have gone so far so far as to assert that he was prepared to see Canada bankrupted if it meant saving the British Empire from destruction, a sentiment echoed by the Australian Labor politician Andrew Fisher, who declared that 'Australia would defend Britain to our last man and our last shilling'.[3]

The Dominions' menfolk rushed to the recruiting stations determined to serve King and Country. Australia offered 20,000 men, New Zealand 8,000 and Canada a further 20,000. Wealthy and entrepreneurial Canadians even circumvented official channels by raising their own regiments. One, Princess Patricia's Canadian Light Infantry, was to be immortalised by its exploits on the Western Front. Raised at his own expense by the immensely wealthy Andrew Hamilton Gault at a cost of over C$100,000, he filled its ranks almost exclusively with British ex-servicemen who had migrated to Canada, leaving only 10 per cent of its ranks to be occupied by native-born Canadians. Tragically, however, and with consequences not be fully realised at the time, their enthusiasm was to be cruelly squandered. By May 1915, they had only four officers and 150 men left out of the 1,098 who had departed so cheerfully from Canada only a few weeks before. At the Third Battle of Ypres in 1917, they won two Victoria Crosses but lost 80 per cent of her officers and 60 per cent of her Other Ranks. The tide of enthusiasm was beginning to turn as the war lost its early romantic appeal and the newspapers filled with lists of the dead. Conscription had to be considered as the supply of ready and willing volunteers began to dry up, but this only served to polarise the country. It became a major election issue in 1917 when Meighan introduced two bills into the Ottawa Parliament, but in splitting the country it also failed in its aim. The Canadian call-up of 1 October 1917 received a lamentable response, and of the 331,934 men summoned to fight, 310,376 applied for an exemption. Clearly, the notion of fighting in noble causes on the battlefields of Europe was losing its appeal.

Newfoundland had contributed the Royal Newfoundland Regiment to the war effort and it, too, suffered horrendous casualties. At Beaumont Hamel, on 1 July 1916 – the first day of the Somme – the regiment suffered 90 per cent casualties. Nevertheless, another 600 volunteers were found to fill its ranks, but by April 1918 it practically ceased to exist as a functioning fighting unit. The stoic Dominion's supply of men was drying up and she simply had no more to give.

Australia can be said to come of age in the vicious cauldron of the Dardanelles Campaign at Gallipoli. The ANZACS were en route to France when the decision to attack the Turks at Gallipoli was made. They were therefore unfortunate enough to be at the right place at the wrong time, and were held in Egypt until they were needed to take part in the fateful campaign. The privations of the Australians, alongside the New Zealanders, British and French, still cause rancour in some quarters to this day, but there is no denying the awful statistics. Some 860 Australians were lost in the first six days of the campaign. One battalion went into action on the afternoon of 25 April 1915 with over 30 officers and 900 men, and within four days it had been reduced to nine officers and 400 men. Between 6 and 13 August, of 50,000 men fighting in Suvla Bay, 16,000 had become casualties.

The Western Front chewed up yet more of Australia's youth. The 5th Australian Division was engaged in the attack on Fromelles near Aubers on 19/20 July 1916, by which time they had suffered 7,000 casualties; between 23 July and 3 September 1916, the 1st ANZAC Corps suffered 23,000 casualties securing the village of Pozières and its commanding ridge. On 26/27 September 1917, during the Third Battle of Ypres, the 4th and 5th Australian Divisions launched an attack against Polygon Wood. Total Australian losses were almost 7,000.

Thus, as the war progressed, the Dominions' contributions became more and more crucial to victory. The costs were horrendous, and their views and opinions increasingly had to be taken into account. At the end of 1916, when Lloyd George became Prime Minister he proposed the formation of an Imperial War Cabinet to bring the Empire's war effort under a single direction. However it did not come into being until November 1917 and another year was to elapse before it met, by which time the Dominion Prime Ministers, led by Canada's Borden, insisted that under no circumstances would it supersede the decision-making powers of their respective parliaments. The sacrifices of the war meant that the post-war constitutional relationship between the UK and the Dominions would be changed forever. Imperial unity could no longer be predicated upon an enduring relationship of parent and child. The Dominions had 'come of age' in the Great War and their political leaders were determined to have their newfound status acknowledged, the earliest manifestation of which was their right to send plenipotentiaries to the peace conference as representatives in their own right.[4] The move was intended to reconcile the 'unity of the Empire towards the rest of the world with the equality and independence of its component nations',[5] but in truth it had actually created a dichotomy.

The Imperial Conference of March 1921 sought to formalise this arrangement, but the British maintained their position that the Foreign Office in Whitehall was and ought to remain the single conduit for a unified imperial foreign policy and strategy. A Colonial Office paper issued in advance of the conference urged 'better and more continuous communication between London and the Dominion capitals', a subject which was and would remain a cause of some irritation, and be brought into sharp relief in the forthcoming crisis in Turkey.

The Australian Prime Minister William Hughes had complained that he received information about the British governments' decisions from the newspapers before the telegrams arrived from London, and urged that 'a practical and sure way of bridging the apparently impossible chasm which divides ... the Empire from united action' had to be found. He went on to say that '... while we cannot come here regularly, we must have a voice in the management of the affairs of the Empire ... it affects the very existence of the Empire.'[6]

Lloyd George agreed with Hughes, but returned to his conviction that those affairs should only be managed through the Foreign Office. There was therefore some common ground, but by no means was the notion of London serving as the Imperial Foreign Office unanimously accepted. Each Dominion had evolved and developed in quite distinct ways and were at varying stages of political development, and had contrasting strategic interests that did not require the same solutions. William Hughes' Australia, for example, was thousands of miles away and was reliant upon the Royal Navy for its protection. It was a young country yet to find its feet on the world stage, and was looking with some concern at the growth of a powerful Japanese empire. New Zealand was in a similar situation and if anything was even more dependent upon the Royal Navy to protect its lines of communication and secure its integrity. South Africa was the most powerful presence in southern Africa, with few enemies of its own but mindful of its strategic position as a key staging post on the route to India. The defeat of Germany had not just removed a major threat, but her participation in the war had assigned to the Dominion mandates of her own, which she now wished to defend and develop. Canada however, a vast territory, self-governing since 1867 and with the longest undefended border in the world with the neighbouring United States, had no real enemies. She naturally viewed her strategic interests differently from her partners in Asia and Africa, and had politicians who were not afraid to articulate those interests.

One such man was William Lyon Mackenzie King, born in Berlin (later renamed Kitchener), Ontario in 1874. He came to personify the shift in Dominion attitudes that was slowly evolving since the end of the war. The grandson of the infamous William Lyon Mackenzie, who led an abortive rebellion against the British in 1837, he had studied economics and government at the University of Toronto before joining the civil service and finally entering politics. His socialist credentials won him the seat of Waterloo North Ontario for the Liberals in 1908, and when the war created deep schisms over the issue of conscription he played a role in opposing the move. He was fully aware that from

Canada, out of a population of under eight million, 600,000 had served at home and abroad, of whom some 61,000 men were killed, and another 172,000 wounded. He was determined that his country would reap the rewards to which such a sacrifice entitled her people. He single-mindedly pursued his radical agenda after the coming of peace and developed a considerable following within his party. When the party leader, Wilfrid Laurier, died in February 1919, he was elected in his place.

When the Liberals won the election of 1921, King was determined to use his premiership to pursue an independent foreign policy for his country within the Empire, regardless of the pontifications of British politicians. He was therefore to follow a strategy that would inevitably place him on a collision course with Whitehall. Being aware of the growing sense of autonomy demonstrated by the Dominions both in the world arena and at imperial meetings, London's apparently off-hand treatment of their partners in general and Churchill's clumsy handling of the September telegram in particular appears all the more inept. By sending it on a Saturday he apparently overlooked the fact that, with a weekend looming, the recipients were unlikely to be at their desks to receive the appeal first-hand. They would therefore almost certainly learn of its contents from a civil servant or, even worse, in the newspapers, as Australia's William Hughes had already noted with some irritation.

This is exactly what happened, and Mackenzie King only learnt of the telegram from a reporter from the *Toronto Star* newspaper who accosted him in the street to gauge his reaction, before he had either a chance to consider its contents or consult his Cabinet. Equally surprised was the recently installed Governor-General of Canada, Lord Byng of Vimy, who was to play a defining role in the ensuing constitutional crisis. Born in 1862 to an aristocratic family, Byng joined the Royal Hussars in 1883, serving in the Sudan in 1884, and in the Boer War of 1899–1902. In October 1914 he was placed in command of a cavalry division and then served in the Dardanelles. Following this, he was promoted to lieutenant-general and in 1916 was given command of the Canadian Division on the Western Front. Here he demonstrated rare gifts of leadership and skill in his deployment of the Canadian troops he commanded, and they proudly wore the epithet 'Byngs' Boys' as a consequence. This was graphically illustrated on 9 April 1917, when British and Canadian troops attacked the German-held Hindenburg Line at Arras and Vimy. It was a victory won at tragic human cost: a total of nearly 11,000 men fell in the assault, including 3,500 dead. Nonetheless the scale of loss was far smaller than had previously been experienced in similar actions, and this was due almost entirely to Byng's meticulous planning and preparation.[7] In August 1918 he led his troops on a massive offensive towards Bapaume, which foiled the Germans' attempt to make a last stand behind the Hindenburg Line, and went on to make signal contributions towards the final defeat of the German Army.

Byng's appointment as Governor-General of Canada broke several conventions and set the pace for the future. Firstly, the Canadian government was consulted on his appointment for the first time, as previously the British government alone decided whom they would send – appointments that were not always popular. Consequently, his selection was widely approved by the Canadians, who, in the words of one general, 'literally adored' him, and he was not going to let them down.[8] He also selected Canadian officers as his aides-de-camp,[9] a step which brought the previously aloof office closer to the people, and further enhanced his popularity. Even Mackenzie King was moved to remark that he believed that 'both Lord and Lady Byng are going to be most popular and acceptable', in stark contrast to his predecessor Lord Devonshire, who was considered aloof and detached.[10]

Constitutionally, the role was that of interlocutor between the Crown, the British government and the Dominion governments, explaining British policy and securing Dominion cooperation with it. Byng, however, was not a man to be treated as a pawn, as he made clear upon his appointment when he began to press for change and insisted that 'I will not act as their [the British government's] ambassador'.[11] Although he confided to Arthur Meighan upon taking office, 'I've never done anything like this you know, and I expect I'll make mistakes,'[12] he wasted little time in getting to know the people, and embarked upon a series of tours where he met many of his former comrades-in-arms. It was while he was engaged in these duties that the telegram arrived, but he decided not to rush back to Ottawa in order to avoid speculation that the crisis was greater than it was. When he did finally return he made it known that he approved of the line taken by King, a stance fully reflected in the replies he submitted to the British government.

Following the initial communication from London, Byng attempted to further clarify the Dominion's new position in a telegram to Churchill on 18 September. Gone was the automatic assurance of Dominion loyalty to the Mother Country; his reply was now couched in more guarded and measured tones. He advised Churchill that it was 'the view of the government that public opinion in Canada would demand authorisation on the part of parliament, as the necessary preliminary to the despatch of a contingent to participate in the conflict in the Near East'. To further underline his government's position, he went on to insist that 'we will welcome the fullest possible information in order to decide upon the advisability of summoning parliament'.[13] Ottawa wanted an explanation from London before even putting the wheels in motion which might, or might not, lead to the government sanctioning any involvement in the present crisis.

In an attempt to redeem the situation, a contrite Churchill sought to assure the Governor-General and the Ottawa government on 19 September that what Britain needed at this delicate stage was not 'an immediate decision to send troops' but a public assurance that Britain could enjoy her moral support, and 'a statement that Canada will stand by the Empire' if action against the Turkish Nationalists was considered necessary.[14] Not too much on the face of it, to ask of a loyal ally and friend, but it cut no ice with Byng. He simply reiterated that the Canadian government could take no measures or make any announcements until and unless Parliament was consulted first.

One colleague, the Minister of Marine and Fisheries, Ernest Lapointe, was perhaps more combative than King and complained that the British should never have made so public a request in the first place. He was of the opinion that both the French and English language newspapers were 'very critical' of Britain and that these accurately reflected the public mood. He warned King that the government position should be 'non-committal',[15] something that would certainly fall far short of what London had hoped for, and went on to warn perceptively that he did not believe either France or Italy were going to be embroiled in any adventure against Turkey, and implied that they ought not to be either unless the merits of any involvement were very clearly spelled out. Meanwhile, a chastened Churchill was trying to soothe ruffled feathers by asserting that the British government's faux pas was little more than a 'defect in procedure' rather than arrogance or presumption.[16] Mackenzie King was unmoved and Lapointe pointed out that it was not the timing that was at issue, but the tone and content of the original communication.[17]

Mackenzie King too was busy testing the water, both of public opinion and in his own Cabinet. As he confided to his diary on 17 September, he had been angered by the content of the telegram which he felt had not, as Churchill had claimed to Byng, been hastily drafted due to the pressure of time but instead 'to play the imperial game' and to 'test out centralisation versus autonomy as regards European wars'.[18] He felt, as Byng had made clear to Churchill, that Parliament had the last word, and anyway would not agree to send men to Turkey. He had a very good feel for the developing public mood and was confident that 'the French Canadians and … the maritime provinces will be opposed' to the sending of troops.[19] Underpinning his position was the fear of arousing further public discord on top of the serious social consequences of the post-war slump and unemployment. Any perceived attempt at involving the country in such a distraction as a European war could reopen wounds not yet properly healed since the highly damaging Conscription Crisis. Nevertheless, King did not wish, publicly at any rate, to appear to have dismissed the British request out of hand, but, as *The Times* reported, simply advised London that 'the communication from the British government is not sufficiently informative to enable Canada to reach a decision' and that such a decision, as Byng had already explained, would have to await such clarification.

King's conviction that the French Canadians and the Maritime Provinces would support his stand nonetheless had to be weighed up against those provinces where there was still a very strong sense of affinity with the United Kingdom. *The Times* described how 'the veterans of Toronto have telegraphed the Prime Minister ... offering to raise a battalion here within a week. The officers of the 19th Alberta Dragoons have offered to mobilise their regiment,' and 'the Royal Canadian Regiment has offered its services.'[20] He also recognised the need to 'satisfy Jingo sentiment', whilst some Cabinet members felt that they ought at least to respond favourably to the telegram whilst retaining the right to decide for themselves the part they would play.[21]

Nevertheless, the thirteen Cabinet meetings that took place on the following day served if anything to reinforce King's conviction. He confided to his diary that night how he found all those present at the meetings of one voice in opposing Canadian involvement and had even gone so far as to admit that 'all were inclined to feel [the] whole business an election scheme of Lloyd George and company', serving to underline just how much suspicion there was now of the London government's motives and intentions.[22] Canada's stand could not have contrasted more with that of New Zealand, whose Governor-General, Admiral Jellicoe, wired London on 20 September assuring them of the Dominion's almost unanimous support. Although the Labour Party had moved an amendment that any decision to go to war should be decided by a referendum, it was overruled by 57 votes to 7, and over 5,000 men had already registered to fight in Turkey if called upon to do so.[23] The following day, news that 12,000 ex-officers and men and 300 nurses had volunteered for recall to fight in the Near East was transmitted to London, further buoying the government's morale and helping to offset the attitude of the Canadians.[24]

In South Africa, of course, the British government had to contend with the predictable reaction of the Dutch Boers, still seething from their defeat in 1902 and their compulsory incorporation in the Union of South Africa. Jan Smuts was apparently on a tour of the Union at the time the telegram was despatched, and bearing in mind the predictable political turmoil should his response favour one side or the other, he managed to avoid even sending an official reply. However, as in Canada, the official position did not necessarily reflect feeling in the country at large. The English descendants were naturally more sympathetic to the appeal from London than the Dutch, though not altogether overconfident that it might be replied to positively. Indeed, the *Times of Natal* could only express its hope 'that the invitation will meet with a ready response', but conceded that it 'doubts however it has been received with that vivid and spontaneous enthusiasm which was always the case in the past at any time of Britain's need'.[25] The journal's editor would have been greatly encouraged therefore by the heartening news from Johannesburg that 'numbers of men came forward today to enlist for the Near East',[26] joining the lines of private individuals in Canada and New Zealand ready to answer the call.

Lloyd George, encouraged by such reports, wrote to King George and suggested that he might consider sending a message of appreciation to the Dominions that had responded favourably to the telegram, but this proposal met with a guarded response. The King-Emperor would hardly wish to show favouritism between his various subjects and risk underlining the growing sense of disunity the crisis was creating. After giving Lloyd George's suggestion some thought, Lord Stamfordham replied to the Prime Minister on 20 September. He expressed the King's deep misgivings that 'his doing so may give rise to an invidious discrimination between them and the other Dominions who, so far have not offered assistance'.[27] Fortunately for future Imperial goodwill, the idea was quietly allowed to drop.

This was perhaps just as well, as the issue was tricky enough as it stood without London exacerbating the situation. Like Mackenzie King, Australia's Prime Minister, William Hughes, made his views all too clear, but privately. As Beaverbrook put it, Australia said 'Yes' and 'No' to the telegram.[28] In public, as *The Times* of 18 September reported, 'Mr Hughes ... and the government ... wishes to associate itself in whatever action is deemed necessary to ensure the freedom of the straits ... and is prepared if circumstances require to send a contingent of Australian troops.' However, he was savagely rebuked by Mr John McGirr of the New South Wales Labor Party, who described his assurances as 'audacity and effrontery, and objects to the dragging of Australians into every European brawl'.[29] Although Hughes received some support from Earle Page, the leader of the Country Party, who endorsed his sentiments, the Federal Labour leader Matthew Charlton was 'entirely opposed the sending of a contingent unless the peoples of Australia is consulted in a referendum'.[30]

Irrespective of such outspoken opposition, Hughes was determined to embrace imperial unity to the wider world. On 30 September he announced to the Australian House of Commons that 'Australia's attitude was unqualified and needed no restatement ... we want Kemal to remember this. We stand for peace. We want the Turks to have a fair deal, but if war is to come, Kemal must not forget what entry into the conflict by Australia means.'[31]

In private, Hughes attitude could not have contrasted more to the public persona he had adopted at the risk of such political opprobrium. It was he, after all, who had pointedly referred in 1921 to the need to improved communications so that individual countries could not be put on the spot, and recent events appeared to fly in the face of undertakings made by Britain to improve, not exacerbate the problem. He warned Lloyd George that, 'a Dominion ought not to be stampeded into action by premature press statements'.[32] He complained that, although updates on the Greek-Turkish war had been received, 'from time to time ... no information suggesting that the Empire was likely to be involved in hostilities ... have come to hand.' On the contrary he insisted, the very fact that Britain was going to face off the Nationalists, 'came as a bolt from the blue' to the Australian government. He pointed out that even at this stage the British government had not made it plain just what the Turkish Nationalists were doing that justified any action being taken, and that 'the Commonwealth Government found itself in [a] most embarrassing position being asked not to decide between peace and war because the British government had already made the decision', but that as she had now told the press she had been invited to participate, 'we could [not] in all the circumstances say we would not do so'. Hughes went on to argue that 'the Dominions ought to be consulted <u>before</u> any action is taken or irrevocable decisions made by Britain', because 'then and then only can our voices be heard and our counsels heeded'. Emphasising Australia's continued commitment to the Empire, he conceded that '[it] is one and indivisible or it is nothing', but warned that if Britain made decisions on her own and invited the Dominions 'to be associated' with them only 'after they had been done', then any talk of a common Imperial foreign policy was no more 'than empty air', a position which 'gravely imperils the unity of the Empire'. Hughes also resented being made to appear as British puppets 'by declaring ourselves in favour of one policy today and in a months' time compelled by a change of government in Britain to favour quite another'. All this was, he said, due to his country not being properly consulted: 'What we are entitled to is a real share in moulding foreign and Imperial policy'.

Hughes was also well aware of the motives prompting the outbursts of his political opponents, where memories of the Dardanelles were still raw. 'The Australian people are sick of war,' he warned London, and it was his firm belief that unless vital national interests were at stake, war was 'not only a blunder but a crime'. He had no time for the aspirations of Mustapha Kemal, he said, but he equally had no time for the territorial ambitions of the Greeks, for whom they were not prepared to risk 'one Australian soldiers' life'. He insisted that the Empire 'should not be asked to join in an unjust or unnecessary war', reminding Lloyd George pointedly that Australia had already been through one 'dreadful ordeal' and that 'in a good cause we are prepared to venture our all, in a bad one, not a single man'. He also asked what the League of Nations was doing to intervene in the crisis, considering that the whole reason it had been established in the first place was to 'maintain peace'. If it was unable to help resolve the crisis he insisted, then it ought perhaps to make way for an organisation that could.

He insisted that if any justifiable amendments or modifications to Sevres could be made to meet Turkish Nationalist demands and avoid war, 'they ought to be offered now before hostilities commence'. He also went public on 20 September and stressed that 'Australia's ambition was limited to the freedom of the Dardanelles and the preservation of the invulnerability of the peninsular ... beyond that,' he warned, 'we think we ought not to go.'[33]

In Canada, Mackenzie King rode out the crisis, succeeding in mollifying those who advocated fuller support for Britain, and those like Lapointe who urged what would amount to a refusal to participate. Those individuals throughout the country who had expressed their willingness to fight were not called upon to do so, and in fact the crisis had blown over before Parliament was convened to vote on the issue. Nevertheless, it was a close run thing. Constitutionally the Dominion's duties and legal obligations in such emergencies were unclear, but he was sure of his own strong convictions. These are revealed in his diary, in which he confided solemnly that 'it is not right to take this country into another European war, and I shall resist [such a step] to the uttermost ... if membership of the British Empire means participation by the Dominions in any and every war in which Great Britain becomes involved, without consultation, conference or agreement of any kind in advance, I can see no hope for an enduring relationship'.[34] He reiterated his determination to steer Canada away from an Imperial Foreign policy in a letter to a friend shortly after the crisis, when he wrote:

Anything like centralisation in London, to say nothing of a direct or indirect attempt on the part of those in office in Downing Street to tell the people of the Dominions what they should or should not do, and to dictate their duty in matters of foreign policy, is certain to prove just as injurious to the so-called 'imperial solidarity' as any attempt at interference in questions of a purely domestic concern.[35]

On 2 January 1923, Mackenzie King made a statement in the House of Commons in Ottawa in an effort to draw a line under the issue, in which he pointed out:

We have felt and feel very strongly that, if the relations between the different parts of the British Empire are to be made of an enduring character, this will only be through a full recognition of the supremacy of parliament, and this particularly in regard to matters which may involve participation in war. It is for parliament to decide whether or not we should participate in wars in different parts of the world, and it is neither right nor proper for any individual or for any group of individuals to take any steps which in any way limit the right of parliament in a matter which is of such great concern to all the people of this country.[36]

Australian Prime Minister Stanley Bruce, who had succeeded Hughes, endorsed this philosophy when he insisted:

> We have to try to ensure that there shall be an Empire foreign policy which, if we are to be in any way responsible for it, must be one to which we agree and have assented ... we cannot blindly submit to any policy which may involve us in war ...[37]

Therefore, even though none of the Dominions were required to send a single man to Chanak or fire a single shot at the Turkish Nationalists, the crisis at Chanak had a profound effect on imperial relations and 'ultimately vindicated the independence of the Dominions'.[38] Britain could now add to India the list of those once staunch imperial associates whose unreserved devotion could no longer be taken for granted in her hour of need.

9

STOP THIS NEW WAR

On 19 October, 1922 a cabal of Conservative MPs met to decide the fate of the now shaky Coalition government, of which they formed the majority party and which had by now appeared to have outlived its usefulness. Underlying this decision was the desire to see the end of the political career of David Lloyd George, under whom they had been chafing for months and from whose dominance they were desperate to be freed. Head of the Coalition and its Prime Minister since the First World War, he was a man who, following a succession of crises and domestic and foreign policy decisions, was now 'unable to capture and hold public confidence'.[1] The fact that the Conservative element of the government was meeting so soon after the crisis with Turkey was no coincidence, and despite the fact that trouble had been brewing for some time on one issue or another, they quite simply no longer trusted him or the reckless adventurism that had almost dragged the country into another war.[2]

The camel's back had indeed become heavily weighed down ever since the coalition's startling electoral success of December 1918, in which they won 478 seats in the House of Commons. Some 335 of these were Conservative, so despite his resounding victory Lloyd George was heavily dependent upon their goodwill and support. This factor was to have a substantial bearing on subsequent developments, but first let us consider some of the straws, of which the adventure in Turkey would prove arguably to become the last. He had started to lose his sheen when the so-called 'Honours Scandal' came to light during the height of the First World War and he was implicated in the sale of peerages in exchange for cash to provide funds for his party.[3] His nominations were brought into question, and his reputation tarnished, being depicted as 'devious', 'unscrupulous', and of engendering every feeling 'except trust'. Indeed, his personal qualities in general left something to be desired, and such was his ruthlessness that he had very few real friendships upon which to call. In the words of one arch critic, 'he shed his friends like the ermine sheds its winter coat',[4] a quality that would find him lacking allies when he really needed them. It was partly this personal distrust that intensified the move to oust him.[5]

There were more problems closer to home following the sudden return to a peacetime economy. Having declared that returning servicemen would find 'Homes fit for Heroes' to live in, economic and political realities had instead turned such undertakings into a 'a faded mockery',[6] and increased the appeal of the Liberals' nearest rival for working-class votes, the Labour Party. It was soon obvious that a country geared to the demands of war would find outlets for its manufactures drying up as peace returned. Deteriorating industrial relations followed close on the heels of layoffs and wage cuts, and when the unions went on strike during 1919–1920 matters threatened to go into complete freefall. The unedifying sight of striking policemen joining picket lines and carrying placards demanding better pay and conditions persuaded many in government that action needed to be taken, and quickly.

When the dole queues grew to some two million men, the burden on the Exchequer, starved of tax returns and with war debts to pay, increased to the point where cuts in unemployment benefit had to be considered. This was a view endorsed by the Conservatives in the Coalition, but Lloyd George's resistance to this solution sowed discord in the party ranks and gave his opponents further cause to want to see the back of him.

When the seventy-three Irish Sinn Feiners who had been elected to the House of Commons chose instead to remain in Dublin and declare an independent Irish Republic, Lloyd George faced yet another crisis which he could not hope to win. Urged to take positive action, he authorised punitive operations by the British Army and specially recruited auxiliaries and 'Black and Tans', named after a well-known pack of hounds in County Limerick. These men were essentially unemployed ex-soldiers who had become inured to violence, and for whom the upheavals in Ireland found a welcome outlet. Their criminal activities served to alienate the ordinary Irish populace still further, and were met with violence in equal measure until a state of near-civil war had broken out. Law and order was breaking down as the government's hold on the island became more and more tenuous and even the presence of over 40,000 British soldiers. Police and auxiliaries could not calm the situation. Indeed, in many cases they exacerbated it. The bloodshed reached appalling degrees of savagery and it was clear that only compromise could end the killing which had by 1921 totalled over 1,200 Irishmen and women and approximately 800 soldiers and policemen. In a speech at Carnarvon on 9 October 1920, Lloyd George had boasted that 'we have murder by the throat', but he had already come to the conclusion that he would have to meet the Nationalists halfway, despite resistance from members of his own Cabinet and military men such as Sir Henry Wilson.[7] Others viewed negotiation as little more than outright treachery, but opinion in Britain was becoming increasingly hostile to the war as the killing and brutality continued. The accommodation that Lloyd George came to with the Nationalists created an Irish Dominion, the 'Free State', but retained six of the northern counties in the United Kingdom. It not only outraged his avowedly Unionist backbench Conservative MPs but brought civil war to Ireland and in the long run satisfied no one. On 31 October 1921, thirty-two diehard Conservative MPs supported a motion of no confidence in the handling of the affair, but the division of the island of Ireland proceeded, heralding over sixty more years of violence and misery.[8]

Nor could he garner much consensus in his handling of foreign diplomacy, and his ignominious and short-lived participation in the so-called Allied 'Intervention' in Russia, earned him few plaudits. The Red Army overwhelmed their White adversaries and by the end of 1919 it was all over. The decision to withdraw support was further prompted by Labour's hostility to the action, and by stirring up working-class opposition they threatened to take even more votes from the Liberals. A conference convened in Genoa to discuss German war reparations too ended in dismal failure. Although he had hoped that a successful outcome would 'restore his star to the zenith', it instead served to further blot his copybook.[9] The United States declined to attend and France refused all compromise with respect to the payment of German reparations. Indeed, its only successful outcome was to bring a much-resented rapprochement between Germany and Russia who, as the despised black sheep of the international community, sought solace in each other's estrangement. Lloyd George thus returned from his 'last foreign excursion empty-handed' and much maligned.[10]

As we have seen, there was also growing concern at government policy in India, where the Montagu–Chelmsford Reforms in particular were causing dismay among Conservatives. One outspoken hardliner, Sir William Joynson-Hicks, called any such measures to acquiesce to Indian demands for self-government 'the criminal betrayal of every white man and woman in India',[11] and in February 1922 he passed a motion of censure against the Secretary of State Lord Montagu, which was supported by ninety MPs.[12]

Clearly the cards were gradually becoming stacked against the increasingly besieged Prime Minister, and his litany of policy decisions were now to be fatally compounded by his stubborn support of the Greeks and the policies that he chose to adopt towards the defeated Turks. At the very time when support for Greece formed the lynchpin of his policy in Turkey he would alienate the overwhelming majority of Conservative MPs, who had been pro-Turk since Disraeli and who viewed his machinations with dismay.[13]

As we know, Lloyd George's 'one irreconcilable critic' was Lord Montagu, who had been instrumental in ensuring the Prime Minister was aware of the damage his policy in Turkey was doing to Muslim sentiment in India.[14] He was, in Lord Beaverbrook's words, 'bitterly and unalterably opposed to Lloyd George's support of Greek claims and pretensions',[15] and this issue came to a head at the beginning of March 1922. The Viceroy of India, Lord Reading, sent another anxious telegram to Lord Montagu, in which he reiterated the necessity of agreeing to compromises with the Nationalists. Without consulting the rest of the Cabinet, Montagu decided to publish the telegram, unaware or not minding that such an overt criticism of government policy from one of the Empire's senior figures could be extremely embarrassing and damaging. Lord Curzon in particular was about to embark on delicate negotiations in Paris, and the publication of such dissent placed him in an intolerable position. It gave, he claimed, the impression that British foreign policy was being dictated not in London but by 'a subordinate branch of the British government 6,000 miles away' [in India].[16] He insisted that unless Montagu was removed from his post he would resign, telling Lloyd George that unless he were 'publicly repudiated in both Houses of Parliament, I should decline to go to Paris and some other Foreign Secretary had better take my place.' Lloyd George also greatly resented the Secretary of State's constant interference, and judged this to be an ideal opportunity rid himself of this singular source of irritation. On 9 March he demanded his resignation for action 'totally incompatible with the collective responsibility of the Cabinet to the Sovereign and Parliament'.[17] Montagu reluctantly acceded to the demand, but unfortunately the matter was not allowed to rest.

He was naturally aggrieved at the way he had been treated and, apparently the worse for drink, candidly voiced his attitude to a journalist from *The Evening Standard*. He then proceeded to give a speech in his Cambridge constituency in which he vilified his colleagues, and claimed that Curzon had written him a 'plaintive, hectoring, bullying, complaining letter' over the issue.[18] Curzon demanded to see a copy of the alleged correspondence, but Montague declined and the Foreign Secretary proceeded to give his side of the story to the House of Lords on 14 March. Although Curzon vindicated himself and showed that Montagu was motivated largely by hubris, it did not serve Lloyd George or the government well. The unsavoury episode gave the growing ranks of dissenters on the backbenches further cause to feel that the Coalition was losing its way,[19] and prompted another motion by Joynson-Hicks which condemned its lack of 'definite and coherent principle' in dealing with such high matters of state.[20]

The momentous speech he gave in the Commons on 4 August, in which he blithely praised his Greek allies, was taken as further proof that he was losing touch with reality. Secretary of State for War, Lord Derby, wrote to Bonar Law condemning this apparently 'insane love of the Greeks' and pleaded 'how could you expect the Turks to negotiate with a man who could make such a speech?'[21] On 1 September he announced that he had decided that the time had now come to break with the Coalition. More bad news followed when the Conservative Chief Whip, Leslie Wilson, who had been taking soundings of his fellow MPS, warned the party leader Austin Chamberlain that over 180 of them were prepared to stand as independent Conservatives at the next election rather than to go before the electorate a second time on a Coalition ticket. This was followed by a note from Conservative Party Chairman, George Younger, to Austin Chamberlain on 16 September which warned that Bonar Law was also unhappy about the future and was seriously reconsidering his position with respect to the status of the Coalition.

Indeed, in the country at large a groundswell of anti-war sentiment was beginning to develop. The government had failed completely in their efforts to stir up a war spirit or to persuade the population that such a stance was justified under any pretext whatsoever. The British people wanted peace but believed increasingly that they were being propelled into an unnecessary war through the verbose outpourings of Lloyd George.[22] His warlike posturing particularly rankled a population that had lost faith in its politicians after years of empty promises and was now disillusioned by life in an austere post-war world. These views were stridently articulated by elements within the national press. On 18 September the *Daily Mail* printed the chilling headline 'STOP THIS NEW WAR'. The newspaper accused the government of having deliberately employed intemperate language in the communiqué of the 16th to 'provoke a disastrous and costly war' and of having committed 'every conceivable blunder' in its policy in Asia Minor. It was now compounding the felony by threatening to 'add further vast expenditure to the nations' burdens' to fight 'a mad war'. It even called upon the Dominions to 'flatly refuse' to participate in the 'disastrous military exercise', which it alleged Lloyd George had concocted to cover up his own 'irreparable blunders'. It went on to ask why the government was so 'eager for a deadly war in the

East?', concluding that it was Lloyd George's 'last desperate throw in a struggle which must inevitably lead to his own downfall'.[23]

Lord Lovat Fraser was even more scathing in his criticism of the Prime Minister, claiming that 'no man is more directly responsible for the misery and devastation in Asiatic Turkey than Mr Lloyd George', he accused him of being 'headstrong, obstinate and entirely contemptuous of advice', of urging the Greeks on 'when the whole of his ministerial colleagues were against him', and of acting unconstitutionally and in such a manner that had Cabinet responsibility prevailed then 'he would never have been allowed to back the Greeks year after year'.[24]

Anti-war meetings were held throughout London and the provinces, where crowds called upon the government to end their warmongering and instead use their influence to bring the Greeks to the negotiating table. Disquiet too was rising further to the surface among the ranks of the Trades Union movement. The *Daily Mail* carried reports of 'widespread protests' against the war and of organisations such as the works committee of Poplar Borough Council passing motions in which they 'emphatically protest against the country's entrance into any war' and their indignation at 'the bellicose attitude of the government and the sending of troops to Constantinople';[25] sentiments echoed by organisations such as the National Association of Unions in the Textile Trade, which promised 'to take any and every means necessary to frustrate this mad and idiotic policy'. In the Yorkshire city of Bradford the Lord Mayor announced his intention of calling a meeting to protest against the 'proposed war', and as far afield as Washington in the United States Senator Lodge of the Foreign Relations Committee stated that more bloodshed would be 'a disgrace beyond words'. Equally vehement was the *New York World and Philadelphia Public Ledger* which accused the British government of 'sabre rattling'. In Germany, Britain's growing discomfort, reported the *Daily Mail*, was being met with 'signs of joy',[26] and in India, the highly critical *Times of India* accused the government of 'using a steam hammer to crack a nut'. Moreover, the *Bombay Chronicle* went so far as to call for 'every Muslim, Indian, Christian and Englishman who cares for justice and fair play' to 'protest against the biased attitude of the British Government', which was 'contrary to all the hopes of Asia and of Islam'.

On top of this deluge of criticism from around the world, Lloyd George faced personal confrontation from his critics. On 21 September he received a deputation of some thirty members of the General Council of the Trades Union Congress. They included the redoubtable dockers' leader Ben Tillett, who said he was 'cognisant of the vested interests, and the cross purposes of the vested interests', which were at play in the current crisis, but was emphatic in his view that the working class was 'absolutely antagonistic to the war'.

Confident that it had its finger on the pulse of the nation, *The Daily Mail* escalated its demands. On the morning of the 21st it demanded the British 'GET OUT OF CHANAK' entirely, and insisting that 'public opinion in Great Britain grows sterner and more emphatic every day. Our people will not tolerate another war in the Near East' it asserted, and appealed to the nation 'to insist that the government must stop beating their war drums.'[27] It also went on to quote former Foreign Secretary Lord Grey's dire prediction that 'we may be heading for disaster' unless the government drew back from the brink. However, as Lord Beaverbrook put it so succinctly, 'Lloyd George decided to be strong at the wrong time and for the wrong reasons,'[28] and he was to be severely punished for it. Sensing Lloyd George's growing isolation, and eager to dissociate himself from what had become a seriously unpopular policy, even Curzon was prompted on the 27th to admit to the Cabinet that he did not 'hold quite such strong views on the retention of Chanak as some of his colleagues'.[29] Openly anti-war sentiments were now being voiced by other senior politicians, and on 2 October Arthur Griffith-Boscawen, the Secretary of State for Agriculture, wrote to Curzon and Chamberlain insisting:

I am certain the average Englishman is dead against war in general ... I don't believe the country cares anything about Thrace and Constantinople and Conservatives generally would prefer to see the Turks there rather than the Greeks ...[30]

On 6 October former Prime Minister Herbert Asquith finally spoke out against the government. In a scathing indictment published in all the newspapers the following day he lampooned their handling of the crisis and summed up its foreign policy as being quite simply amateurish.[31] Asquith's critique coincided with Andrew Bonar Law's own deep misgivings contained in a letter published in *The Times* on the following day. He insisted that the British could not hope to keep the Turks out of Constantinople on their own, stating prophetically, 'We cannot alone act as policeman of the world,'[32] in an assessment Lord Beaverbrook called 'a root and branch condemnation of the Chanak policy'.[33] It also served to encourage those Conservatives who wished to precipitate the end of the Coalition and read Bonar Law's sentiments as a sign that he would be prepared at the very least to stand against Lloyd George in a leadership contest and perhaps pull them out of the arrangement altogether.[34] Conservatives were further inspired by the announcement by Reginald Clarry of his intention to stand as an independent Conservative at the Newport by-election, due to be held on 18 October – a prospect Lloyd George admitted could destroy the Coalition if it resulted in a Conservative victory.[35]

If such a move was being considered, then now was the moment to act. Lord Beaverbrook went so far as to assert that Lloyd George 'foolishly believed that a state of war against Turkey would unite Conservative and Coalition Liberals, silence the opposition parties and justify an appeal to the electors with a whopping majority for his leadership'.[36] If so, it was a cataclysmic misjudgement, the consequence of which would all too soon manifest itself.

With a General Election due to be called, timing was crucial, and if the Conservatives were to take Reginald Clarry's lead and campaign on their own ticket, Lloyd George had to be dispensed with as a prerequisite. For that to happen the Coalition had to be dissolved, and before *that* could take place a majority of Conservative MPs had to be convinced that this was the only way forward.

However, despite the warning bells and clear hostility of so many Conservatives to such an idea, a meeting of Cabinet ministers on 10 October agreed that the election should be fought on 15 November as a Coalition, and there was little dissent to this arrangement.[37] President of the Board of Trade, Stanley Baldwin in fact opposed this stance, stating unequivocally that Lloyd George had now become 'an albatross around the party's neck', and that he for one would refuse to serve under him again, while Leslie Wilson urged the party to go to the polls alone and with their own leader.[38] Curzon at this time had more pressing business, and with the negotiations at Mudania in full swing he was worried that an election could compromise the delicately balanced proceedings. He had nevertheless his own axe to grind, becoming increasingly unhappy at Lloyd George's unorthodox conduct of foreign affairs. His methods, eschewing Cabinet responsibility in favour of personal advisers and his own instinct, had caused Curzon increasing resentment. Combined with his bullish and overbearing manner he had long become irksome to Cabinet colleagues, who felt excluded from the key decisions. This habit of excluding Curzon had been a feature of his dealings with the Greeks,[39] a defining moment being his secret negotiations in March 1921 that were unknown to the Foreign Office and actually at odds with the decisions of the Cabinet. That very week, Curzon had discovered to his dismay that the Prime Minister had been engaging in secret negotiations with the Italians. Perhaps he pondered the only way to restore the balance of power in Cabinet and return to consensus politics would indeed be the end of the Coalition. Others naturally held a contrary view. Churchill stubbornly held to the defence of the Coalition as the only positive course of action for the country, accusing Baldwin and anyone else who dared to challenge the primacy of the Prime Minister of base disloyalty. Conservative leader Austen Chamberlain was also fulsome in his defence of the status quo. With such solid backing from the higher echelons of both parties, opponents of the pact faced an uphill climb.

Then, almost overnight, the entire political landscape was transformed as the result of a blunder of epic proportions. It came at the hands of the Prime Minister himself. Despite the developing storm, when a little quiet circumspection might have been called for, he doggedly persisted in his attacks on the Turks and the French, condemning both in a speech in Manchester on 14 October – the very day that the Mudania Convention was due to come into force. It was naturally a highly sensitive stage in Britain's diplomacy with Turkey by anyone's standards, but not apparently in Lloyd George's estimation. He chose this very moment to accuse the Turks of being cut-throats and barbarians, the French of being perfidious cowards and to insist that he alone had acted all along in the role of peacemaker. Furthermore, he contrasted his own dogged defiance of the Turks with Foreign Secretary Lord Grey's alleged appeasement of the Germans in 1914, 'which ended in the most disastrous war this world has seen',[40] whilst his 'amateurish' diplomacy had been proven to be the very policy that had 'brought peace'.[41] Not only did the speech threaten to seriously embarrass the British delegates to the forthcoming peace negotiations, but the Prime Ministers' utterances flew right in the face of received wisdom and made a mockery of everything that had been striven for by men such as Curzon. It was a calumny that finally convinced him to confront Lloyd George and clear the fetid political air once and for all. In exasperation, he submitted a letter of resignation to the Prime Minister, who begged him instead to hold on for at least a few more days, and obligingly Curzon stepped back from the brink, which gave his boss a breathing space whilst the drama in the Westminster village unfolded.

Meanwhile, Churchill hosted a dinner on 15 October, to which both Liberal and Conservative Ministers were invited. He felt that if the Coalition was to survive it required the unstinting loyalty of all of its members to Lloyd George as a prerequisite. Curzon decided that he could not attend the meeting, which was taken as proof of his sitting on the fence, but in fact he had already decided to tender his resignation if the Cabinet agreed upon an election before the Turkish peace conference was held, and had advised Chamberlain accordingly. Suddenly another dramatic twist in the complex saga unfolded when on the 16th Churchill was suddenly taken ill with acute appendicitis and was almost immediately bedridden. Suddenly, Lloyd George was divested of one of his closest allies just at the moment when his political survival was most precariously balanced.

Having as promised held off in his resignation, Curzon went to see Lloyd George on 17 October in a confrontation that failed to mollify his growing concerns. It was, he recalled, 'one of the most curious'[42] audiences he had ever had with his old master as he was begged not to desert his 'old comrade in arms',[43] or to forget 'the great scenes in comradeship of the war'.[44] He then launched into a tirade of self-justification of his actions, trying to vindicate his policies and his strategies and asserting that he had been right all along and everyone

else wrong. Curzon used this tirade of misrepresentation to give vent
to his longstanding resentment of the Prime Minister's domination of
foreign affairs. Throughout the entire crisis, he alleged, Lloyd George
had said one thing in public and another in private, encouraging the
Greeks to pursue their disastrous adventure in Anatolia and having
no exit strategy when it all went wrong, as so many people had
told him it would. Lloyd George denied the charges and proceeded
to call the Greeks mendacious.[45] For his part, Curzon repeated his
offer of resignation and advised Lloyd George that he should act as
his conscience dictated, to which the Prime Minister responded that
all would be over one way or the other on the 19th, after which he
would like as not be resigning anyway.[46] With this exchange Curzon
departed not only perplexed, but also slightly concerned that the
Premier had finally lost his grip. What ensued was inevitable.

Conservative MPs had been busy plotting his downfall, testing the
political water and garnering the support of their colleagues. All that
remained was for a vote to be taken and the decision to be made.
The momentous meeting was arranged at the Carlton Club for the
19th, the same morning the result of the Newport by-election was
announced and Clarry had won with a majority of 2,090 votes. As
the *Daily Mail* reported the following day, the motion before the
assembled MPs was

> that this meeting of the Conservative members of the House of
> Commons declares its opinion that the Conservative Party, while
> willing to cooperate with the Coalition Liberals, should fight the
> election as an independent party, with its own leader and its own
> programme.[47]

In the debate that followed there were still those who wanted to keep
the Coalition intact, but there were still other, more influential voices.
One speaker, Sir Henry Craik, told the meeting that he believed the
party had been 'led on a slippery, dangerous and doubtful path' on a
journey it was now wise to terminate.[48] Stanley Baldwin then spoke,
and his words were to be among the most damning. Whilst conceding
that Lloyd George was, without a doubt, a 'dynamic force', he added

that such a force could be, and was in his case anyway a 'terrible thing'.[49] It had split the Liberals and was now threatening the same fate for the Conservatives. He went on:

I should like to give you just one illustration to show what I mean by the disintegrating influence of a dynamic force. Take Mr Chamberlain and myself. He is prepared to go into the wilderness if he should be compelled to forsake the Prime Minister, and I am prepared to go into the wilderness if I should be compelled to stay with him.[50]

His view was supported by Bonar Law, who had already done the Prime Minister a great deal of harm with his letter to *The Times* and now spoke outright of the need to fight the next election alone. Both men spoke as one when they insisted that the Conservatives must now 'dissociate themselves from a Prime Minister no longer worthy of their trust'.[51] Against such a formidable array of voices more conciliatory arguments stood little chance, even the urgings of Arthur Balfour, who expressed his view that only a Coalition government could face the challenge of post-war reconstruction and an emerging Labour Party failed to sway the assembly.[52] Chamberlain naturally spoke in favour of the Coalition, but he was too 'unconvincing' to sway anybody,[53] and then when he claimed there was no difference of policy between the two wings of the Coalition he was met by strong murmurs of dissent,[54] interspersed by cries of 'Ireland', 'Egypt', 'India' and 'Newport'.[55]

In the vote taken at the end of the meeting, those for continuing with the Coalition numbered 87, those against 187. The die was cast, the Coalition dead and Lloyd George on his way out. The *Observer* newspaper, once regarded as Lloyd George's Sunday read, called openly for his resignation, which he duly tendered to the King that afternoon. Bonar Law was appointed leader and he was invited to form a government comprised of the majority Conservative MPs. Here came a man of a refreshingly different personality and political style to his predecessor. His more finely honed grasp of the public mood, particularly his own party's desire for a 'sense of quietude, caution and balance',[56] could have been no better expressed than when he promised the nation 'tranquillity and freedom from adventures and commitments both at home and abroad'.[57] It was music to the electorate's ears. The ordinary man and woman in the street cared not a whit who controlled the Straits, or whether Smyrna was called Izmir or the other way round; very few bothered whether the Greeks had Thrace or it was part of Turkey, and the fate of minorities in Anatolia was of not the slightest interest. The Conservative stance echoed such sentiments, and they were to be amply rewarded as a result.

With the political demise of Lloyd George and the dissolution of the Coalition, the end, for the time being at least, of another political giant had come. Winston Churchill too was 'without an office, without a seat, without a party' and, thanks to a short stay in hospital, 'without an appendix'.[58] Politicians of course never dare admit the error of their ways, and on 10 November, when he was on the campaign trail in Dundee, he insisted stubbornly that the Turkish crisis was 'a near war which [the government] had endeavoured to stop'. He claimed that this had been achieved and that far from shying away from his part in the episode, he was 'proud to have participated in [it]'.[59] His electors, however, were nowhere near as convinced, and in the election that followed he came third, hardly polling enough votes to save his deposit. For the Conservatives it was a resounding success. They had returned to power for the first time since 1905, winning 38 per cent of the poll with 5,200,000 votes, gaining 344 seats. Labour came second with 4,000,000 votes and 142 seats. The National Liberals won 62 seats and the Liberals 53. It was a defining moment for which the crisis in Turkey alone could not take the entire credit, but it had certainly played a considerable part. By antagonising his colleagues and 'pushing on with an extreme anti-Turk policy' to a point of fanaticism that few Liberals and virtually no Tories could reasonably accept, Lloyd George had become the architect of his own downfall. For this he had paid the ultimate political price.[60]

Nonetheless, there remained the unfinished business of negotiating the final peace with Turkey. It remained to be seen if a Conservative administration could meet the challenge any better than a Coalition one, and a Conservative Prime Minister discharge his duty to secure peace any more effectively than a Liberal.

10

NONE OF US CAN PRETEND THAT THE TREATY IS A GLORIOUS INSTRUMENT

Responsibility for resolving this vexed question had now fallen within the orbit of Lord Curzon, whose role in the Chanak Crisis had been significant. Despite the machinations of his overbearing boss Lloyd George, he had nevertheless walked a fine line between peace and war. Now, having survived the downfall of the Lloyd George Coalition, he was to undertake what was arguably the greatest political challenge of his long career. Curzon was well-travelled, erudite, intelligent and highly successful, one of the youngest ever Viceroys of India and, with the possible exception of his decision to divide Bengal, one of her most outstanding. He was very proud, self-confident, somewhat aloof and, many of his contemporaries felt, arrogant. But he was also a man of his time, one of conviction who would decide upon the merits of a course of action and stick to it. His reappointment as Foreign Secretary and his selection as leader of the British delegation to the small Swiss resort of Lausanne would prove to be inspired. However, before the conference could begin there were still hurdles to overcome, and not just from the British side of the diplomatic divide.

For the British and for Curzon in particular this was to be a peace negotiation like no other. He freely admitted that he faced an uphill struggle and confided with considerable prescience to the British ambassador to Berlin, 'Hitherto we have dictated our peace treaties. Now we are negotiating one with the enemy who has an army in being while we have none, an unheard of position,'[1] but one which the British were largely to blame for bringing about. Horace Rumbold was to serve as his deputy at Lausanne, and although he expected at first to give the Turks 'a real good blow on the head',[2] realpolitik was to mean matters developed slightly differently and the negotiations would test their diplomatic skills to the utmost. He was soon to admit that they faced a long haul. Writing to Lancelot Oliphant, Assistant Secretary to the Foreign Offices' Eastern Department, on 28 October, Rumbold acknowledged that 'the situation here is critical ... and will remain so throughout the peace conference', which he conceded 'may break down' so complex and demanding did he foresee it being.[3] Curzon of course also knew that he would not just have his work cut out for himself with the Turks. Bitter experience had amply demonstrated that his French 'Allies' could not be trusted to play a straight bat. However, he was about to embark on delicate negotiations, and he did not want to take the risk that they would act true to form and try to throw a massive spanner in the works. The Turks of course were banking on the same inter-Allied factionalism that had served them so well to date, and so Curzon had to devise a scheme to avoid such a scenario. As he pointed out to King George:

Poincare wants to get me to Lausanne ... without any previous conversations or understanding with the Allies ... in order (1) to save himself from being forced into a quarrel with the Turks, owing to their impossible behaviour, and (2) to put me in a position where ... deserted as usual by France and Italy I shall be beaten on every point and forced either to conclude a humiliating peace or to break up the Conference ... I will not fall into this trap. I do not mean to go until I have some clear idea whether Allied unity means something or absolutely nothing. Whether in fact we are going to stand out on any point, or whether I am to get on to my stomach and crawl. If this latter, I had sooner crawl in Downing Street than before the eyes of the world at Lausanne.[4]

In other words he was determined to establish his terms of reference before he sat across the table from the Nationalists. Were they going to sell the British out as they had done at Chanak, or were they going to act in good faith? There was only one way to find out. Consequently, on the way to Lausanne he paid a visit to the new French President, Alexandre Millerand, and an agenda was agreed which Curzon hoped would prevent the Turks running rings round them. The French and the Italians too, still obsessed with protecting their privileges and economic advantages, needed to demonstrate a degree of circumspection if they were to ensure that the negotiations did not leave their overriding concerns off of the agenda altogether. Curzon, on the other hand, had no interest whatsoever in preserving those privileges; what mattered to him was the freedom of the Straits. This, after all, was what the whole confrontation in the Neutral Zone had been about – a confrontation that the French had failed to tender any support for. If they expected the British to jeopardise their hard-won peace in order to restore colonial arrangements, they would find themselves in for a big surprise. In any case, whatever the British and French had in mind, the abolition of the Capitulations were the mainstay of Nationalist policy, and they were determined not to return from Lausanne without ensuring they were gone once and for all. It had all the makings of a jamboree, unless Curzon could guarantee otherwise.

The Nationalists meanwhile were seeking closure on the issue of the Sultanate, and the right of the Ottoman government to negotiate on behalf of Turkey. Their successes to date had demonstrated overwhelmingly that it was they and not the weak and enfeebled government in Constantinople that had defeated the Greeks and forced the Allies to renegotiate the abortive Treaty of Sevres. They were in no mind to stand by the sidelines now. Consequently, Defence Minister Refet was despatched to Constantinople to persuade the Sultan to sack his lackeys and recognise the government in Ankara. He spent several hours with the vacillating Sultan, who made it obvious from the outset his own interests and not those of the country were his first priority. He demonstrated his aptitude for obtuseness and obfuscation by refusing to take the broad hint that events had now overtaken him, and that it was for the best if he simply resigned himself to the inevitable. Mehmet VI hinted that he might consider a coalition of both governments, but Refet was equally unyielding.

There was no room in Turkey's brave new world for men who had so meekly lain down in the face of repeated Allied humiliations. Refet emphasised that to keep his throne the Sultan had to accept two conditions: one, that he assume the role of a purely constitutional monarch, acting on the advice of his Ministers; the other, to sack his government in Constantinople. Mehmet however insisted that if he disregarded the advice of his own ministers and dismissed his government against their wishes, by Refet's own standards, that would in itself be unconstitutional. In the face of such sophistry, Refet realised that he was unlikely to get any further and he cabled Kemal that the obstinate Sultan was still 'far from our way of thinking'.[5] Mustapha decided that if the Sultan chose not to go then he needed to be pushed, and to this end embarked upon a subtle campaign of quiet but effective intimidation.

The Allies knew only too well by now that their days in the city were numbered and were not too inclined to rock the boat. When Rumbold received an entreaty from the Yildiz Palace, in which the panicking Sultan informed him of his plight and his need for reassurance and extra protection, Rumbold found himself in a dilemma. He could not be seen to be partisan for fear of angering the Nationalists, but Mehmet was still the monarch and was entitled to protection. All this confusion served to do was leave the constitutional, not to mention physical, future of the Sultan in a state of limbo. Then, somewhat ineptly, the invitation to the conference was issued. However it was not just sent to the Nationalist government at Ankara but also to the defunct government sitting in Constantinople. Even before the invitation had been issued, it had become quite obvious that the fate of the Divine Porte was hanging in the balance. Now that the Nationalist army had forced the Allies to the negotiating table and were now in direct contact with them, there was no longer anything constructive for the Ottoman government to do. Compounding Mehmet's intransigence was the now ridiculous joint invitation to Lausanne, but it did give Mustapha the excuse he needed to finally take affirmative action.

On 1 November 1922 Ankara issued a statement announcing that the Constantinople government, which included the office of the

Sultan, had in fact 'lapsed' on 16 March 1920 after the occupation of the capital by the Allies, and having prorogued itself, had left Ankara as the only legitimate seat of government. The office of Caliph was, for the time being at least, to be retained but separated from the office of Sultan, and offered to someone 'worthy and fitting'.[6] Finally the penny had dropped, and the government in Constantinople realised that the game was up. Matters came to a head on 4 November when Prime Minister Tefik Pasha resigned. The following day all the Ottoman ministries were shut down, and on the 10th Mehmet attended Friday Prayers as Sultan for the final time.

The Sultan, having at last recognised that the end of his dynasty was imminent, made final arrangements to depart quietly from the country before he was thrown out bag and baggage by the Nationalists. He contacted Rumbold again, this time begging for safe passage out of the country. His succinct *cri de coeur* ran as follows:

> Considering my life in danger in Constantinople, I take refuge with the British Government, and request my transfer as soon as possible from Constantinople to another place.[7]

The British duly obliged, deciding that the sooner he went the sooner the problem he posed would be resolved. All that remained was for the Sultan to be secreted out of the city without anyone knowing, so a cunning plan was hatched. At around 0400 on 17 November, after an early morning breakfast of bacon and eggs,[8] Harington and a few close confidantes set about putting the into action. Under the disguise of an early morning drill by British soldiers in the pouring rain, the Sultan was taken from his palace and rushed through the streets of his former capital in the back of an army ambulance before being smuggled aboard the British warship HMS *Malaya*. But he was not entirely alone, and with an eye for his future comforts managed to take with him for company his doctor, valet, bandmaster, two secretaries, two eunuchs, and all the plunder they could carry between them from the royal treasury. However, before departing he placed into the care of a stunned Harington 'his five wives',[9] with the request that he ensure their safekeeping. These loose ends tied up, and now a private citizen, he sailed into obscurity to live out the few remaining years of his life in exile. He died just four years later, with the vacancy that he so hastily left behind him never to be filled.

With this little drama concluded the Nationalists stood as the legitimate, indeed only, authority to send a Turkish delegation to Lausanne.

Once they had concluded their deliberations, the British and French delegations made their way together to Switzerland and the relatively sanguine surroundings of Lausanne. On the way they encountered one of Europe's new breed of statesmen, one who had only recently arrived on the European stage and was waiting to make his mark. That man was the Italian Benito Mussolini, and he was planning to use the conference as a platform for his own self-publicity. En route, the delegation received a note from the new Fascist Prime Minister, in which he insisted that they pay him a visit before proceeding to the conference. They agreed to the 'invitation' in the interests of Allied solidarity but for their pains were subjected to a typically Mussolini-esque tirade, in which the new boy puffed himself up and made all manner of pompous and outrageous demands, including recognition as an equal delegate at the conference. Despite making a good impression on some of those who encountered him – Lady Rumbold for instance seems to have found him 'most impressive and Napoleonic'[10] – he generally succeeded only in astounding the British and French with his capacity for buffoonery. While Mussolini made a fool of himself in front of the Press surrounded by his mob of Blackshirt thugs, Curzon prepared for the long haul ahead.

Fortunately for the British delegation, neither Mussolini nor Poincare remained in Lausanne for long once the conference opened, leaving him and his able lieutenant Horace Rumbold behind to shoulder the burden as senior Allied negotiators. Curzon had been handed the opportunity of a lifetime, the chance to do what suited him best, to dominate the proceedings and run the show in what he considered to be Britain's best interests. The senior French and Italian delegates present, M. Barre and Marchese Garroni respectively, were no match for the erudite and skilful Curzon, and the Greek delegate Venizelos was no longer the statesman he had once been, 'diminished', in Harold Nicolson's words, 'by the position of impotence in which he was placed'.[11] Having seen his outlandish dreams turn to dust, and with no room for manoeuvre, he was more or less left with no choice but to accept whatever the British and Turks agreed between them. Also represented in various capacities were Japan, Rumania and the Kingdom of the Serbs, Croats and Slovenes, thankfully later abbreviated to Yugoslavia. They were in effect little more than observers, though, as the only players that mattered were the Turks and the British. Curzon was therefore in his element. As Sir Horace Rumbold explained to King George on 18 December:

> Lord Curzon is the life and soul of the Conference and supplies all the driving power. I shudder to think what would have happened if he had not been there.[12]

Curzon himself, as we have seen following Mudania, was under few illusions of the challenge that lie ahead. 'Lausanne will be a long and desperate struggle,' he admitted, and 'the chances against a success are so great that my shares will go down' should he return empty-handed.'[13]

However, he would meet in Mustapha Kemal's man on the spot, Ismet Inonu, someone who would very nearly prove his equal as a negotiator, as the two sides tried to outmanoeuvre one another in the uninspiring surroundings of the dining room of the Hotel du Chateau, 'with its shoddy ceiling, its ironwork chandeliers' and 'its general *table d'hote* atmosphere'.[14] Neither did first impressions allow particularly favourable judgments to be made by either party. Curzon examined his counterpart at their first meeting and thought Ismet looked 'more like an Armenian lace seller than a Turkish General',[15] whilst Turkish delegate Slatin Pasha, is said to have observed that Curzon, 'with his smooth cheeks and frock coat', more closely resembled 'a court eunuch' than a British statesman.[16] However, the proceedings soon disabused either side of the notion that it was going to be an exchange between an Armenian lace seller and a court eunuch. For his part, Curzon's patronising and apparently haughty attitude was largely blamed on the intemperate atmosphere that dominated the proceedings,[17] and

Ismet would later remark that it was 'always the English voice, and the English fist banging on the table'.[18] However, he was as equally adept at raising the temperature of the room as his adversary, and in fit of utter exasperation Curzon protested, 'You remind me of nothing as much as a music box. You play the same old tune day after day until we are heartily sick of it – sovereignty, sovereignty, sovereignty.'[19]

In this highly charged and tense atmosphere, the effectiveness of Curzon's negotiating skills were generally making their mark, and the Press wrote glowing accounts of his progress. His attention to the job in hand was only rarely interrupted by unwelcome distractions, such as when his inebriate valet disappeared in a fit of pique, having inconsiderately hidden all of Curzon's trousers. In another, the brace he had to wear because of a near crippling back problem broke, leaving him in considerable discomfort whilst he waited for a replacement to be sent from home.

The Italians meanwhile, egged on from Rome by the tiresome Mussolini, proved a major source of irritation, threatening to leave the conference if they were not given their sphere of influence or a Mandate over former Ottoman territory. One might have assumed that after their earlier debacles they had all but given up such aspirations, but in any case Curzon had seen enough of so-called Italian diplomacy after his brief encounter with Mussolini. So he decided to call their bluff, and told them they could walk out if they wanted to; it would have no bearing on the outcome of the conference one way or the other, anyway. Their bluff having been called, the Italians decided to remain, no doubt hoping to pick up a few scraps as the negotiations progressed.

The new British Prime Minister, Bonar Law, was also taking a studious interest in the proceedings. Having made promises to the British public of future peace and stability in foreign affairs, he was concerned lest the negotiations meet any hurdles that may prevent a swift conclusion of the conference and risk a resumption of hostilities. Paramount amongst these was the fate of Mosul, the oil-rich region that had been included as expected in the newly constituted British Mandate of Mesopotamia. He was quite adamant, he wrote to Curzon on 8 January, that 'we should not go to war for the sake of Mosul', a position endorsed by newspapers such as the *Daily Express* with headlines such as 'No War to Defend Mosul'.[20] Such a lack of support from London ran counter to the need to convince the Turks that Britain was still prepared to fight if the need arose. Instead Rumbold had to admit, that whilst 'in the last resort the Turks would not shrink from the use of force ... the mere thought of force is repugnant to Bonar Law's mind',[21] and would serve as a severe impediment to their negotiating position.

With this ringing encouragement, Curzon proceeded with his exhausting labours, and on 23 January the issue had come up on the agenda. Discussions centred primarily upon the question of defining its parameters, a subject made more difficult by the mixed ethnicity of its population, which included Arabs, Kurds, Nestorian Christians and Turks. However, the subject upon which the crucial status of the region hinged was its oil.

Curzon opened the discussions by inviting Ismet to present his country's justification for having Mosul incorporated within the new Turkish state. This he proceeded to do, but the Turkish claim rested on ethnographic statistics of dubious provenance. Having travelled widely in the region and written an authoritative work on Iran and her neighbours, the expertise he had accumulated enabled Curzon to counter Ismet's arguments almost statistic for statistic, in 'what was perhaps the most brilliant, the most erudite, the most lucid exposition which even he had ever achieved'.[22] Curzon won the argument, if not Turkish acceptance of it. Therefore, as neither would give way they reached a predictable impasse. After considerable rancour and with a stalemate looming, both parties finally, and the Turkish side very reluctantly, agreed to submit the issue to the League of Nations for arbitration; if they failed to reach an agreement within nine months, the League would be allowed to adjudicate. The Turks were, at the end of the day, pragmatists and although the National Assembly castigated Ismet for his stance on the subject, his position was thoroughly endorsed by his boss Mustapha. He recognised perhaps more than any of his colleagues and comrades the enormous strides that had been made over the last few months alone, and in the face of such victories he conceded, 'Is it reasonable to continue the war for

Mosul?'[23] Clearly, the securing of a Turkish state was a tough enough challenge without fighting for territory that now lay far beyond their national borders. Rumbold was probably correct therefore when he had assured Lord Stamfordham on 11 January that 'I am inclined to think that we shall solve the still outstanding difficulties in some sort of fashion',[24] and Mosul did eventually pass to Iraq. This crucial compromise had, it transpired after all, allowed the conference to continue to work its way through the remainder of the demanding agenda. In this atmosphere of almost claustrophobic wheeling and dealing, the two sides worked their way through a host of issues until, once Curzon had resolved those of paramount concern to Britain, he wanted to wind up the proceedings and announced that he intended to have the draft treaty submitted for signature. He added that he intended to depart for home on 4 February whether it was signed or not. Having spent eight weeks in the town, working long hours negotiating during the day followed by the demands of his red Despatch Box in the evenings, all in terrible pain from his back, he was exhausted.

Not surprisingly, the French failed to see things in quite the same light. Denied satisfaction during the previous two months of talks, and seeing the whole matter being effectively wrapped up with their concerns regarding economic and legal matters left unresolved, they resorted to their favourite tactic, prevarication and delay. They insisted that the treaty could not yet even be said to be in draft stage, and was subject to further review. Curzon however remained unmoved, and refused to give way. He was especially determined when the French urged more leeway in Turkey's demands just so they might secure some Turkish accommodation of their narrow concerns. At this point Curzon could conceivably have made a separate peace with the Turks and have left the French in the lurch, but it was much to his credit that he failed to take this possibly tempting option. Ismet, according to Curzon, also tried to squeeze more concessions right up to the last minute: 'Like a true Turk … [he] thought he could still catch me before I turned the corner of the street in order to have a final transaction over the price of the carpet,'[25] and prepared to depart as planned.

Nevertheless, Ismet still had to consult with his masters in Ankara, and here matters were looking decidedly perilous. Returning to the new capital he faced furious deputies who castigated both Ismet and Mustapha over their handling of the negotiations, and especially the compromise over Mosul. Many argued for the fighting to be resumed rather than let the city and its surrounding oil reserves be surrendered, and such arguments continued for a week, with the still significant anti-Mustapha faction seeing their best opportunity yet to topple him. It seemed at one point this might be achieved when a leading enemy of Kemal's disappeared and was later found dead and he was implicated in his murder, but Rumbold remained confident that things were now reaching a conclusion and was sure that Mustapha would be able to influence the assembly in Ankara. He wrote rather scathingly to Sir Lancelot Oliphant on 5 March that 'all the ignorant gas-bags at Ankara are having a run for their money',[26] but would eventually toe the line. Meanwhile, Ismet was packed off once again to Lausanne to wrap things up.

By the time the conference reconvened on 23 April 1923, Rumbold had replaced Curzon as head of the British delegation. It was now his task to address the outstanding issues, mainly relating to the economy, finance and the judiciary; once they were resolved, the treaty could be signed and everyone could go home. As he had assured Lord Stamfordham on 13 March, he no longer anticipated even 'the risk of war',[27] and the outstanding issues could be resolved without too much further contention.

The French delegation, of course, had still to receive satisfaction on the outstanding and still-burning issue of the Turkish national debt. Curzon, as we have seen, had originally refused to entertain their concerns, but after weeks more of endless wrangling Rumbold reluctantly agreed that much of it could now be addressed outside the conference. In the interim reparations were to be waived and economic concessions frozen, and in exchange a few temporary 'legal advisors' were to remain to oversee French interests. With this compromise finally agreed, the time arrived at last to sign the final draft treaty. The document was presented to the assembled delegates for signature on 24 July.

To finally reach this denouement so many compromises had to be made that it had become, according to Rumbold, 'not a glorious instrument, but the least unsatisfactory terms possible'.[28] However, Rumbold was confident it would be signed. After all, as he wrote to Curzon on 28 April, 'they [the Turks] seem really keen to get a settlement this time ... their army is no longer what it was, they are stony broke and in urgent need of peace'.[29] It covered all the salient points and most of the delegates could live with it. Most importantly of all, it removed any possibility of further conflict. The killing was now over; the barbed wire could finally be rolled up and removed from the battlefields.

It was, or so the preamble stated, intended to 'bring to a final close the state of war which had existed in the East since 1914',[30] and '[the signatories] being anxious to re-establish the relations of friendship and commerce which are essential to the wellbeing of their respective people, and considering that these relations must be based on respect for the independence and sovereignty of States'.

Its main provisions confirmed Turkey's frontier with Syria and settled the demarcation lines of Turkey's frontiers with Bulgaria and Greece, while a Boundary Commission would arbitrate in the event of any disagreements. It also confirmed Turkish sovereignty over Imbros, Tenedos and The Rabbit Islands, and any islands less than 3 miles from the Asiatic coast. In exchange, the Turks agreed to guarantee the rights of non-Muslims on the islands. Greek aircraft were forbidden to fly over the Anatolian coast, and no Turkish aircraft were to fly over the islands of Mytilene, Chios, Samos or Nikaria.

Turkey recognised the Treaties of Peace and additional conventions concluded between the Allies and the other Central Powers, and recognised the frontiers of Germany, Austria, Bulgaria, Greece, Hungary, Poland, Rumania, the Kingdom of the Serbs, Croats and Slovenes and Czechoslovakia whilst renouncing extra territorial jurisdiction over any nationals of any territory placed under the sovereignty or protection of the Allies, or of any nationals of a territory detached from Turkey.

The natives of Morocco, Tunisia and Libya were now to be officially acknowledged as the nationals of France and Italy respectively, and Turkey also renounced sovereignty over Egypt and The Sudan. Turkey also recognised the British annexation of Cyprus, while Turkish nationals on the island were given two years to opt for Turkish nationality, but having done so would have to leave the island within twelve months. For her part, Turkey was released from 'all undertakings and obligations' with respect to the Ottoman loans guaranteed on the Egyptian Tribute, and these were transferred to the Egyptian public debt. Turkey also undertook 'to assume full and complete protection of life and liberty to all inhabitants of Turkey without distinction of birth, nationality, language, race or religion'. She also guaranteed freedom of religion, as well as the freedom of movement and the right to emigrate. All Turkish nationals were to enjoy the same civil and political rights as Muslims, equality before the law, employment rights and freedom of the press. Minorities were also given the right to use their own languages in the press, in courts of law, and to have equal access to government funds and subsidies. Greece undertook to confer the same rights to Muslim minorities in her territory. Whether or not such promises would survive the drying of the ink on the treaty remained to be seen.

The Ottoman public debt and Turkey's obligation to repay shares of the debt for which 'other States are liable' was also addressed, and 'a Council of the Ottoman Debt' was given three months to determine 'the amounts of the annuities for the loans payable by each of the States concerned, and [who] shall notify to them [of] this amount'. Disputes arising were to be referred to an arbiter appointed by the Council of the League of Nations. A Commission meanwhile would meet in Paris to decide upon the method of carrying out the distribution of the nominal capital of the Ottoman public debt as well as other tiresome fiscal considerations. Numerous articles covered who should pay, how much, in what proportions based upon when the country concerned ceased to be part of the Ottoman State, what their share would have been, and involving all manner of complicated calculations and formulas in the hope of arriving at an equitable agreement.

The treaty even included an extensive list containing each of the original loans, the date that they had to be repaid, the date they were signed, the interest rate and the bank which issued the loan. Some had to be repaid much sooner than others; for example, the Osmani Loan, made in April 1890, had to be repaid by 1931, whereas the Baghdad Series III, made in June 1908 by the Deutsche Bank, still had until 2010 to be repaid. In all there were some thirty such loans made to finance the building of the docks, arsenals and warships, irrigation works and other such projects that had placed Ottoman Turkey in hock to the Allies in the first place. Many had been made by the Ottoman Imperial Bank, which of course was owned by France. No wonder she was so anxious.

Turkey and the Allies apart from Greece agreed to renounce 'all pecuniary claims for the loss and damage suffered respectively by Turkey and the said Powers ... as the result of acts of war, or measures of requisition, sequestration, disposal or confiscation'. This was either because it would have taken forever to calculate the respective obligations or because they just wanted to wipe the slate clean.

Turkey also had to renounce any rights to the gold handed over to the Allies by Germany and Austria towards their reparations payments. She also had to agree not to claim from the British government or its nationals 'the repayment of the sums paid for the warships ordered in England by the Ottoman Government', which were requisitioned by the British in 1914 and which were partly to blame for escalating the hostilities between the two countries. Turkey henceforth abandoned 'all claims in the matter'.

Whilst Greece was compelled to recognize her obligation to pay for the damage caused by the invasion of Anatolia, as a quid pro quo Turkey also had to acknowledge the 'financial situation' of Greece resulting from 'the prolongation of the war and from its consequences', and renounce 'all claims for reparations against the Greek Government'. In other words on this matter, too, they agreed to call it quits.

On property rights, the treaty undertook that whilst 'the States in favour of which territory was or is detached from the Ottoman Empire after the Balkan Wars or by the present Treaty, shall acquire, without payment, all the property and possessions of the Ottoman Empire situated therein, the recipients of Turkish civil and military pensions who acquire under the present Treaty the nationality of a State other than Turkey, shall have no claim against the Turkish Government in respect of their pensions.' It failed, however, to explain where such pensioners were to get their incomes from in future.

One article also covered the rights and obligations of Greece, Rumania and the Serbs-Croats-Slovenes and Turkey to 'undertake mutually to facilitate ... to search on their territory for, and the restitution of, moveable property of every kind taken away, seized or sequestered by their armies or administrations in their respective territories', so it could be returned to its rightful owners. Whether this would translate into actual action is subject to conjecture – or wishful thinking.

Greece also agreed that any debts arising out of any contracts concluded 'in districts in Turkey occupied by the Greek army' would have to be paid back by the Greek government which, bearing in mind the nature of their short-lived if eventful occupation, was not particularly generous of them.

Articles also covered subjects ranging from debt repayments interrupted by the war, life assurance premiums, marine insurance, fire and other insurances; industrial, literary and artistic property; and Turkey's obligation to honour treaties, conventions and agreements entered into by the Ottoman government over many years. These ranged from a Convention of 1884–1887 regarding the protection of submarine cables, to those of 1904, 1910 and 1921 safeguarding the suppression of white-slave traffic.

Another element of the final treaty addressed issues relating to 'Communications and Sanitary Questions', by which Turkey further undertook to abide by recent Conventions relating to freedom of transit and the transportation of goods by rail that dated back to 1890. Under a further section Turkey undertook to 'take such measures as are appropriate in accordance with the provisions of international sanitary questions'. Curzon's and Rumbold's staffs, not to mention Ismet's, were nothing if not thorough.

Such mundane but important issues arising from drainage or irrigation being in one state as the result of the new borders, and the machinery running them being in another was also addressed.

Turkey even had to renounce any claims of sovereignty 'over the whole or part of such [communications] cables as no longer land on her territory', but could still lay claim where 'at least one end remains in Turkish territory'. Each of the signatories also had to recognise the abolition of all foreign post offices in Turkey. Such painful minutiae was of course necessary because this treaty, unlike Sevres, was largely dealing with a new government, not to mention an entirely new geographic entity to the one which went to war in 1914.

The issue of prisoners of war was also dealt with, although 'the exchange of prisoners of war and interned civilians detained by Greece and Turkey respectively' formed the terms of a separate agreement. This treaty allowed for 'prisoners of war and interned civilians awaiting disposal or undergoing sentence for offences against discipline' to be repatriated, and their property to be returned.

The delegates agreed to 'cause to be respected and maintained' all war cemeteries and graves in their territory, and to allow the erection of memorials. They also agreed, 'subject to the requirements of public health', to allow the bodies of servicemen to be returned to their own countries, whilst further agreeing to provide each other with lists of prisoners of war and interned civilians who died in captivity, as well as the location of their graves.

As had also become agreed custom in Belgium and France, Turkey agreed to grant 'in perpetuity the land within Turkish territory' where war graves and cemeteries were situated, and to give 'free access' to such sites. The Greek government also agreed to the same provisions where circumstances 'affected their territory'. Sadly, as the war in Iraq revealed, this undertaking failed to stand the test of time.

A key achievement was the acceptance by the Turks of a Straits Convention, a major British goal embodied in Article 23. It stated that 'the High Contracting Parties are agreed to recognise and declare the principle of freedom of transit and of navigation, by sea and by air, in time of peace as in time of war, in the strait of the Dardanelles, the Sea of Marmara and the Bosphorus, as prescribed in the separate Convention signed this day [the date that the Treaty of Lausanne was signed], regarding the regime of the Straits. This Convention will have the same force and effect in so far as the present High Contracting

Parties are concerned as if it formed a part of the present Treaty.' It survived for thirteen years.

On 30 January a much darker chapter in the negotiations was opened when the delegates agreed upon an agreement euphemistically entitled a 'Convention Concerning the Exchange of Greek and Turkish Populations'. In essence it sought to resolve once and for all the burning question of Greece and Turkey's longest running sore, that of their respective minority populations. On the face of it this was a pertinent and logical step, but in its execution it was to thrust tens of thousands of helpless civilians into a maelstrom of misery and despair as they were compulsorily uprooted from the homes they had lived in for generations and were forced to seek new lives in what were, to them at least, completely alien lands.

The plan was essentially the brainchild of a Norwegian, Fritjof Nansen, who had been the League of Nations Commissioner for Refugees since 1919. The proposal appealed to the Greeks as a way of resolving their dire overcrowding problem, as the influx of some 700,000 refugees from Turkey could at least partly be offset by the departure of a like number of Muslims, thus freeing up their resources for the newcomers. A similar voluntary undertaking had already been agreed and included in the peace treaty with Bulgaria, by which some 92,000 Bulgarians and 46,000 Greeks were exchanged. Only two sets of populations were to be spared this ordeal, the Greek inhabitants of Constantinople and the Muslim inhabitants of Western Thrace. Everyone else, regardless of their wishes, were to move in what was referred to as 'a compulsory exchange of Turkish nationals of the Greek Orthodox religion established in Turkish territory, and of Greek nationals of the Muslim religion established in Greek territory'. Furthermore, the irrevocable nature of the exchange was underlined by Article 7's emphasis that 'the emigrants will lose the nationality of the country which they are leaving, and will acquire the nationality of the country of their destination'. There was obviously no provision for a change of heart and definitely no going back.

As practically all of the Greeks from West Anatolia had left the country already, the plan mainly affected those of Central Anatolian

Greek Orthodox (Greek and Turkish speaking) and the Pontic Greeks. The convention gave the respective minorities five months, until 1 May 1923, to make their moving arrangements and to plan for their exiles. They were then faced with the prospect of those long forced marches already so graphically and painfully described by the pen of Ernest Hemingway.

This, the least publicised but nevertheless perhaps one of the most far reaching in humanitarian terms of all the undertakings given at Lausanne, was to cast a shadow over what overall was a magnificent diplomatic achievement. Although it did not form a part of the final treaty, it did, as explained in Article 19, 'have the same force and effect between the High Contracting Parties as if it formed part of the Treaty to be concluded with Turkey', and 'it shall come into force immediately after the ratification of the said Treaty by the two High Contracting Parties'.

In putting his signature to it, Venizelos had finally conceded that his dream of a Greek empire in Anatolia was dead, and could never be resurrected.[31] For his part, Ismet had brought to fruition the long cherished dream of a unitary Turkish state, free at last of the loose ends of the extinct Ottoman Empire. Arguably Curzon's greatest diplomatic achievement, it had resolved a crisis that had threatened to embroil the entire region in a catastrophic war. For all his skill, he had nonetheless been unable to impose a treaty on the Nationalists. He had not been dealing with a bankrupt government but with a determined and highly motivated foe with everything to play for.

Ten weeks after the treaty was signed, the last Allied troops left Constantinople, among them General Harington. He later recalled how 'the evacuation was a great test of staff work and was carried out without a hitch from start to finish'.[32] It was indeed an enormous exercise in logistics, as the Army had considerable quantities of materiel to dispose of before they departed, much of which was deposited into the eager hands of the Turks, including two British fire engines 'with which they were delighted', Harington noted with satisfaction.[33]

Perhaps typically for the British, the departure was accompanied by considerable pomp and ceremony, 'the most amazing demonstration

I have ever known', according to Harington.[34] In front of thousands of cheering onlookers, the departing officials saluted the Turkish flag and were then escorted by a Colour Party of Guardsmen to the dockside.[35] He then transferred to the warship HMS *Marlborough,* whose band played 'Auld Lang Syne' as she slowly slipped her moorings and steamed away. He had earlier written to Ismet Pasha, expressing his sincerest good wishes for the future and trusting that they had parted as friends, 'we shall carry away with us many happy memories of Turkey and we hope we shall carry away the respect of the Turkish nation with whom we have come into contact'.[36] Ismet too had departed from the long and arduous chapter, elated at his achievement. He naturally returned to a hero's welcome in Ankara, where he announced that the treaty left his beloved country

> a homogenous, unified homeland; within it, freedom from the obligations imposed by foreigners and from privileges of a nature creating a state within a state, freedom from imposed financial obligations; a free rich homeland with a recognised absolute right of self-defence ... [37]

For the Greeks, however, the humiliation was too much, and many of those politicians and generals blamed for the debacle faced show trials, at the end of which they were summarily executed. G. Ward Price expressed his conviction that 'as time goes by this treaty will stand as the most important milestone in the whole recent course of the relations of East and West', predicting quite rightly that 'it establishes a precedent that will influence all our future dealings with Asiatic nations' and concluding that those old ideas of Turkey as the sick man of Europe 'are rendered out of date by the peace in Lausanne'.

Lloyd George not surprisingly saw the treaty in less glowing terms. He had staked his career and his very political survival on support for the Greeks, so when it all turned to dust his bitter comments could have been expected. His view of the treaty reflected this when he remarked:

> It is no wonder that Ismet has a smile on his face ... when all was over, reports from Ankara state that the peace is hailed as a

great Turkish triumph, and so it is ... The Pact of Mudania was not Sevres, but it certainly was better than Lausanne ... From Sevres to Mudania was a retreat ... From Mudania to Lausanne was a rout ...[39]

The treaty received condemnation from other sources as well. One French newspaper, *L'Clair,* claimed that 'the prestige of the west is reduced to dust', while the *Echo de Paris* condemned it simply as 'a treaty of defeat'.[40] Nevertheless, Turkey's achievement was undoubtedly monumental. On 28 July, *The Times* published the Aga Khan's message to the Muslim world in which he exclaimed:

For the first time in history a treaty has been signed on behalf of a Mohammedan nation upon absolutely equal terms with the Great Powers of the West. The treaty reflects the greatest credit upon the steadfast leadership of Ghazi Mustapha Kemal. The freedom obtained by the Turkish state is complete.[41]

It was a sentiment shared as sincerely by non-Muslims. Lt-Col A. C. Yate declared in the *Asiatic Review* of January 1924:

His [Mustapha's] demonstration that a vanquished state could deal with the victors on its own terms, tear up the Treaty of Sevres, and substitute the very different Treaty of Lausanne, was a tonic to the disaffected nationalists of the Arab world, Egypt and Persia; for years to come the thought of it will cheer them whenever it crosses their minds.[42]

Whatever its long-term effects, the Treaty of Lausanne saw the turning of the final page in a drama which had lasted as long as the First World War itself, and in many respects brought even greater pathos and tragedy. If negotiated four years earlier it could have avoided untold misery, the destruction of hundreds of towns and villages throughout Anatolia and Thrace, the extinction of ancient communities and the ruin of millions of lives through homelessness, exile, and genocidal hysteria.

WE CANNOT ALONE ACT AS POLICEMAN OF THE WORLD

The dramatic events that had stunned the world were now, to all intents and purposes, concluded – but not necessarily, however, the subsequent fortunes of those who had played such key roles in shaping them. The disgraced Enver Pasha, architect of much of Turkey's downfall, had ignominiously fled Constantinople on the night of 2 November 1919 on board a German ship. It took him to the Crimea and thence to Berlin. The man generally held as being largely culpable for Turkey's failure in the war was to elude the justice of his countrymen and disappear into obscurity. He re-emerged briefly, only to face an ignominious end trying to stoke futile anti-Soviet uprisings in the Caucasus in August 1922.

Mustapha Kemal, still basking in the glory of his historic achievement, soon embarked upon the reform of those institutions indispensable to a modern Turkish state. Turkey was officially declared a republic in October 1923, with himself as President, and this step was followed in March 1924 by the abolition of the Caliphate, the very institution that so many Muslims around the world had attempted to preserve. The first steps were then taken to suppress once and for all the pervasive influence of the Muslim clerics, and in April 1924 the religious courts were closed. Four years later Islam would cease entirely to be the nation's state religion. Mustapha's determination to turn Turkey into a Western-style secular society went so far as to abolish the *de rigueur* fez in 1925. In 1926 a civil code gave equal rights to women and in November 1928 the Latin alphabet was adopted. In April 1930 women were allowed to vote in local elections and the first female judges were also appointed to the judiciary. Four years later, women were allowed to vote in parliamentary elections and to stand as representatives. In 1931 international weights and measures came into use, and the following year Turkey was admitted to the League of Nations, underpinning her status as a fully fledged independent sovereign state.

Surnames were adopted in 1934, and Mustapha took the name of Ataturk, or 'Father of the Turks'. It was certainly an apposite choice. Mustapha Ataturk had achieved much for his people, and he was a national hero by the time of his death from cirrhosis of the liver in 1938, his hard drinking having finally caught up with him. His reforms had not been welcomed everywhere, but such was his strength of character that he was able to realise most if not all of his goals. After his death, Turkey continued to modernise. She had her problems, most serious of all the economic consequences of ejecting thousands of Greek and Armenian entrepreneurs, businessmen and traders. Their departure deprived the new Turkey of an invaluable human resource that, like the expulsion of the Ugandan Asians by Idi Amin in the 1970s, was only acknowledged after it was too late. To offset such shortfalls the Turkish government toyed with various socialist-style schemes, few of which bore fruit.

Remaining neutral throughout the Second World War, her new President Ismet Inonu, having adopted the place of his victories against the Greeks as his surname, led her through an era of relative stability. Turkish neutrality also brought great benefits to British interests following a rapprochement achieved between the two countries in the 1930s. One of the few blots on her copybook was the ruthless suppression of her Kurdish and Armenian minorities, who she continues to view as a threat to the integrity of her hard-won statehood to this day.

The contrast with her former adversary Greece, however, could not have been starker. Eleutherios Venizelos followed his fall from grace in 1920 with intermittent returns to politics throughout the

1920s and 1930s. He was then implicated in an abortive anti-royalist coup in March 1935 that resulted in civil war and his exile to France. He died there, largely unmourned, shortly afterwards. However, he has enjoyed a posthumous resurgence in more recent years, having airports named after him and postage stamps printed in his honour, his role as perhaps Greece's greatest patriot serving only to highlight her failed attempt at becoming a major world power.

The years following Greece's miserable adventure in Turkey proved to be politically, economically and socially disastrous. She depended for many years upon loans and foreign aid, whilst dictatorship arrived at the end of the civil war with the establishment of a right-wing government under General Metaxas, the man whose early warnings against the Turkish misadventure went largely ignored. It survived until the Italian invasion of 1940, but even after her liberation by Britain in 1944 she faced many more years of turmoil, civil wars and coups.

The huge population exchanges that resulted from the Greek departure from Turkey and the loss of Eastern Thrace caused untold social and economic misery. All of a sudden the quaysides of Greek ports were inundated, and their councils faced the challenge of providing shelter and food for over a million refugees, an unprecedented humanitarian disaster only resolved after many years of effort. Not least was the problem posed by assimilating cultures which in Turkey may have been clearly Hellenic in character, but in Greece seemed alien and foreign. Turkey's loss would eventually prove to be Greece's gain as these naturally industrious communities formed the nucleus of a social class that would in years to come be a great asset to the economic fabric of the country. From farmers to industrialists, these entrepreneurial and energetic new citizens would transform the country, and one in particular would go on to become one of the world's foremost shipping magnates. Aristotle Onassis fled Smyrna after the Turkish occupation of September 1922, but eventually returned to Greece, forging the huge commercial empire that bore his name and eventually made him reputedly the world's richest man.

Tragic Armenia, tortured by Turkish racial and religious enmity and intolerance, and promised salvation by the Allies too, was to be abandoned. Promised independence and freedom on the one hand, but increasingly viewed as an obstacle to a rapid solution to Turkish intransigence on the other, she was left to her fate. The Treaty of Sevres had given the task of defining the borders of the new state to the US, and a military mission headed by General James Harbord was despatched by President Wilson to make an evaluation of the status of the country. His report made bleak reading, admitting that it was indefensible and as a consequence unviable. Only the assurance of an Allied Mandate and military guarantees of protection could have prevented rapid Turkish reoccupation, but neither was forthcoming. As the United States declined the offer of a mandate over the troubled country, and none of the Allies would commit troops for her protection, she lay helpless. The Armenian Republic survived just two short years as a sovereign state before Turkish and Soviet forces invaded simultaneously and she ceased to exist. There was nothing the Allies or the League of Nations could or would do to resist the act. Only the fate of one of those responsible for the massacres could have demonstrated any sense of justice. Talaat Bey, who is accused of having signed the orders for the deportations in 1915, fled to Germany after the war, but was tried in absentia by the Ottoman government. He was found guilty but, having perhaps understandably declined to return to Turkey to face his punishment, he was instead gunned down in a Berlin street in 1921 by an Armenian patriot.

The lesson of Armenia, or rather the forgotten lesson, went even deeper. Political expediency and indifference soon eradicated the memory of the wider world to her bitter sufferings, so much so that when later Hitler was planning his own 'Final Solution' he was able to refer to the fate of the Armenians as a precedent. 'Who still talks nowadays of the extermination of the Armenians?' he is said to have remarked, when the possible consequences of his own genocide were questioned.[1]

The Turkish war also brought into sharp relief the bitter resentment felt by Italy at the manner in which she was shortchanged by her allies. Offered anything she wanted to enter the war on their side, she ended up with scraps, breeding a bitterness that demagogues like Benito Mussolini found easy to exploit. Italy's emergence from

Lausanne with nothing to show for her posturing simply reinforced his ideological revanchism. In August 1923, when three Italian officials who were engaged in delineating the Albanian-Greek border were murdered under suspicious circumstances, Italy automatically accused the Greeks of having been complicit in the killings. She issued a series of humiliating demands that the Greek government rejected. Subsequently, in a bellicose show of nationalistic fervour, Mussolini ordered the Greek island of Corfu to be occupied until they came to terms. The two sides faced an impasse that was resolved only when the League of Nations became involved and the matter was referred to the Council of Ambassadors. As a result of their deliberations the Italian demands were watered down, but the Greeks were still required to apologise and pay a heavy fine. Mussolini and his fascist sidekicks felt suitably assuaged to accept the decision and withdrew their forces from Corfu. Twenty years later, the disastrous Italian invasion of their hated neighbour appeared to bring the issue full circle.

In 1935, Italy embarked upon the invasion of Ethiopia, seen by Mussolini as a way of salving his growing megalomania and anger at being sidelined in world affairs. His predisposition towards foreign adventure was compounded by the imposition of sanctions by the League of Nations, and eventually a hostile Britain and France left him with no alternative, as he saw it, but to throw in his lot with Hitler.

In India, Muslim nationalism, stirred by the perceived threat posed to the Caliphate, galvanised Mahatma Gandhi's independence campaign, and it gathered such momentum that the British would find it impossible to resist. India's slow progress towards constitutional reform, interspersed by riots and the imprisonment of leaders like Gandhi and Nehru, could ultimately have only one outcome. In 1930, the Simon Commission recommended self-government for the Indian provinces, and two Round Table Conferences were convened in 1930 and 1931 in an attempt to reach a long-term solution. But progress was slow in the face of strong opposition from politicians such as Winston Churchill, who did all he could to block constitutional reform.

Despite obstruction and delay, The Government of India Act was passed in 1935. It was a major step but made only limited concessions, excluding defence and foreign affairs. The Second World War then witnessed the 'Quit India' campaign, orchestrated by Gandhi and his supporters, and Dominion Status was promised once the war with Japan was won. In 1945, the new Labour government accelerated the process, and in August 1947 the two sovereign states of India and Pakistan emerged at last.

The older Dominions continued to re-evaluate their relationships with the United Kingdom as events underlined the need for independent foreign policies. The precedent set by Canada over the Chanak Crisis was fortunately not followed by massive ructions between Ottawa and London, but it was not long before the notion of a unified Imperial Foreign Policy was abandoned. The Washington Naval Conference, convened between November 1921 and February 1922 to discuss naval disarmament in the Pacific, was to provide the precedent they needed to assert their new-found autonomy. Attended by the UK, its deliberations were also clearly of great importance to Canada, Australia and New Zealand, having their own security interests in the region, but they were not invited to attend. It left them in little doubt where they now stood. When the same thing then happened at Lausanne and no Dominion representatives were present, Mackenzie King commented that while Canada took 'no exception' to having not been invited to the conference, it also implied that she was under no obligation to be bound by it either.

In March 1923, Canadian representatives travelled to Washington to negotiate a modest treaty of their own, designed to protect the Pacific halibut fishing industry; the British government, they decided, need not be invited. It had been accepted protocol for the British ambassador in Washington to counter-sign such documents. On this occasion, however, Governor-General Byng advised the British ambassador that the 'signature ... by Mr Lapointe alone will be sufficient and ... it will not be necessary for you to sign as well'. Britain raised objections, but the Canadians threatened to install their own ambassador to Washington if London insisted, and the British reluctantly backed down.

When Mackenzie King attended the 1923 Imperial Conference, he was determined to put an end once and for all, as he saw it, to 'a centralising imperial policy, both politically and militarily'. Lord

Curzon, however, was still of a mind that British foreign policy was 'not of these islands alone, but that of the Empire'. This philosophy had already been overtaken by events, and Mackenzie King now had his victory over the signing of the Halibut Treaty to prove it.

When, two years later, Britain, France and Germany met at Locarno in 1925 to guarantee the borders of Western Europe, Article IX of the final document specified that the British signature imposed no obligations on the Dominions to associate themselves with it in any way. Long gone were the halcyon days when edicts were issued from London and the Dominions loyally fell in behind.

Once they were recognised as separate members of the League of Nations, the Dominions concluded that it was only logical to consider establishing their own diplomatic missions abroad. Canada, as usual, took the lead and proceeded to install representatives in countries it considered important to her national interests. She appointed an ambassador to Washington in 1927, another to France in 1928, and a third to Tokyo the following year.

Another constitutional anomaly was the role of the Governor-General. As we have seen, when each Dominion was established, a Governor-General was appointed and despatched from Britain to act as the representative of both the Crown and the government. He was usually a distinguished politician or member of the royal family or, as in Byng's case, a former soldier. Mackenzie King proposed separating this dual function. Subsequently, in 1928 the resident High Commissioner was to act as the diplomatic representative of the UK, whilst the Governor-General's role was restricted to that of the Sovereign's personal representative. Australia adopted this convention in 1931 and New Zealand followed suit in 1939.

The Imperial Conferences held in 1926 and 1930 were used by the Empire's least enthusiastic members, the Irish Free State and the Union of South Africa, to further clarify their status, which was finally enshrined in the 1931 Statute of Westminster as

> autonomous communities within the British Empire, equal in status, in no way subordinate one to another in any aspect of their domestic or external affairs, though united by a common

allegiance to the Crown, and freely associated as members of the British Commonwealth of Nations.

This landmark confirmed that Britain was no longer at the heart of a huge, unified world state, but at best the senior partner of an international community that was free to come or go much as it pleased, the only real proviso being that each member recognised the British monarch as Head of State.

Nevertheless, Britain's relationship with her Dominions, later known as Realms, varied widely. As we have seen, both the Irish Free State and the Union of South Africa were the most antipathetic to membership of the Empire. The Irish Republic was proclaimed in 1949 after incremental constitutional amendments, which rendered the monarch almost redundant in all but name. By the protocols of the time, she was not allowed to rejoin the Commonwealth, and left that year. The Union of South Africa became a republic following a referendum in 1960, and only rejoined when the Apartheid regime came to an end in the 1990s.

By contrast, Canada did not formally repatriate all her lawmaking powers until 1982 when the Canada Act was passed by the Westminster Parliament. Likewise, the Australia Act in 1984 performed the same function, removing the last vestiges of British sovereignty.

Viscount Byng, the man who could largely be credited with facilitating the Canadians' gradual move to true statehood, remained as her Governor-General until 1926. Despite one constitutional glitch, the so-called 'King-Byng' affair in which he came to blows with Mackenzie King over the right to dissolve parliament and call an election, he departed as arguably her most popular Governor-General. Upon leaving his beloved Canada in 1926, he went on to serve as Commissioner of the Metropolitan Police and was promoted to the rank of field marshal. He eventually retired to his home in Thorpe-le-Soken, Essex, and died in 1935 at the age of seventy-three. His wife, Lady Byng, returned to Canada and ended her days there in 1949.

After his resignation in 1922, Lloyd George's career went into virtual free fall. He continued to lead an eviscerated Liberal Party from 1926 to 1931, and then lead the Independent Liberals. However he had made too many enemies and alienated too many influential political figures ever to hope to be given a senior role in government, and he never held office again. He took a high profile role in opposing Hitler and shared Churchill's efforts in resisting appeasement, but he was destined to sit out the Second World War on the back benches, watching the movers and shakers below prosecute the war with the same vigour and determination he had exercised twenty-five years before. His contribution was finally recognised in 1945, when he received an earldom. He died the same year.

Lausanne was to prove Curzon's swansong. Soon after he returned to the UK, his already failing health went into terminal decline, and he died, a prematurely old and frail man of sixty-six, on 20 March 1925. Curzon had served his country in various capacities throughout his adult life, but had often been the subject of envy and scorn. His efforts at Lausanne, and his determination to resolve at last what had become a thorn in the British side, was to bring him well-deserved praise and recognition. Even in Turkey, the country he often treated with apparent aloof disdain and some contempt, his role in creating a new nation is still remembered with respect and not a little affection.

Churchill fared rather better than his contemporaries. After losing his seat in the 1922 election, he left the Liberals and was elected as the 'constitutional anti-socialist' candidate for Epping in 1924. He became Chancellor of the Exchequer shortly afterwards, a post he held until 1929. He rejoined the Conservatives in 1925, but his views on India and Germany saw him increasingly out of step with conventional wisdom. He then passed into what became known as his 'Wilderness Years', from 1929 to 1939, when he returned to office in triumph as First Lord of the Admiralty and then in May 1940 as Prime Minister. After leading the country to victory in 1945, he again fell from grace, but returned in 1951 to a world he barely recognised. No longer the world statesman he once had been, his views were now more out of step than ever, and he reluctantly retired to paint and write in 1955. He died in 1965, mourned by the generation who shared his times, and a younger one that benefited from the fruits of their sacrifices.

He did, however, have the last laugh on Mackenzie King. His own political career blossomed, holding office from 1935 to 1948. During the Second World War, Canada played host at what became known as the Quebec Conferences, held in 1943 and 1944, where the British and

US planned wartime strategy. Mackenzie King had tried to give the impression that he was participating in the highest circles, a participant rather than merely the host, but Churchill, perhaps recalling his own snub twenty years before, ensured that he was left in no doubt as to his very junior role. He was excluded from all the strategic decision-making, and was lucky to be included in the publicity photos with Churchill and Roosevelt – something that he clearly bitterly resented.

Sir Horace Rumbold proceeded from Lausanne to present his credentials as ambassador to Madrid, a post he held from 1924 to 1928, before being appointed ambassador to Berlin from 1928 to 1933. In this capacity he was to play a crucial role in warning the British government of the growing menace posed by the Nazis, which he articulated in a series of despatches and which were widely acknowledged as being of immense value in allowing the British to assess the increasing danger of the new regime. He retired in 1933 and died after just eight years of retirement in 1941.

Anglo-French relations, badly affected both before and during the Chanak Crisis, continued to decline throughout the 1920s and 1930s. In addition to the fallout from Turkey, two other key and seemingly intractable problems, German reparations and French national security, beset Anglo-French relations. With the war won, British interest in both issues waned very quickly. On reparations, public opinion was moving against the belief that Germany alone was to blame for the war, and consequently that she alone ought to shoulder the cost for it, while British national security had apparently been assured by the German defeat. Germany was no longer the pre-eminent threat and a return to the pre-war status quo was inevitable, as Lord Hardinge explained to Curzon on 1 May 1920:

> Nothing can alter the fundamental fact that we are not liked in France, and never will be, except for the advantages that the French people may be able to extract from us ...[2]

Lord Curzon too saw that the wartime alliance was rendered defunct now the threat from Germany was removed, and that the old frictions were now emerging:

We have been brought, for reasons of national safety, into alliance with the French, which I hope will last, but their national character is different from ours, and their political interests collide with ours in many cases. I am seriously afraid that the Great Power from whom we may have most to fear in the future is France.[3]

French actions had certainly done little to allay such fears. She wanted her money and she was determined that Germany would never again be in a position to violate her borders. Her economy, like so many other nations, had been severely damaged by the conflict, so she was relying on reparations as she had Turkey's debts to make up the shortfall. When Germany defaulted on her reparations payments, France marched her troops into the Ruhr in January 1923. The occupation would continue until the Germans paid up, but only Belgium and Italy supported the action, and Britain was opposed. The Germans, like the Turks before them, were encouraged by this disunity and took the confrontation to the wire, whilst within the Ruhr itself the miners went on strike, depriving the French of the very coal they needed to keep their factories open. The French were outraged that the British, who watched French militarism with concern, had opposed their decisive action; a Europe dominated by France had never seemed any more attractive a prospect than had one dominated by Germany. Britain and the US favoured resolution of the reparations issue through what became known as the Dawes Plan, allowing Germany to borrow the money she needed to meet her obligations, whilst a Reparations Agency ensured fair play. However, it was also dependent on France not seeking to recover her money by force. Months of negotiation and delay followed, and the occupation of the Ruhr continued.

In 1924 a new British Labour government came to power in Britain under Ramsay MacDonald, and France elected a new Leftist Coalition under Edouard Herriot. It seemed that these two governments ought to be able to come to some accommodation. The new French Premier met the Prime Minister in London to see what could be arranged, hoping to link reparations with national security. A conference was convened to discuss the plan later that year, and agreement was reached by which French evacuation would proceed and Germany would commence payments backed by loans. The French subsequently evacuated the Ruhr in 1925, but this failed to resolve the underlying issues.

Britain had now firmly adopted a neutral policy towards France and she strongly resisted any binding treaty of commitment. Instead, she agreed to act as guarantor to a German sponsored Franco-German mutual security pact, which became the Treaty of Locarno, and bound all the signatories to honour the borders as determined by the Treaty of Versailles. Europe finally began to settle down.

The unpopular Versailles Treaty became a target for the new Nazi Germany after Hitler came to power in January 1933. Concerted Anglo-French action would be essential if the Nazi regime's revisionist demands were to be resisted effectively. Instead, the bitter legacy of Versailles continued to fester, preventing any genuine cooperation. Britain, chastened by the Chanak Crisis and its fallout, was in no position to check Hitler until it was too late. She was disinterested in Europe until the arrival on the scene of Neville Chamberlain, and needed all her waning energies to address the numerous problems arising in the Empire, particularly in India and the Middle East. As for the problems in the world at large, Britain had come to accept that, as Bonar Law had prophesised, she could no longer act alone as the world's policeman.

Finally, despite having been drawn up to resolve such issues, the Treaty of Versailles was so inherently unfair that it could not hope to last in the form in which it was agreed in 1919. The need to satisfy French demands for reparations and security led to it being tweaked around the edges and superseded by other agreements that would ultimately render it null and void.

What might have been the outcome, therefore, if Versailles itself had been a properly negotiated treaty like Lausanne? If nothing else, it would have denied the Nazis the gift of an election manifesto presenting the German electorate with a simplistic solution to complex economic and social issues. Versailles was just as impossible to enforce as Sevres, but blind nationalism and an irrational desire for vengeance forced its imposition against all logic and common sense. The outcome was a gradual loss of credibility, the treaty being too strict to enforce but its signatories too weak to prevent a new powerful Germany rising from the ashes and ultimately plunging Europe into yet another catastrophic war.

Furthermore, Britain's failure to influence Turkey's choice of regime left a legacy of anti-British sentiment throughout the Middle East. The bloody nose she received at the hands of the Nationalists did not however deter the British from embarking upon further adventures in the region. These enterprises also almost inevitably resulted in further humiliation and retreat.

In Egypt, where Mustapha's victory was so warmly welcomed, internal disorder grew to a level rarely experienced since Britain originally occupied the country. Finally, in response to nationalist-inspired riots and the threat of anarchy, Egyptian independence was recognised in 1922. Despite this, British influence remained through a series of unequal treaties, until the debacle of the Suez Crisis of 1956 finally precipitated the departure of the last British troops from her soil.

Britain accepted the League of Nations' mandate over Mesopotamia, later Iraq, in 1922, but soon faced serious problems. The challenge of reconciling the country's various ethnic groups, especially the recalcitrant Kurds, not to mention nascent nationalism, led to a premature departure; in 1932 the country became independent, though with continued British influence and control, supported by a considerable military presence to protect British interests. The need to protect oil supplies compelled a level of control over the country that resulted during the Second World War to a de facto coup, culminating in the departure of the pro-German Prime Minister and the installation of a more compliant government. Britain maintained a military presence in the country into the 1950s, by which time the atmosphere in the Middle East, fuelled by Abdul Nasser's new brand of ultra-nationalism, compelled the final withdrawal.

In Iran too, traditionally viewed as within Britain's sphere of influence, considerable political authority was exercised for over thirty years, again largely due to the country's considerable oil wealth.

However the hold was also a tenuous one, fraught with troubles in the face of a hostile population and, during the Second World War, a regime again sympathetic to Germany. On this occasion, Britain moved in concert with Soviet Russia, unseating the government and replacing it with a pro-Allied regime. Nonetheless, Britain's hold on the reins of power only finally came to an end in the 1950s, when they were seamlessly handed over to the United States.

Britain's disastrous Mandate over Palestine needs no retelling here. Burdened by the unfortunate undertakings of the Balfour Declaration, the 1920s and 1930s witnessed war between the indigenous Arab population and migrating Jews. The dire situation came to a head following the Holocaust and the flood of Jewish immigrants seeking a country of their own, free from persecution. The rule of law threatened to break down as the British administration sought to resolve the demands of Jew and Arab populations, and Britain finally threw in the towel in 1948 and handed the Mandate back to the United Nations. A State of Israel was immediately declared, bringing its own legacy of tragedy and mutual conflict between the Palestinians and the Israelis.

The British Mandate over Transjordan posed fewer challenges, with the establishment of a compliant and relatively friendly and accommodating ruling dynasty, which survives to this day. It represents perhaps Britain's only long-term success in the region. Nevertheless, even here Nasser's explosive brand of Arab nationalism could not be ignored, and the monarchy has had to walk a tightrope of diplomatic fence-sitting in order to survive as the one remaining British-created kingdom in the Middle East.

Only in the traditionally conservative and insular Gulf States did British influence survive until relatively recently. Kuwait, a British Protectorate from 1899 until 1961, shared similar arrangements with the United Arab Emirates until Britain finally withdrew its forces from the region in 1972. On balance, however, the decades following the debacle in Turkey are a catalogue of political and diplomatic retreat and failure lasting half a century.

NOTES

1 The rest of Europe do me as much harm as they can
1. Mango, A., *Ataturk* (London: John Murray, 1999), p. 48.
2. Turkology Update Leiden Project Working papers Archive, Dept of Turkish Studies, Leiden University, 'Greek and Turkish Refugees and Deportees, 1912–1924'.
3. Civitas 99, 'Considerations upon the Armenian Genocide' (12 May 2005), pp. 3–4.
4. Palmer, A., *The Decline and Fall of the Ottoman Empire* (London: John Murray, 1992), p. 199.

2 I am not ordering you to attack; I am ordering you to die
1. Housepian, M., *Smyrna 1922: The Destruction of a City* (Faber and Faber, 1972), p. 39.
2. Gilbert, M., *Winston S. Churchill, Vol. III: 1914–1916* (London: Heinemann, 1971), p. 190.
3. Walder, D., *The Chanak Affair* (London: Hutchinson, 1969), p. 24.
4. Carlyon, L. A., *Gallipoli* (Doubleday, 2001), p. 41.
5. Kinross, P., *Ataturk: The Rebirth of a Nation* (London: Phoenix, 1993), p. 66.
6. Gilbert, *Churchill, Vol. III*, p. 192.
7. Tuchmann, B., *August 1914* (London: Papermac, 1980), p. 142.
8. Walder, *The Chanak Affair*, p. 27.
9. Macfie, A. L., *The End of the Ottoman Empire: 1908–1923* (London: Longman, 1998), p. 127.
10. Carlyon, *Gallipoli*, p. 45.
11. Ibid, p. 46.
12. Macfie, *The End of the Ottoman Empire*, p. 126.
13. Ibid, p. 141.
14. Mansel, P., *Constantinople – City of the World's Desire, 1453–1924*, p. 373.

15. Mango, *Ataturk*, p. 137.

16. James, R. R., *Gallipoli* (London: Pan, 1965), p. 11.

17. James, ibid, p. 48.

18. Carlyon, *Gallipoli*, p. 73.

19. James, *Gallipoli*, p. 65.

20. Mango, *Ataturk*, pp. 146–147.

21. Balakian, P., *The Burning Tigris – A History of the Armenian Genocide* (Pimlico, 2005), p. 200.

22. Balakian, ibid, p. 200. See Appendix 5 for a detailed account of the Armenian genocide.

23. Mango, *Ataturk*, p. 185. Also translatable as 'We're in the shit'.

24. Sonyel, S., *Ataturk: The Grand Turk* (London: Cyprus Turkish Association Publication), p. 19.

25. *The Times*, 7 January 1918.

26. Mango, *Ataturk*, p. 189.

27. Miller, G., *Straits – British Policy Towards the Ottoman Empire & the Origins of the Dardanelles Campaign* (University of Hull Press, 1997), ch. 31.

28. Macfie, *The End of the Ottoman Empire*, p. 179.

29. Macfie, ibid, p. 177.

30. Lloyd George, D., *War Memoirs* (London: Oldham Press, 1934), p. 1974.

31. Lloyd George, ibid, pp. 1976–7.

32. Nicolson, *Curzon: The Last Phase* (1934), p. 117.

33. *Source Records of the Great War, Vol. VI*, ed. Charles F. Horne (National Alumni, 1923).

34. Ibid.

35. Macfie, A. L., *Ataturk* (Longman, 1994), p. 51.

36. Kinross, *Ataturk*, p. 136.

3 In the event of a total or partial partition of Turkey

1. Dockrill, M. & J. Douglas Goold, *Peace without Promise: Britain and the Peace Conference, 1919–1923* (Batsford Academic and Educational, 1981), p. 142.

2. Nicolson, *The Last Phase*, p. 83.

3. Ibid, p. 85.

4. Heinrich, P. C., 'Italy and the Repudiation of the 1917 St Jean de Maurienne Agreement', *The Journal of Modern History*, 48 (2) (June 1976), p. 106.

5. Ibid., p. 99.

6. Walder, *The Chanak Affair*, p. 60.

7. Smith, M. L., *Ionian Vision: Greece in Asia Minor 1919–1922* (Allen Lane, 1923), p. 70.

8. Nicolson, H., *Peacemaking: 1919* (London: Methuen, 1964), p. 251.

9. Nicolson, *The Last Phase*, p. 97.

10. Smith, *Ionian Vision*, p. 11.

11. Ibid., p. 16.

12. Ibid, p. 17.

13. Walder, *The Chanak Affair*, p. 37.

14. Smith, *Ionian Vision*, p. 41.

15. Ibid, p. 53.

16. Lecture 14 of 25 on Modern Balkan History (The Balkans in the Age of Nationalism), Steven W. Sowards (www.lib.msu.edu).

17. Walder, *The Chanak Affair*, p. 65.

18. 'Papers Relating to the Foreign Relations of the United States: The Paris Peace Conference 1919, Vol. 3', p. 872, quoted in Cohen & Major, *History in Quotations* (London: Cassell, 2004), p. 806.

19. Nicolson, *The Last Phase*, p. 96.

20. Walder, *The Chanak Affair*, p. 66.

21. Ibid, p. 66.

22. Sowards, Modern Balkan History.

23. Walder, *The Chanak Affair*, p. 41.

24. Nicolson, *Peacemaking*, p. 251.

25. MacMillan, M., *Peacemakers – The Paris Conference of 1919 and its Attempt to End War* (London: John Murray, 2001), p. 363.

26. Dockrill & Goold, *Peace without Promise*, p. 188.

27. Smith, *Ionian Visions*, pp. 74–5.

28. Glenny, M., *The Balkans 1804–1999: Nationalism, War and the Great Powers* (Granta, 1999), pp. 348–9.

29. Erhan, C., 'Greek Occupation of Izmir and Adjoining Territories: Report of the Inter-Allied Commission of Inquiry, May–September 1919' (Ankara: Centre for Strategic Research, 1999).

30. Macfie, *The End of the Ottoman Empire*, p. 183.

31. Kinross, *Ataturk*, p. 140.

32. Glenny, *The Balkans*, p. 382.

33. Lord Beaverbrook, *The Decline of Lloyd George* (London: Collins, 1963), p. 153.

34. Dockrill & Goold, *Peace without Promise*, p. 188.

35. Ibid, p. 184.

36. Sharp, A., *The Versailles Settlement – Peacemaking in Paris 1919* (Macmillan, 1994), p. 163.

37. Palmer, *Ataturk* (1991), p. 49.

38. Dockrill & Goold, *Peace without Promise*, p. 191.

39. Smith, *Ionian Vision*, p. 79.

40. Gidney, J. A., *A Mandate in Armenia* (1967), p. 113.

41. Housepian, *Smyrna*, p. 64.

42. Smith, *Ionian Vision*, p. 80.

43. Kokkinos, D., *History of Modern Greece* (Athens: Melissa Editions, 1972).

44. Walder, *The Chanak Affair*, p. 70.

45. Smith, *Ionian Vision*, p. 89.

46. Ibid, p. 90.

47. Housepian, *Smyrna*, p. 66.
48. Walder, *The Chanak Affair*, p. 70.
49. Glenny, *The Balkans*, p. 383.
50. Balakian, *The Burning Tigris*, p. 325.
51. Sonyel, *Ataturk*, p. 23.
52. Walder, *The Chanak Affair*, p. 76.
53. Erhan, 'Greek Occupation of Izmir and Adjoining Territories'.

4 *Let us march, friends!*

1. Sonyel, *Ataturk*, p. 28.
2. Macfie, *The End of the Ottoman Empire*, p. 186.
3. Mango, *Ataturk*, p. 225.
4. Ibid, p. 225.
5. Sonyel, *Ataturk*, p. 26.
6. Ibid, p. 28.
7. CAB 21/203. Memorandum by the Secretary of State for War, Winston Churchill, to the cabinet, dated 18/11/19. p. 4.
8. Kinross, *Ataturk*, p. 170.
9. Sonyel, *Ataturk*, p. 30.
10. Kinross, *Ataturk*, p. 155.
11. Sonyel, *Ataturk*, p. 31.
12. Mango, *Ataturk*, p. 224.
13. Sonyel, *Ataturk*, p. 31.
14. Ibid, p. 32.
15. Ibid, p. 33.
16. Ibid, p. 34.
17. Housepian, *Smyrna*, p. 86.
18. Nicolson, *Peacemaking*, p. 248.
19. CAB21/203, memo from Churchill to Cabinet, dated 18/11/19. Appendix A, p. 6.
20. CAB21/203, ibid p. 6.
21. Sonyel, *Ataturk*, p. 33.
22. Smith, *Ionian Vision*, p. 116.
23. Palmer, *The Decline and Fall of the Ottoman Empire*, p. 52.
24. Macfie, *Ataturk*, p. 75.
25. CAB21/203, ibid, p. 7.
26. CAB21/203, ibid, p. 8.
27. Kinross, *Ataturk*, p. 195.
28. Macfie, *Ataturk*, p. 86.
29. Ibid., p. 87.
30. Nicolson, *The Last Phase*, p. 247.
31. Kinross. *Ataturk*, p. 196.
32. Cabinet Papers, CAB 21/203, Memorandum on the Nationalist Movement in Turkey, 20 October 1919 et sec.

33. Cabinet Papers, CAB 21/203. Earl Curzon to Earl Granville, October 21, 1919 [144506].

34. Sonyel, *Ataturk*, p. 47.

35. Smith, *Ionian Vision*, p. 113.

36. Ibid, p. 107.

37. Foreign Office Papers, FO608/107. (WCP. 92, 1589-384/1/3).

38. Foreign Office Papers, FO608/107. Memo from Allenby to Foreign Office (0144/5123).

39. Foreign Office Papers. FO608/107. Telegram from Lord Derby to Lord Curzon No. 394.

40. Foreign Office Papers, FO608/107. Various correspondence.

41. Bell, P. M. H, *France and Britain, 1900–1940: Entente and Estrangement* (Routledge, 1996), p. 126.

42. MacMillan, *Peacemaking*, p. 406.

43. Kinross, *Ataturk*, p. 201.

44. Sonyel, *Ataturk*, p. 47.

45. Ibid., p. 49.

46. Mansel, *Constantinople*, pp. 392-3.

47. Zurcher, E. J., *Turkey: A Modern History* (London: IB Tauris, 1994), p. 158.

48. Ibid, p. 159.

49. Ibid.

50. Macfie, *The End of the Ottoman Empire*, p. 195.

51. Sonyel. *Ataturk*, p. 57.

52. Macfie, *Ataturk*, p. 100.

53. Dockrill & Goold, *Peace without Promise*, p. 174.

54. Walder, *The Chanak Affair*, p. 82.

55. Dockrill & Goold, *Peace without Promise*, p. 214.

56. Gilbert, M., *Sir Horace Rumbold: Portrait of a Diplomat 1869–1941* (London: Heinemann, 1973), p. 224.

5 The Greeks were nice chaps too

1. Gilbert, *Churchill*, p. 486.

2. Ibid.

3. Smith, *Ionian Vision*, p. 123.

4. Palmer, *The Decline and Fall of the Ottoman Empire*, p. 254.

5. Smith, *Ionian Vision*, p. 124.

6. Macfie, *Ataturk*, p. 101.

7. Housepian, *Smyrna*, p. 91.

8. Gilbert, *Churchill*, p. 488.

9. Harington, Gen. Sir C., *Harington Looks Back* (London: John Murray, 1940), p. 109.

10. Smith, *Ionian Visions*, p. 131.

11. Housepian, *Smyrna*, p. 92.

Notes

12. Morgan, K., *Consensus and Disunity: The Lloyd George Coalition 1918–1922* (OUP, 1986), p. 319.

13. Smith, *Ionian Visions*, pp. 165–6.

14. Palmer, *The Decline and Fall*, p. 255.

15. Walder, *The Chanak Affair*, p. 96.

16. Gilbert, *Rumbold*, p. 225.

17. Ibid, p. 228.

18. Ibid, p. 229.

19. Sonyel, *Ataturk*, p. 63.

20. Smith, *Ionian Vision*, p. 190.

21. Sonyel, *Ataturk*, p. 63.

22. Zurcher, *Turkey*, p. 160.

23. Macfie, *Ataturk*, p. 117.

24. Sonyel, *Ataturk*, p. 65.

25. Mango, *Ataturk*, p. 311.

26. Kinross, *Ataturk*, p. 265.

27. Ibid.

28. Smith, *Ionian Visions*, p. 183.

29. Mango, *Ataturk*, p. 311.

30. Sonyel, *Ataturk*, p. 65.

31. Gilbert, Rumbold, p. 237.

32. Ibid., p. 238.

33. Smith, *Ionian Vision*, p. 202–3.

34. Dockrill & Goold, *Peace without Promise*, p. 220.

35. Smith, *Ionian Vision*, p. 207.

36. Ibid., p. 200.

37. Kinross, *Ataturk*, p. 267.

38. Smith, *Ionian Vision*, p. 226.

39. Walder, *The Chanak Affair*, p. 152.

40. Gilbert, *Rumbold*, p. 242.

41. Glenny, *The Balkans*, p. 387.

42. Horton, G., *The Blight of Asia* (Bobbs-Merrill Co., 1926).

43. Holland, R., *The Pursuit of Greatness: Britain and the World Role 1900–1970*, p. 101.

44. Gilbert, *Rumbold*, p. 245.

45. Nicolson, *The Last Phase*, p. 264.

46. Morgan, *Consensus and Disunity*, p. 320.

47. Smith, *Ionian Vision*, p. 251.

48. Gilmour, D., *Curzon* (London: Papermac,1994), p. 540.

49. Harington, *Harington Looks Back*, p. 110.

50. Smith, *Ionian Visions*, pp. 244–6.

51. Ibid., p. 246.

52. Gilbert, *Rumbold*, p. 249.

53. Smith, *Ionian Visions*, p. 273.

54. Morgan, *Consensus and Disunity*, pp. 321–2.

55. Holland, *The Pursuit of Greatness*, p. 101.

56. Smith, *Ionian Vision*, p. 283.

57. Owen, F., *Tempestuous Journey: Lloyd George, His Life and Times*, p. 632.

58. Harington, *Harington Looks Back*, p. 110.

59. Nicolson, *The Last Phase*, p. 270.

60. Mango, *Ataturk*, p. 342.

61. Smith, *Ionian Vision*, p. 295.

62. *The Times*, 4 September 1922.

63. *The Times*, 5 September 1922.

64. Walder, *The Chanak Affair*, p. 168.

65. *The Times*, 7 September 1922.

66. *The Times*, 9 September 1922.

67. Anonymous Account of the Burning of Smyrna (Misc. 97/Item 1473) Imperial War Museum Department of Documents.

68. Papers of T. W. Bunter (87/22/1), Imperial War Museum Department of Documents.

69. Papers of M. M. Carus Wilson (77/185/1) Imperial War Museum Department of Documents.

70. Hemingway, *Snows of Kilimanjaro* (Arrow, 1952), pp. 30–1.

71. McMeekin, S., *The Ottoman Endgame*, p. 472.

72. Ibid., p. 473.

73. *Daily Mail*, 11 September 1922.

74. *Daily Mail*, 13 September 1922.

75. *The Times*, 12 September 1922.

76. Housepian, *Smyrna*, p. 155.

77. Kinross, *Ataturk*, p. 325.

78. *Daily Mail*, 16 September 1922.

79. Housepian, *Smyrna*, p. 167.

80. *The Times*, 15 September 1922.

81. Papers of Major-General G. N. Wood CB, CBE, DSO, MC (78/31/1) Imperial War Museum Department of Documents.

82. Owen, *Tempestuous Journey*, pp. 646–7.

83. Harington, *Harington Looks Back*, p. 149.

6 You will get no cooperation from us

1. Keay, J., *India: A History* (London: HarperCollins, 2000), p. 480.

2. Chadha, Y., *Rediscovering Gandhi* (London: Century, 1997), p. 244.

3. Lloyd George, *War Memoirs*, p. 2005.

4. Walder, *The Chanak Affair*, p. 30.

5. Miller, G., *Straits*, p. 505.

6. FO144506.

7. MacMillan, *Peacemakers*, p. 414.

8. Kinross, *Ataturk*, p. 298.

9. Payne, R., *The Life and Death of Mahatma Gandhi* (New York: Smithmark, 1995), p. 346.

10. Edwards, M., *The Myth of the Mahatma Gandhi, the British and the Raj* (London: Constable), p. 202.

11. Chadha, *Rediscovering Gandhi*, p. 244.

12. Payne, *Gandhi*, p. 347.

13. Wolpert, S., *Gandhi's Passion – The Life and Legacy of Mahatma Gandhi* (Oxford University Press, 2001), p. 107.

14. Macfie, *The Eastern Question*, p. 65.

15. Chadha, *Rediscovering Gandhi*, p. 245.

16. Payne, *Gandhi*, p. 348.

17. Chadha, *Rediscovering Gandhi*, p. 241.

18. Gilbert, *Churchill*, pp. 477–8.

19. Macfie, *The Eastern Question*, p. 66.

20. Cabinet Papers. Letter from the Aga Khan to Lord Montagu. CAB/21/184.

21. CAB/21/184.

22. Palmer, *The Decline and Fall of the Ottoman Empire*, p. 252.

23. *The Islamic Review*, April 1920, p. 139. Courtesy of the Woking Mosque website.

24. Chadha, *Rediscovering Gandhi*, p. 246.

25. Wolpert, *The Chanak Affair*, p. 107.

26. Payne, *Gandhi*, p. 349.

27. Wolpert, *Gandhi's Passion*, p. 110.

28. Ibid, p. 108.

29. Chadha, *Rediscovering Gandhi*, p. 248.

30. Ibid, p. 247.

31. Ibid, p. 247.

32. Clement, C., *Gandhi: Father of a Nation* (London: Thames and Hudson/New Horizons, 1996).

33. Gilbert, *Churchill*, p. 498.

34. Ibid.

35. Ibid., p. 499.

36. Judd, D., *Lord Reading: Rufus Isaacs, First Marquess of Reading, Lord Chief Justice and Viceroy* (London: Weidenfeld and Nicolson, 1982), p. 201.

37. Hyde, H. M., *Lord Reading: The Life of Rufus Isaacs, First Marquess of Reading* (London: Heinemann, 1967), p. 379.

38. Judd, *Lord Reading*, p. 205.

39. Payne, *Gandhi*, p. 350.

40. Judd, *Lord Reading*, pp. 206–7.

41. Shri B. R. Nanda, *Gandhi: A Pictorial Biography* (www.mkgandhi.org/biography).

42. Judd, *Lord Reading*, p. 206–7.

43. Hyde, *Lord Reading*, p. 362.

44. Payne, *Gandhi*, p. 357.

45. Judd, *Lord Reading*, p. 223.

46. Ziegler, P., *Mountbatten* (London: Guild Publishing, 1985), p. 61.

47. Walder, *The Chanak Affair*, p. 157.

48. Hyde, *Lord Reading*, p. 368.

49. Ibid, p. 364.

50. Mehta, V., *Mahatma Gandhi and His Apostles* (London: Andrew Deutsch, 1977).

51. Low, D. A. I., 'Government of India and the First Non Cooperation Movement – 1920–1922', *The Journal of Asian Studies*, 25 (2) (Feb. 1966), p. 241.

52. Judd, *Lord Reading*, p. 224.

7 All talk was of war

1. Owen, *Tempestuous Journey*, p. 633.

2. Cabinet Papers. CAB 23/31. Minutes of Meeting held at 10 Downing St. on 7/12/22.

3. Ibid.

4. Gilbert, *Churchill*, p. 821.

5. *The Times*, 11 September 1922.

6. Papers of Col J. C. Petherick, containing Brigadier-General D. I. Shuttleworth's report on his activities at Chanak (66/130/1), Imperial War Museum Department of Documents, et sec.

7. Cabinet Papers, CAB23/31, Minutes of meeting held 15 September.

8. Morgan, *Consensus and Disunity*, p. 322.

9. Gilbert, *Churchill*, p. 825.

10. Ibid., p. 826.

11. CAB23/31, ibid.

12. *The Times*, 18 September 1922.

13. *The Times*, 16 September 1922.

14. Gilbert, *Churchill*, p. 831.

15. *The Times*, 18 September 1922.

16. Ibid.

17. Gilbert, *Churchill*, p. 831.

18. Owen, *Tempestuous Journey*, p. 648.

19. Gilbert, *Rumbold*, p. 262.

20. CAB 21/241. Curzon to Cabinet, 22/09/22 (4213).

21. Nicolson, pp. 273–4.

22. Gilbert, *Churchill*, p. 833.

23. Nicolson, Harold, *King George V* (London: Constable & Co. Ltd, 1984), p. 369.

24. CAB 23/39. Minutes of Meeting held at 10 Downing Street.

25. Gilbert, *Churchill*, p. 835.

26. CAB 21/241. Minutes of meeting held at No. 10 Downing Street.

27. CAB 21/241. Cable from W. Tyrell to Lord Curzon (CP. 2417 No. 474).

28. Gilbert, *Rumbold*, p. 264–5.

29. *The Times*, 22 September 1922.

30. Mango, p. 351.

31. Ibid., p. 352.

32. Nicolson, *The Last Phase*, p. 275.

33. Walder, *The Chanak Affair*, p. 271.

34. *The Times*, 26 September 1922.

35. Ibid.

36. Shuttleworth's report.

37. Gilbert, *Churchill*, p. 836.

38. CAB 21/241.

39. Shuttleworth.

40. Shuttleworth.

41. Shuttleworth.

42. Cabinet Papers CAB 21/241. Cable from General Harington to Lord Cavan 2609/22.

43. Gilbert, *Churchill*, p. 837.

44. Gilbert, *Rumbold*, p. 267.

45. Gilbert, *Churchill*, p. 839.

46. CAB24/241. Minutes of meeting held at Downing Street on 27/09/22.

47. Gilbert, *Churchill*, p. 841.

48. Ibid.

49. Owen, *Tempestuous Journey*, p. 649.

50. CAB21/241. Cabinet: The Greek Army. Note by the Secretary of State for War (4247), 30/09/22.

51. CAB 21/241 (4240).

52. *The Times*, 29 September 1922.

53. Gilbert, *Churchill*, p. 842.

54. Walder, *The Great Chanak*, p. 259.

55. CAB12/241. Cabinet Cable to Harington.

56. CAB23/31. Minutes of meeting held at Downing Street.

57. CAB 21/241.

58. Owen, *Tempestuous Journey*, p. 648.

59. Gilmour, *Curzon*, p. 545.

60. Ibid., p. 546.

61. Gilbert, *Churchill*, p. 849.

62. Ibid.

63. Ibid.

64. CAB 23/31. Minutes of Cabinet Meeting held at No.10 Downing Street, 1/10/22.

65. Ibid.

66. Ibid.

67. Gilbert, *Churchill*, p. 852.

68. Harington, *Harington Looks Back*, p. 151.

69. Gilbert, *Churchill*, p. 853.

70. Ibid., p. 854.

71. Harington, *Harington Looks Back*, p. 118.

72. Gilmour, *Curzon*, p. 547.

73. Harington, *Harington Looks Back*, p. 118.

74. Ibid., p. 119.

75. Gilbert, *Churchill*, p. 857.

76. Hemingway, quoted in *History in Quotations*, ibid, p. 807.

77. Harington, *Harington Looks Back*, p. 124.

78. Ibid.

79. Walder, *The Chanak Affair*, p. 317.

80. Harington, *Harington Looks Back*, p. 126.

81. Walder, *The Chanak Affair*, p. 319.

82. Harington, *Harington Looks Back*, p. 151.

83. Gilbert, *Rumbold*, p. 273.

84. Gilbert, *Churchill*, p. 861.

85. Ibid.

86. Nicolson, *King George V*, p. 369.

87. Harington, *Harington Looks Back*, p. 144.

88. Ibid.

89. Ibid., p. 281.

90. Ibid.

91. Gilbert, *Churchill*, p. 862.

8 *In a good cause we are prepared to venture our all*

1. A. J. P. Taylor, *English History, 1914–1918* (1982), p. 249.

2. Carlyon, *Gallipoli*, p. 109.

3. Ibid.

4. Butler, L. and H. Jones, *Britain in the Twentieth Century 1900-1939*, vol. 1 (Oxford: Heinemann, 1994), p. 233.

5. Barnett, C., *The Collapse of British Power* (Gloucester: Alan Sutton, 1987), p. 173.

6. Ibid, p. 177.

7. Neillands, R., *The Great War Generals on the Western Front 1914–1918* (London: Robinson, 1998), pp. 330–40.

8. Williams, *Byng of Vimy: General and Governor General* (Leo Cooper, 1983), p. 267.

9. Ibid, p. 268.

10. Ibid, p. 274.

11. Ibid, p. 273.

12. Ibid, p. 271.

13. Documents on Canadian External Relations, vol. 3, 1919-1925, Department of External Affairs. Telegram from Byng to Churchill, 18/09/22, p. 78, document 106.

14. Ibid., telegram from Churchill to Byng, 19/09/22, p. 79 document 109.

15. Ibid., telegram from Lapointe to Mackenzie King 19/09/22, p. 78, document 108.

16. Ibid., telegram from Churchill to Byng, 11/10/22 p. 82–83, document 115.

17. Beaverbrook, *Decline of Lloyd George*, p. 161.

18. Mackenzie King Archives, Diary entry for 17/09/22 (Transcript). National Archives of Canada.

19. Mackenzie King Archives, Diary entry for 17/09/22 (Transcript). National Archives of Canada.

20. *The Times*, 17 September 1922.

21. MK diary entry for 18/09/22.

22. MK diary entry for 18/09/22.

23. Owen, *Tempestuous Journey*, pp. 640–1.

24. Walder, *The Chanak Affair*, p. 253.

25. *Daily Mail*, 20 September 1922.

26. *Daily Mail*, 20 September 1922.

27. Owen, *The Chanak Affair*, p. 643.

28. Beaverbrook, *Decline of Lloyd George*, p. 161.

29. *The Times*, 19 September 1922.

30. *The Times*, 18 September 1922.

31. *The Times*, 30 September 1922.

32. Prime Minister's Department, correspondence file, alphabetical series. Turkey-Near East Cables, c.1922, Commonwealth Archives Office: CRS A981, item Turkey 4. Copy of telegram sent by the Prime Minister to Lloyd George, et seq.

33. *The Times*, 20 September 1922.

34. Canadian Department of External Affairs, vol. 1: The Early Years, 1909-1946. Papers of WL Mackenzie King.

35. Barnett, *Collapse of British Power*, p. 182.

36. 'Documents on Canadian Foreign Policy, 1917–1939' (Toronto: Oxford University Press, 1962), pp. 87–94.

37. Barnett, *Collapse of British Power*, p. 183.

38. Mowat, C. L., *Britain Between The Wars, 1918–40* (London: Methuen, 1955).

9 Stop this new war

1. Beaverbrook, *Decline and Fall of Lloyd George*, pp. 34–35.

2. Jenkins, R., *Asquith* (London: Collins, 1964).

3. Beaverbrook, *Decline and Fall*, p. 17.

4. Ibid., p. 35.

5. Blake, R., *The Conservative Party from Peel to Thatcher* (London: Fontana Press, 1985), p. 208.

6. Taylor, *English History*, p. 246.

7. Mowat, *Britain between the Wars*, p. 77.
8. Kinnear, M., *The Fall of Lloyd George: The Political Crisis of 1922*, p. 84.
9. Morgan, *Consensus and Disunity*, p. 302.
10. Taylor, *English History*, p. 247.
11. Judd, *Lord Reading*, p. 214.
12. Ibid.
13. Morgan, *Consensus and Disunity*, p. 324.
14. Ibid., p. 321.
15. Beaverbrook, *Decline and Fall*, p. 38.
16. Gilmour, *Churchill*, p. 539.
17. Judd, *Lord Reading*, p. 213.
18. Gilmour, *Churchill*, p. 539.
19. Mowat, *Britain between the Wars*, p. 137.
20. Ibid.
21. Morgan, *Consensus and Disunity*, p. 322.
22. Taylor, *English History*, p. 249.
23. *Daily Mail*, 18 September 1922.
24. Ibid.
25. *Daily Mail*, 20 September 1922, et sec.
26. *Daily Mail*, 19 September 1922, et sec.
27. *Daily Mail*, 21 September 1922.
28. Beaverbrook, *Decline and Fall*, p. 162.
29. Morgan, *Consensus and Disunity*, p. 324.
30. Ibid., p. 325.
31. Gilbert, *Churchill*, p. 858.
32. Butler & Jones, *Britain in the Twentieth Century*, p. 227–8.
33. Owen, *Tempestuous Journey*, p. 654.
34. Gilbert, *Churchill*, p. 859.
35. Ibid., p. 863.
36. Beaverbrook, *Decline and Fall*, p. 187.
37. Taylor, *English History*, p. 250.
38. Gilbert, *Churchill*, p. 863.
39. Gilmour, *Curzon*, p. 554.
40. Owen, *Tempestuous Journey*, p. 655.
41. Gilbert, *Churchill*, p. 865.
42. Ibid., p. 553.
43. Owen, *Tempestuous Journey*, p. 657.
44. Gilmour, *Curzon*, p. 554.
45. Ibid.
46. Ibid.
47. *Daily Mail*, 20 October 1922.
48. Walder, *The Chanak Affair*, p. 325.
49. Taylor, *English History*, p. 250.

50. Kinnear, *Fall of Lloyd George*, p. 127.
51. Lynch, M., *Lloyd George and the Liberal Dilemma* (London: Hodder & Stoughton, 1993), p. 103.
52. Blake, *The Conservative Party*, p. 208.
53. Morgan, *Consensus and Disunity*, p. 349.
54. Owen, *Tempestuous Journey*, p. 658.
55. Gilbert, *Churchill*, p. 867.
56. Holland, *The Pursuit of Greatness*, p. 102.
57. Mowat, *Britain between the Wars*, p. 145.
58. Jenkins, R., *Churchill*, p. 376.
59. Gilbert, *Churchill*, p. 881.
60. Morgan, *Consensus and Disunity*, p. 344.

10 None of us can pretend that the treaty is a glorious document

1. Gilmour, *Curzon*, p. 556.
2. Kinross, *Ataturk*, p. 355.
3. Gilbert, *Rumbold*, p. 276.
4. Nicolson, *King George V*, p. 373.
5. Kinross, *Ataturk*, p. 347.
6. Ibid., p. 348.
7. Mansel, *Constantinople*, p. 407.
8. Harington, *Harington Looks Back*, p. 130.
9. Ibid., p. 131.
10. Gilbert, *Rumbold*, p. 281.
11. Nicolson, *Curzon*, p. 290.
12. Nicolson, *King George V*, p. 373.
13. Nicolson, *Curzon*, p. 284.
14. Ibid, p. 307.
15. MacMillan, *Peacemakers*, p. 463.
16. Walder, *The Chanak Affair*, p. 337.
17. Zurcher, *Turkey*, p. 168.
18. Kinross, *Ataturk*, p. 355.
19. MacMillan, *Peacemakers*, p. 463.
20. Nicolson, *Curzon*, p. 351.
21. Gilbert, *Rumbold*, p. 281.
22. Nicolson, *Curzon*, p. 334.
23. Mango, *Ataturk*, p. 367.
24. Gilbert, *Rumbold*, p. 281.
25. Dockrill & Goold, *Peace without Promise*, p. 243.
26. Gilbert, *Rumbold*, p. 287.
27. Gilbert, *Rumbold*, p. 288.
28. Kinross, *Ataturk*, p. 370.
29. Gilbert, *Rumbold*, p. 289.

30. Treaty of Lausanne, text of, et sec.
31. Walder, *The Chanak Affair*, p. 341.
32. Harington, *Harington Looks Back*, p. 138.
33. Ibid.
34. Ibid, p. 139.
35. Walder, *The Chanak Affair*, p. 360.
36. Harington, *Harington Looks Back*, p. 140.
37. Sonyel, *Ataturk*, p. 84.
38. *Daily Mail*, 24 July 1923.
39. Sonyel, Ataturk, pp. 85–86.
40. Ibid., p. 85.
41. Ibid.
42. Ibid., p. 86.

11 We cannot alone act as policeman of the world

1. *New York Times*, 24 November 1945.
2. Bell, *France and Britain*, p. 159.
3. MacMillan, *Peacemakers*, p. 384.

APPENDICES

Appendix 1: The Treaty of Sevres
The following are extracts from the Treaty of Sevres, and are cited here as an illustration of the punitive nature of the first treaty signed with the Ottoman government in August 1920. They give the reader a good appreciation of just why its provisions were rejected by Mustapha Kemal and the Nationalists.

Article 36
Constantinople
Subject to the provisions of the present Treaty, the High Contracting Parties agree that the rights and title of the Turkish Government over Constantinople shall not be affected, and that the said Government and His Majesty the Sultan shall be entitled to reside there and to maintain there the capital of the Turkish State.

Nevertheless, in the event of Turkey failing to observe faithfully the provisions of the present Treaty, or of any treaties or conventions supplementary thereto, particularly as regards the protection of the rights of racial, religious or linguistic minorities, the Allied Power reserve the right to modify the above provisions, and Turkey hereby agrees to accept any dispositions which may be taken in this connection.

The Straits
Article 37.
The navigation of the Straits, including the Dardanelles, the Sea of Marmara and the Bosphorus, shall in future be open, both in peace and war, to every vessel of commerce or of war and to military and commercial aircraft, without distinction of flag.

These waters shall not be subject to blockade, nor shall any belligerent right be exercised nor any act of hostility be committed within them, unless in pursuance of a decision of the Council of the League of Nations.

Article 62.

Kurdistan

A Commission sitting at Constantinople and composed of three members appointed by the British, French and Italian Governments respectively shall draft within six months from the coming into force of the present Treaty a scheme of local autonomy for the predominantly Kurdish areas lying east of the Euphrates, south of the southern boundary of Armenia, as it may be hereafter determined, and north of the frontier of Turkey with Syria and Mesopotamia.

Article 64.

If within one year from the coming into force of the present Treaty the Kurdish people within the areas defined in Article 62 shall address themselves to the Council of the League of Nations in such a manner as to show that a majority of the population of these areas desires independence from Turkey, and if the Council then considers that these peoples are capable of such independence and recommends that it should be granted to them, Turkey hereby agrees to execute such a recommendation, and to renounce all rights and title over these areas.

Article 65.

Smyrna

The provisions of this Section will apply to the city of Smyrna and the adjacent territory defined in Article 66.

Article 68.

Subject to the provisions of the Section, the city of Smyrna and the territory defined in Article 66 will be assimilated, in the application of the present Treaty, to territory detached from Turkey.

Article 69.

The city of Smyrna and the territory defined in Article 66 remain under Turkish sovereignty. Turkey, however, transfers to the Greek Government the exercise of her rights of sovereignty over the city of Smyrna and the said territory. In witness of such sovereignty the Turkish flag shall remain permanently hoisted over an outer fort in the town of Smyrna. The fort will be designated by the Principal Allied Powers.

Article 70.

The Greek Government will be responsible for the administration of the city of Smyrna and the territory defined in Article 66, and will effect this administration by means of a body of officials which it will appoint specially for the purpose.

Article 71.

The Greek Government will be entitled to maintain the city of Smyrna and the territory defined in Article 66 the military forces required for the maintenance of order and public security.

Article 81.

The Greek administration will have the right to regulate and tax the consumption of salt at Smyrna and within the territory defined in Article 66.

Article 83.

When a period of five years shall have elapsed after the coming into force of the present Treaty the local parliament referred to [in Article 72.] may, by a majority of votes, ask the Council of the League of Nations for the definitive incorporation in the Kingdom of Greece of the city of Smyrna and the territory defined in Article 66. The Council may require, as a preliminary, a plebiscite under conditions which it will lay down.

In the event of such incorporation as a result of the application of the foregoing paragraph, the Turkish sovereignty referred to in Article 69 shall cease. Turkey hereby renounces in that event in favour of Greece all rights and title over the city of Smyrna and the territory defined in Article 66.

Section V.

Greece.

Article 84.

Without prejudice to the frontiers of Bulgaria laid down by the Treaty of Peace signed at Neuilly-sur-Seine on November 27, 1919, Turkey renounces in favour of Greece all rights and title over the territories of the former Turkish Empire in Europe situated outside the frontiers of Turkey as laid down by the present Treaty.

The islands of the Sea of Marmara are not included in the transfer of Sovereignty effected by the above paragraph.

Turkey further renounces in favour of Greece all her rights and title over the islands of Imbros and Tenedos. Sovereignty of Greece over the other islands of the Eastern Mediterranean, particularly Lemnos, Samothrace, Mytilene, Chios, Samos and Nikaria, is confirmed.

Section VI

Armenia

Article 88.

Turkey, in accordance with the action already taken by the Allied Powers, hereby recognises Armenia as a free and independent State.

Article 89.

Turkey and Armenia as well as the other High Contracting Parties agree to submit to the arbitration of the President of the United States of America the question of the frontier to be fixed between Turkey and Armenia in the vilayets of Erzurum, Trebizond, Van and Bitlis and to accept his decision thereupon, as well as any stipulation he may prescribe as to access for Armenia to the sea, and as to the demilitarisation of any portion of Turkish territory adjacent to the said frontier.

Article 90.

In the event of the determination of the frontier under Article 89 involving the transfer of the whole or any part of the territory of the said Vilayets to Armenia, Turkey hereby renounces as from the date of such decision all rights and title over the territory so transferred. The provisions of the present Treaty applicable to territory detached from Turkey shall thereupon become applicable to the said territory.

Section VII

Syria, Mesopotamia, Palestine

Article 94.

The High Contracting Parties agree that Syria and Mesopotamia shall, in accordance with the fourth paragraph of Article 22 Part I (Covenant of the League of Nations) be provisionally recognised as independent States subject to the rendering of administrative advice and assistance by a Mandatory until such time as they are able to stand alone.

The determination of the other frontiers of the said States, and the selection of the Mandatories, will be made by the Principal Allied Powers.

Section VIII

Hedjaz

Article 98.

Turkey, in accordance with the action already taken by the Allied Powers, hereby recognises the Hedjaz as a free and independent State, and renounces in favour of the Hedjaz all rights and titles over the territories of the former Turkish Empire outside the frontiers of Turkey as laid down by the present Treaty, and comprised within the borders which may ultimately be fixed.

Section IX

Egypt, Soudan, Cyprus

Article 101

Turkey renounces all rights and title in Egypt. This renunciation shall take effect as from November 5, 1914. Turkey declares that in conformity with the action taken by the Allied Powers she recognises the Protectorate proclaimed over Egypt by Great Britain on December 18, 1914.

Article 109.

Turkey renounces in favour of Great Britain the powers conferred upon his Imperial Majesty the Sultan by the Convention signed at Constantinople on October 29, 1888, relating to the free navigation of the Suez Canal.

Article 112.

Turkey renounces all claim to the tribute formerly paid by Egypt.

Article 116.

Turkey renounces all rights and title over or relating to Cyprus, including the right to the tribute formerly paid by that island to the Sultan.

Section X.

Morocco, Tunis

Article 118.

Turkey recognises the French Protectorate in Morocco, and accepts all the consequences thereof. This recognition shall take effect as from March 30, 1912.

Article 120.

Turkey recognises the French Protectorate over Tunis and accepts all the consequences thereof. This recognition shall take effect as from May 2, 1881.

Section XI

Libya, Aegean Islands

Turkey definitely renounces all rights and privileges which under the Treaty of Lausanne of October 18, 1912 were left to the Sultan in Libya.

Article 122.

Turkey renounces in favour of Italy all rights and title over the following islands of the Aegean Sea; Stampalia, Rhodes, Calki, Scarpanto, Casos, Pscopsis, Misiros, Calymnos, Leros, Patmos, Lipsos, Sini and Cos which are now occupied by Italy, and the islets dependent thereon, and also over the island of Castellorizzo.

Article 136.

A Commission ... shall be set up ... to replace the present capitulatory system in judicial matters in Turkey. This commission may recommend, after consultation with the Turkish Government, the adoption of either a mixed or a unified judicial system.

Article 139.

Turkey renounces formally all rights of suzerainty or jurisdiction of any kind over Muslims who are subject to the sovereignty of any other state.

Part V.

Military, Naval and Air Clauses

Section I.

Military Clauses.

Chapter I.

General Clauses.

Article 152.

The armed force at the disposal of Turkey shall only consist of:

(I) The Sultan's bodyguard

(II) Troops of gendarmerie, intended to maintain order and security in the interior and to ensure the protection of minorities.

(III) Special elements intended for the reinforcement of the troops of gendarmerie in cases of serious trouble, and eventually to ensure the control of the frontiers.

Article 153.

Within six months from the coming into force of the present Treaty, the military forces other than that provided for in Article 152 shall be demobilised and disbanded.

Article 154.

The Sultan's bodyguard shall consist of a staff and infantry and cavalry units, the strength of which shall not exceed 700 officers and men. This strength is not included in the total force provided for in Article 155.

Article 155.

The total strength of the forces enumerated in paragraphs (II) and (III) of Article 152 shall not exceed 50,000 men, including staffs, officers training personnel and depot troops.

Article 165.

The Turkish armed force shall in future be constituted and recruited by voluntary enlistment only.

Article 166.

The length of engagement of non-commissioned officers and men shall be twelve consecutive years.

Article 173.

Within six months from the coming into force of the present Treaty all existing arms, munitions of the various categories and war material in excess of the quantities authorised shall be handed over to the Military Inter-Allied Commission of Control ... The Principal Allied Powers will decide what is to be done with this material.

Article 174.

The manufacture of arms, munitions and war material, including aircraft and parts of aircraft of every description, shall take place only in the factories or establishments authorised by the Inter-Allied Commission ...

Within six months from the coming into force of the present Treaty all other establishments for the manufacture, preparation, storage or design of arms, munitions or any war material shall be abolished or converted to purely commercial uses.

The same will apply to all arsenals other than those utilised as depots for the authorised stocks of munitions.

Article 175.

The importation into Turkey of arms, munitions and war materials, including aircraft and parts of aircraft of any description, is strictly forbidden, except with the special authority of the Inter-Allied Commission ...

The manufacture for foreign countries and the exportation of arms, munitions and war material of any kind is also forbidden.

Article 176.

The use of flame-throwers, asphyxiating, poisonous or other gases and all similar liquids, materials or processes being forbidden, their manufacture and importation are strictly forbidden in Turkey.

Material specially intended for the manufacture, storage or use of the said products or processes is equally forbidden.

The manufacture and importation into Turkey of armoured cars, tanks or any other similar machines suitable for use in war are equally forbidden.

Article 177.

In the zone of the Straits and the islands referred to in Article 178, the fortifications will be disarmed and demolished as provided in that article.

Article 178.

For the purpose of guaranteeing the freedom of the Straits, the High Contracting Parties agree to the following provisions:

(I) Within three months from the coming into force of the present Treaty, all works, fortifications and batteries within the zone defined in Article 179 and comprising the coast and islands of the Sea of Marmara and the coast of the Straits, also those in the Islands of Lemnos, Imbros, Samothrace, Tenedos and Mytilene, shall be disarmed and demolished.

The reconstruction of these works and the construction of similar works are forbidden in the above zone and islands. France Great Britain and Italy shall have the right to prepare for demolition any existing roads and railways in the said zone and in the Islands of Lemnos, Imbros, Samothrace, and Tenedos which allow of the rapid transport of mobile batteries, the construction there of such roads and railways remaining forbidden.

In the islands of Lemnos, Imbros, Samothrace and Tenedos the construction of new roads or railways must not be undertaken except with the authority of the three Powers mentioned above.

The territories of the zone and the islands of Lemnos, Imbros, Samothrace, Tenedos and Mytilene shall not be used for military purposes, except by the three Powers referred to above, acting in concert.

The said Power, acting in concert, shall have the right to maintain in the said territories and islands such military and air forces as they may consider necessary to prevent any action being taken or prepared which might directly or indirectly prejudice the freedom of the Straits.

Article 181.
From the coming into force of the present Treaty all warships interned in Turkish ports in accordance with the Armistice of October 30, 1918, are declared to be finally surrendered to the Principal Allied Powers.

Turkey will, however, retain the right to maintain along her coats for police and fishery duties a number of vessels which shall not exceed:
7 sloops, 6 torpedo boats ...
The authority established for the control of customs will be entitled to appeal to the three Allied Powers referred to in Article 178 in order to obtain a more considerable force, if such an increase is considered indispensable for the satisfactory working of the services concerned.

Sloops may carry a light armament of two guns inferior to 77mm and two machine guns. Torpedo boats (or patrol launches) may carry a light armament of one gun inferior to 77mm. All the torpedoes and torpedo tubes on board will be removed.
Article 182.
Turkey is forbidden to construct or acquire any warships other than those intended to replace the units referred to in Article 181. Torpedo boats shall be replaced by patrol launches.

The vessels intended for replacement purposes shall not exceed 600 tons in the case of sloops; 100 tons in the case of patrol launches.

Except where a ship has been lost, sloops and torpedo boats shall only be replaced after a period of twenty years counting from the launching of the ship.
Article 184.

All warships, including submarines, now under construction in Turkey shall be broken up, with the exception of such vessels as can be completed for commercial purposes.

Article 186.

The construction or acquisition of any submarine, even for commercial purposes, shall be forbidden in Turkey.

Article 191

The Turkish armed forces must not include any military or naval air services. No dirigible may be kept.

Article 195.

On the coming into force of the present Treaty all military and Navale aeronautical material must be delivered by Turkey, at her own expense, to the Principal Allied Powers.

Article 226.

The Turkish Government recognises the right of the Allied Powers to bring before military tribunals persons accused of having committed acts in violation of the laws and customs of war. Such persons shall, if found guilty, be sentenced to punishments laid down by law. This provision will apply notwithstanding any proceedings or prosecution before a tribunal in Turkey, or in the territory of her allies.

The Turkish Government shall hand over to the Allied Powers or to such one of them as shall so request all persons accused of having committed an act in violation of the laws and customs of war, who are specified either by name or by the rank, office or employment held under the Turkish authorities.

Article 230.

The Turkish Government undertakes to hand over to the Allied Powers the person who surrender may be required by the latter as being responsible for the massacres committed during the continuance of the state of war on territory which formed part of the Turkish Empire on August 1 1914.

Article 231.

Turkey recognises that by joining in the war of aggression which Germany and Austria-Hungary waged against the Allied powers she has caused to the latter losses and sacrifices of all kinds for which she ought to make complete reparation.

Article 275.

Turkey recognises that all the treaties, conventions or agreements which she has concluded with Germany, Austria, Bulgaria or Hungary since August 1, 1914, until the coming into force of the present Treaty are and remain abrogated by the present Treaty.

Article 277.

Turkey recognises that all treaties, conventions or arrangements which she concluded with Russia, or with any state or Government of which the territory previously formed part of Russia, before August 1, 1914, or after that date until the coming into force of the present Treaty, or with Roumania after August 15, 1916, until the coming into force of the present Treaty are, and remain abrogated.

Appendix 2: *The Treaty of Lausanne*
The following key Articles illustrate the contrasting nature of the final Treaty signed by Turkey under free negotiation, and the abortive Treaty, signed previously by the Ottoman Government, under duress.

Principal Clauses:

Article 3
The Frontier between Turkey and Iraq shall be laid down in friendly arrangement to be concluded between Turkey and Great Britain within nine months. In the event of no agreement being reached between the two Governments within the time mentioned, the dispute shall be referred to the Council of the League of Nations.
Article 12
The decision taken on the 13th February 1914, by the Conference of London, in virtue of Article 5 of the Treaty of London of the 17th-30th May, 1913 and 15 of the Treaty of Athens of the 1st 14th November, 1913, which decision was communicated to the Greek Government on the 13th February 1914, regarding the sovereignty of Greece over the islands of the Eastern Mediterranean, other than the islands of Imbros and Tenedos and Rabbit Islands, particularly the islands of Lemnos, Samothrace, Mytilene, Chios, Samos and Nikaria, is confirmed, subject to the provisions of the present Treaty respecting the islands placed under the sovereignty of Italy whichform the subject of
Article 14
The islands of Imbros and Tenedos, remaining under Turkish sovereignty, shall enjoy a special administrative organisation composed of local elements and furnishing every guarantee for the native non-Muslim population in so far as it concerns local administration and the protection of persons and property ... The agreements which have been, or may be, concluded between Greece and Turkey relating to the exchange of the Greek and Turkish populations will not be applied to the inhabitants of the islands of Imbros and Tenedos.
Article 15
Turkey renounces in favour of Italy all rights and title over the following islands: Stampalia (Astropalia), Rhodes (Rhodos), Calki (Kharki), Scarpanto, Leros, Patmos, Lipsos (Lipso), Simi (Symi) and Cos (Kos), which are now occupied by Italy, and the islets dependent thereon, and also over the island of Castellorizzo.
Article 17
The renunciation by Turkey of all rights and titles over Egypt and over the Soudan will take effect as from the 15th November 1914.

Article 20

Turkey hereby recognises the annexation of Cyprus proclaimed by the British Government on the 15 November 1914.

Article 22

Without prejudice to the general stipulations of Article 27, Turkey hereby recognises the definite abolition of all rights and privileges whatsoever which are enjoyed in Libya under the Treaty of Lausanne of the 18 October 1912, and the instruments connected therewith.

Article 23

The High Contracting Parties are agreed to recognise and declare the principle of freedom of transit and of navigation, by sea and air, in time of peace as in time of war, in the strait of Dardanelles, the Sea of Marmara and the Bosphoros, as prescribed in the separate Convention signed this day, regarding the regime of the straits ...

Article 28

Each of the High Contracting Parties hereby accepts, in so far as it is concerned, the complete abolition of the Capitulations in Turkey in every respect.

Article 39

Turkish nationals belonging to non-Muslim minorities will enjoy the same civil and political rights as Muslims.

Article 45

The rights conferred by the provisions of the present section on the non-Muslim minorities of Turkey will be similarly conferred by Greece on the Muslim minority in her territory.

Article 58

Turkey ... agrees not to claim from the British Government or its nationals the repayment of the sums paid for the warships ordered in England by the Ottoman Government which were requisitioned by the British Government in 1914, and renounces all claims in the matter.

Article 59

Greece recognises her obligation to make reparation for the damage caused in Anatolia by the acts of the Greek army or administration which were contrary to the rules of war. On the other hand, Turkey, in consideration of the financial situation resulting from the prolongation of the war and from its consequences, finally renounces all claims for reparation against the Greek Government.

Article 128

The Turkish Government undertakes to grant to the Governments of the British Empire, France and Italy respectively and in perpetuity the land within the Turkish territory in which are situated the graves, cemeteries, ossuaries or memorials of their soldiers and sailors who fell in action or died of wounds, accident or disease, as well as those of prisoners of war and interned civilians who died in captivity.

Article 142

The separate convention concluded on the 30th January 1923, between Greece and Turkey, relating to the exchange of Greek and Turkish populations, will have as between these two High Contracting Parties the same force and effect as if it formed part of the present Treaty.

Appendix 3: Resolution Passed by the Sivas Conference, 11 September 1919

'The various parts of the Turkish territory which remained within our frontier when, on the 30th October 1919, the Armistice concluded between the Entente Powers and the Turkish Government was signed, are everywhere inhabited by an overwhelming Muslim majority and form a whole; they cannot be separated and would not, for any reason, detach themselves one from another or from the Ottoman Motherland ...

(1.) To security the integrity of the Ottoman Motherland and our national independence, and preserve the Sultanate and Caliphate, the principle has been adopted as essential of putting into action the forces of the nation and render the will of the nation preponderant ...

(2.) The lawful principle has unanimously been agreed upon to oppose and fight, as in the national martyrdoms on the Aidin, Magnesia and Balekesor fronts, against any penetration in or occupation of any portion of the Ottoman Empire, especially against any movement aiming at the creation, within our country, of an independent Greek or Armenian place ...

(3.) All the non-Muslim elements with whom we live in the same country, having long ago had their equality of rights of every sort fully guaranteed, the grant of such privileges as would break our political supremacy and social equilibrium will not be admitted ...

(4.) Every precaution and decision has been taken to safeguard the Sultanate and Caliphate and the integrity of the country and nation should the Turkish government find itself, under some pressure from outside, compelled to abandon or neglect any portion of our territory ...

(5.) We expect the Allies to totally abandon the idea of breaking our national unity comprised within our frontier of 30th October, 1918, when the Armistice was signed, where the large majority of the population is Muslim and the agricultural and social superiority belongs to the Muslims; to respect its historical, ethnic, religious and geographical rights on those territories, cancel any action that is against the above and thus give a decision based on right and justice ...

(6.) Our nation holds in honour humanitarian and modern aims, and realises our scientific, industrial and economic position and wants. We therefore will accept with pleasure the scientific, industrial and economic assistance of any nation who respects the interior and exterior independence of our state and nation; who, provided that our country is kept untouched, admits the principles of nationality within the frontiers indicated in Article 6; and who does not look forward to an occupation of our country. The early conclusion of a peace on these equitable and human conditions too, for the sake of humanity's safety and peace in the world, is our nation's sincerest desire ...

(7.) At this historical moment when the nations fix their own destinies, it is absolutely necessary that our Central Government too, should submit to the will of the nation; for past acts and corresponding results have proved that not only are the decisions, personal and uncontrolled, of any cabinet not supported by the nation, are disregarded by the nation, and that abroad, too, such a cabinet has, and can have, no credit. Without therefore, letting the nation find itself the means of emerging from the trouble and anxiety in which it is, our central Government must at once convoke the National Assembly without loss of time and thus submit to the control of the National Assembly all decisions concerning the destinies of the nation and country ...

(8.) This federal assembly has, under the name of the Society for the Defence of the Rights of Anatolia and Turkey-in-Europe been formed by the union of the Patriotic and National Societies of the same object that have sprung up from the national conscience in presence of the calamities to which our country and nation are exposed. This society is outside any party influence and absolutely free from all individual ambitions. All our Muslim countrymen are by right members of this society ...

(9.) The Congress held on the 4 September 1919, at Sivas by the Society for the Defence of the Rights of Anatolia and Turkey-in-Europe has elected a Committee to pursue its sacred objective and supervise the main formations and all national formations from village to vilayet headquarters have been reinforced and unified.

Appendix 4: Chronology of Key Events

The following lists the dates of key milestones covered by this book. For purposes of brevity and clarity, only key dates are included.

1038	Seljuk Turks turn against their Persian masters at Battle of Nishapur
1371	Battle of Maritsa River
1389	First Battle of Kosovo
1448	Second Battle of Kosovo
1453	Constantinople falls to the Turks
1499	First Battle of Lepanto
1529	Siege of Vienna
1565	Suleiman the Magnificent lays siege to the island of Malta
1571	Second Battle of Lepanto

1683	Siege of Vienna
1822–1829	First Greek War of Independence
1827	Battle of Navarino
1853–1856	Crimean War
1876	Accession of Abdulhamid II and introduction of Constitution
1877–1878	Russo-Turkish War results in Treaty of San Stefano
1880	Birth of Mustapha Kemal
1897	Turks victorious in war with Greece over Crete
1908	'Young Turk' Revolution
1909	Abdulhamid II deposed, and accession of Mehmet V
1911–1912	Italy-Turkish War
1912–1913	Balkan War
1914	First World War begins
1915	Gallipoli Campaign opens
	Treaty promising Italy territory in return to joining Entente
1916	Gallipoli campaign ends in Allied evacuation
1917	British overrun Mesopotamia and Palestine
	Balfour Declaration
1918	President Wilson's Fourteen Points
	First World War ends
1919	April/May: Italian Greek landings in Anatolia
	15 May: Greeks occupy Smyrna
	19 May: Mustapha Kemal lands at Samsun
	22 June: First Proclamation at Amasya
	5 October: Resignation of Ottoman Govt
	Nov: Khilifat Movement launched in India
	4–11 Sept: First Sivas Conference
	27 Dec: Nationalist HQ established at Ankara
1920	Feb: Turkish Nationalist and Irregular forces attack French in Cicilia
	Mar: Allies occupy Constantinople. Turkey and Soviet Union agree upon eastern border
	Apr: Allies sanction Greek move on the Straits to clear Nationalists
	Apr/May: Turkish Nationalist and Irregular forces occupy Balikessir and Ababazar and advance on Constantinople
	11 May: Mustapha Kemal condemned to death in absentia
	30 June: Non Cooperation in support of Khilifat Movement sanctioned by Indian National Congress
	10 Aug: Ottoman Government sign Treaty of Sevres
	28 Sept: Nationalist forces invade Armenia and capture Kars
	Dec: Allies concede that modifications to Treaty of Sevres justified. Treaty of Gumru settles Turkish Armenia frontier.
1921	6–10 Jan: First Battle of Inonu

Feb/Mar: Conference convened in London to discuss possible modifications to the Treaty of Sevres.

Mar: Treaty of Friendship signed with Soviet Union

1 Apr: Second Battle of Inonu

10 July: Greeks launch offensive in Anatolia

5 Aug: Mustapha appointed C-in-C of Turkish Nationalist army

23–30 Aug: Battle of Sakarya

Sept: Indian National Congress urge Non Cooperation with complete independence as the ultimate goal

20 Oct: French-Turkish Accord signed in Ankara.

17 Nov: Boycott of Indians to visit by the Prince of Wales

1922   26 Aug: Turks launch final offensive against Greece

9 Sept: Turks enter Smyrna

23 Sept: Turks enter Neutral Zone

3–11 Oct: Mudania Conference

31 Oct: Handover of Eastern Thrace to Turkey commences

1 Nov: Abolition of the Sultanate

17 Nov: Sultan Mehmet VI leaves Turkey

21 Nov: Lausanne Conference opens

1923   4 Feb: Lausanne Conference suspended

23 Apr: Conference resumes

24 Jul: Treaty of Lausanne signed

23 Aug: Turkish Nationalist Assembly ratifies Treaty of Lausanne

2 Oct: Allies evacuate Constantinople

13 Oct: Ankara becomes new capital of a new, sovereign Turkey

1924   Mustapha Kemal becomes first President of modern Turkish Republic

Appendix 5: Ethnical Statistics

Ethnical statistics for the zone accorded to Greece under the Treaty of Sevres, showing the conflicting statistics for its ethnographical make-up.

	Greeks	Turks	Others	Total
Greek Figures (1912)	553,000	310,000	91,000	954,000
Turkish Figures (1914)	300,000	540,000	44,000	884,000
American Figures (Dr Magie, 1914)	509,000	470,000	78,000	1,057,000

Appendix 6: The Armenian Genocide

In the interests of textual conciseness, clarity and continuity, the detailed account of the alleged genocide of the Armenians in 1915 is shown here. Citing the prospect of internal rebellion amongst the restless population, the Ottoman government subsequently initiated wholesale arrests and deportations. Whatever the original motive, the decision to remove the entire Christian community degenerated into one of history's worst ever examples of officially sanctioned ethnic cleansing.

The Christian population of Asia Minor could trace its roots back some 2,500 years. In AD 301 the Armenian king converted his entire people to the new religion, and created the worlds' first Christian political state. Until the Nineteenth Century the Armenians were treated as second-class citizens at best and suffered compulsory conversion, the abduction of their children and periodic pogroms. The oppression come to a bloody head in the reign of Sultan Abdulhamid, when in 1894 he sanctioned the most savage round of genocide that reportedly resulted in the deaths of some 200,000–300,000 Armenians.

However, there was no evidence that the population at large had ever been seriously inclined to act against their rulers in any concerted way. A few radical nationalist groups did resort to violence to highlight their plight, but despite increasing hardships the majority elected to remain peaceful and endure their lot quietly. Nevertheless, The Young Turks depicted the entire Armenian population as a threat to the security of their country. Furthermore, the concentration of the greater part of the population on the border with the Russian Empire fuelled this suspicion, prompting a leading light of the party, Dr Zazam, to allegedly announce in a speech at the beginning of 1915 that:

We must liquidate and uproot the Armenians in our lands … no Armenian must remain and the name Armenian must be forgotten. At present we are at war and no other favourable opportunity would offer to us: the interventions of the Great Powers and protests of the press will not attract attention and even if they did would be faced with a fait accompli. This time it will be extermination.[1]

Turkey's policy towards the Armenians was no state secret. In a letter to the German Chancellor, Theobold von Bethmann-Hollweg, the German ambassador Baron von Waggenheim mentioned a conversation between Talaat Bey, Minister of the Interior, and a German doctor in the service of the embassy. He was allegedly told that 'the Porte would like to take advantage of the war in order to radically solve the issue of the enemies within the empire without the hindrance of foreign diplomatic interference'.[2] It was apparent therefore, that the Ottoman Government had conceived a scheme that was much more than a simple removal of citizens of doubtful loyalty.

On 24 April, 1915, on the day before the Allied assault upon the Dardanelles, the arrest and rounding up of the Armenian population of Constantinople commenced – thousands of people who could not pose any conceivable threat to Turkish operations in the Caucasus. Meanwhile Armenian soldiers serving in the Ottoman army were disarmed and reassigned to service in auxiliary units, where they would allegedly be worked to death. Enver's brother-in-law, Jevdet Bey reportedly exposed the ultimate objective of these operations when he announced proudly that not a single man, woman or even infant Armenian would be left alive, 'not one so high!' pointing at his knee.[3]

From May to July 1915 the government turned its attention to the greater mass of the Armenian population itself. Erzurum, Bitlis, Van, Diarbekir, Trebizond, Sivas and Kharput, saw their citizens rounded up and forced marched to Aleppo, hundreds of miles to the south. Denied food, shelter or adequate water, every mile was a living hell. Local populations were encouraged to make each faltering step as agonizing as possible, and rapes and other abuses accompanied them with every step.[4] Winston Churchill, in his seminal work, *The World Crisis*, recorded how:

> In 1915, the Turkish Government began, and ruthlessly carried out, the infamous general massacre and deportation of Armenians in Asia Minor ... The clearance of the race from Asia Minor was about as complete as such an act, on a scale so great, could be. It is supposed that about one and a half million Armenians were involved, of whom more than half perished. There is no reasonable doubt that this crime was planned and executed for political reasons.[5]

Between August 1915 and July 1916, the hapless Armenians were moved to the Dardanelles, from where they were then marched into the middle of the desert in even more distant Mesopotamia, where they could be seen 'winding in and out of every valley and climbing up the sides of every mountain.[6] Riddled by disease, exacerbated by the heat of the sun and lacking food or water, they had been herded from one miserable location to the other. One foreign witness was US Consul Leslie Davis who recalled seeing Armenian victims:

> ... in rags and many ... almost naked ... emaciated, sick, diseased, filthy, covered with dirt and vermin ... driven along for many weeks like herds of cattle, with little to eat ... There were few men among them, most of the men having been killed ... A number of dead women and children lay here and there ...[7]

He also remarked how:

> Any doubt that may have been expressed in previous reports as to the Government's intentions in sending away the Armenians have been removed and any hope that may have been expressed as to the possibility of some of them surviving have been destroyed. It has been no secret that the plan was to destroy the Armenian race as a race.[8]

The *New York Times* headlines also made it clear what was happening. On 28th April 1915 they read 'Appeal to Turkey to Stop Massacres – ambassador Morgenthau instructed to make representations on request of Russia.' Such stories could only serve to reinforce the growing awareness of the deaths, clearly being carried out behind the fog of war and the Allied Powers finally issued a Joint Declaration through the United States on May 29, 1915 stating that:

> For about a month the Kurd and Turkish populations of Armenia has been massacring Armenians with the connivance and often the assistance of Ottoman authorities. Such massacres took place in middle April at Erzurum, Dertchum, Eguine, Akn, Bitlis, Mush, Sassun, Zeitun and throughout Cilicia. Inhabitants of about 100 villages near Van were all murdered. In that city the Armenian quarter is besieged by Kurds. At the same time in Constantinople the Government ill-treats inoffensive Armenian population. In view of those new crimes of Turkey against humanity and civilisation, the Allied governments announce publicly to the Sublime Porte that they will hold personally responsible for these crimes all members of the Ottoman Government and those of their agents who are implicated in such massacres.'

In a confidential telegram US ambassador to Turkey, Henry Morgenthau warned the Secretary of State on 16 July 1915, that:

> Deportation of and excesses against peaceful Armenians is increasing and from harrowing reports of eyewitnesses it appears that a campaign of race extermination is in progress under a pretext of reprisal against rebellion. Protests as well as threats are unavailing and probably incite the Ottoman government to more drastic measures as they are determined to disclaim responsibility for their absolute disregard of Capitulations and I believe nothing short of force which obviously the United States are not in a position to exert, would adequately meet the situation. Suggest you inform belligerent nations and mission board of this.

Germany had its own witnesses in Anatolia. Dr Martin Niepage, the leader of the German Missionary Movement in the Ottoman Empire recalled later how:

> When I returned to Aleppo in September 1915, from a three month holiday at Beirut, I heard with horror that a new phase of Armenian massacres had begun which were far more terrible than the earlier massacres under Abdul-Hamid, and which aimed at exterminating, root and branch, the intelligent industrious and progressive Armenian nation, and at transferring its property to Turkish hands. Herr Grief, of Aleppo reported corpses of

violated women laying about naked in heaps on the railway embankment
at Tell-Abiad and Res-el-Ain ... Herr Spiecker of Aleppo had seen Turks
tie Armenian men together, fire several volleys of small shot with fowling
pieces into the human mass, and go off laughing while their victims slowly
perished in frightful convulsion ... We feel it is our duty to draw attention
to the fact that our educational work will forfeit its moral basis and the
esteem of the natives, if the German Government is not in a position to put
a stop to the brutality with which the wives and children of slaughtered
Armenians are being treated here ...[9]

Britain's Viscount James Bryce was then tasked by the Government to investigate.
He concluded that the Turkish Government was entirely complicit in the
massacres and that this was a state sponsored exercise in mass murder. He noted
in his report how:

It would seem that three-fourths or four-fifths of the whole [Armenia] nation
has been wiped out, and there is no case in history, certainly not so since the time
of Tamerlane, in which any crime so hideous and upon so large a scale has been
recorded.[10]

He further stated that:

Our hearts are sick with the sights and stories of abject terror and suffering.
The extermination of the race seems to be the objective, and the means
employed are more fiendish than could be concocted locally. The orders
are from headquarters, and any reprieve must be from the same source.[11]

Liman von Sanders, however, as commander of the Fifth Army, did his best
to prevent these excesses from taking place around the port city of Smyrna,
in Western Anatolia,[12] but there was a limit to what they could do for fear of
alienating their allies. At this time the Germans still saw Turkey as a valuable ally,
so the efforts of officers such as von Sanders could only be local and unofficial.
Arthur Zimmermann, state secretary of the German Foreign Office admitted as
much in October 1915:

The Foreign Office and the Imperial representative agencies in Turkey have,
of their own volition, already done all that was possible by diplomatic
means, to mitigate the sufferings of the Armenians. To bring about a break
with Turkey on account of the Armenian question we did not and do not
consider appropriate ... [13]

It was all the harder to challenge the Turks at a stage in the war when they still
felt confident of victory and immune from the future wrath of her enemies, as
ambassador Morgenthau, confided to his diary on 8 August 1916:

I argued all sorts of ways with him [Talaat Bey] but he said that there was no use, that they had already disposed of three quarters of them, that there were none left in Bitlis, Van, [or] Erzurum, and that the hatred was so intense now that they have to finish it. I spoke to him about the commercial losses and he said that they did not care, that they had figured it out and knew it would not exceed for the banks etc. five million pounds.[14]

As Talaat was to gloat to the ambassador, he was more than satisfied with the outcome, boasting that 'I have accomplished more toward solving the Armenian problem than Abdulhamid accomplished in thirty years'.[15] On 24th August 1916 the *New York Times* ran another headline – 'Armenians Dying in Prison Camps – Hundreds of thousands in danger from Turks ...' but despite international outrage and the consequent clamour for the perpetrators to be brought to book, nothing could be done, especially with the war still being fought and Allied forces still far away from where the worst excesses were being committed. Morgenthau failed to spur his government into action, and he finally returned to the United States, where he headed attempts to raise funds and relief for the Armenians. Only a concerted effort to bring the killers to justice after the war could now assuage the worldwide revulsion at what was taking place under their very noses.

Notes to Appendix 6

1. Civitas '99, Agora papers, p. 6, George Vasan, 12 May 2005
2. Ibid.
3. Housepian, *Smyrna*, p. 41
4. Ibid., p. 42
5. 'Genocide: The Armenian Experience' (The Zoryan Institute for Contemporary Research and Documentation, 2000)
6. Housepian, *Smyrna*, p. 43
7. United States Official Records on the Armenian Genocide 1915–1917, p. 644, doc. NA/RG59/867.4016/392
8. Ibid p. 461, NA/RG59/867.4016/269
9. 'Genocide: The Armenian Experience'
10. Civitas '99, ibid.
11. British Government Report on the Armenian Massacres of April–December 1915 by Lord Bryce
12. Housepian, *Smyrna*, p. 46
13. Macfie, *The End of the Ottoman Empire*, p. 140
14. *United States Diplomacy on the Bosphorus: The Diaries of Ambassador Morgenthau, 1913–1916*, p. 298
15. Balakian, *The Burning Tigris*, p. 157

BIBLIOGRAPHY AND SOURCES

A number of books and other publications have been consulted in the preparation of this work. The list is by no means exhaustive, but represents those publications which have been most useful in my research.

Adelman, P, *The Decline of the Liberal Party, 1910-1931*, (London: Longman, 1981)

Anderson, M, *The Eastern Question*, (London: MacMillan, 1966)

Aziz, K. K., *The Making of Pakistan: A Study in Nationalism* (London: Chatto and Windus, 1967)

Balakian, Peter, *The Burning Tigris: A History of the Armenian Genocide* (London: Pimlico, 2005)

Barnett, Correlli, *The Collapse of British Power* (Gloucester: Alan Sutton, 1987)

Bean, George E., *Aegean Turkey* (Benn Norton, 1979)

Beaverbrook, George, *The Decline and Fall of Lloyd George* (London, 1963)

Bell, P. M. H., *France and Britain 1900–1940* (London: Longman, 1996)

Blake, Robert, *The Conservative Party from Peel to Thatcher* (London: Fontana Press, 1985)

Blake, Robert and Louis Roger, *Churchill: A Major New Assessment of His Life in Peace and War* (Oxford: Oxford University Press, 1993)

Boardman, John, *The Greeks Overseas* (London: Pelican Original, 1964)

Bosworth, R. J. B., *Italy and the End of the Ottoman Empire* (London: M Kent, 1984)

Brewer, David, *The Flame of Freedom: The Greek War of Independence 1821–1833* (London: John Murray, 2001)

Brown, Judith M., *Gandhi: Prisoner of Hope* (Yale, 1989)

Busch, B. C., *Mudros to Lausanne: Britain's Frontier in West Asia, 1918–23* (Albany, 1976)

Bibliography and Sources

Butler, Lawrence and Harriet Jones, *Britain in the Twentieth Century 1900–1939*, vol. 1, Institute of Contemporary British History (Oxford: Heinemann, 1994)

Carlyon, L. A., *Gallipoli* (London: Doubleday, 2001)

Chadha, Yogesh, *Rediscovering Gandhi* (Century, 1997)

Clement, Catherine, *Gandhi: Father of a Nation* (London: Thames and Hudson/New Horizons, 1996)

Dockrill, Michael & J. Douglas Goold, *Peace Without Promise – Britain and the Peace Conferences: 1919-1923* (London: Batsford Academic and Educational Ltd, 1981)

Edwards, Michael, *The Myth of the Mahatma. Gandhi, the British and the Raj* (London: Constable, 1986)

Gilbert, Martin, *The First World War* (London: Harper Collins, 1995)

Gilbert, Martin, *Churchill: A Life* (London: Minerva Edition, 1992)

Gilbert, Martin, *A History of the Twentieth Century – Volume One 1900–1933* (London: Harper Collins, 1999)

Gilbert, Martin, *Sir Horace Rumbold – Portrait of a Diplomat* (London: Heinemann, 1973)

Gilmour, David, *Curzon* (London: Papermac, 1994)

Gleeny, Misha, *The Balkans 1804–1999, Nationalism, War and the Great Powers* (London: Granta Books, 1999)

Harington, C., *Tim Harington Looks Back* (London: John Murray, 1940)

Hemingway, Ernest, *The Snows of Kilimanjaro* (London: Arrow, 1994)

Holland, Robert, *The Pursuit of Greatness, Britain and the World Role 1900–1970* (London: Fontana, 199).

Horton, George, *The Blight of Asia* (Bobbs-Merrill Co., 1926)

Housepian, Marjorie, *Smyrna – The Destruction of a City* (London: Faber and Faber, 1972)

Hyde, Montgomery H., *Lord Reading: The Life of Rufus Isaacs, First Marquess of Reading* (London: Heinemann, 1967)

James, Robert Rhodes, *Gallipoli* (London: Pan, 1965)

James, Lawrence, *The Rise and Fall of the British Empire* (London: Abacus, 1998)

Jenkins, Roy, *Asquith* (London: Collins, 1964)

Judd, Denis, *Lord Reading: Rufus Isaacs, First Marquess of Reading, Lord Chief Justice and Viceroy* (London: Weidenfeld & Nicolson, 1982)

Keay, John, *India: A History* (London: HarperCollins, 2000)

Kinnear, M, *The Fall of Lloyd George* (London: Macmillan, 1973)

Kinross, Patrick, *Ataturk: The Rebirth of a Nation* (London: Phoenix Giant, 1999)

Lewis, Barnard, *The Emergence of Modern Turkey* (Oxford: Oxford University Press, 1961)

Liddell Hart, B. H., *The History of the First World War* (London: Pan Books, 1972)

Lynch, Michael, *Lloyd George and the Liberal Dilemma* (London: Hodder & Stoughton, 1993)

Macfie, A. L., *The Eastern Question 1774–1923* (London: Longman, revised edn 1996)

Macfie, A. L., *The End of The Ottoman Empire: 1908–1923* (London: Longman, 1998)

Macfie, A. L., *Ataturk* (London: Longman, 1994)

Macdonald, Lyn, *1915: The Death of Innocence* (London: Penguin, 1997)

MacMillan, Margaret, *Peacemakers, The Paris Conference of 1919 and Its Attempt to End War* (London: John Murray, 2001)

Mango, Andrew, *Ataturk* (London: John Murray, 2000)

Mansel, Philip, *Constantinople, City of the World's Desire, 1453–1924* (London: John Murray, 1996)

Marwick, Arthur, *Britain in the Century of Total War* (Harmondsworth: Penguin, 1968)

Marwick, Arthur, *World War I* (Open University Press, 1973)

McMeekin, Sean, *The Ottoman Endgame, War Revolution and the Making of the Modern Middle East, 1908–1923* (London: Allen Lane, 2015)

Mehta, Ved, *Mahatma Gandhi and his Apostles* (London: Andre Deutsche, 1977)

Montgomery, A. E., 'The Making of the Treaty of Sevres of 10 August 1920,' *Historical Journal*, 25 (4) (1972).

Morgan, K. O., *Lloyd George* (London: Weidenfeld and Nicolson, 1974)

Morgan, K. O., *Consensus and Disunity – The Lloyd George Coalition Government, 1918–1922* (Oxford: Clarendon Press, 1979)

Mowat, C. L., *Britain Between the Wars, 1918–40* (London: Methuen, 1955)

Neillands, Robin, *The Great War Generals On the Western Front – 1914–1918* (London: Robinson, 1999)

Nicolson, Harold, *King George V* (London: Constable & Co. Ltd, 1984)

Nicolson, Harold, *Curzon: The Last Phase, 1919–1925* (London: Houghton, 1937)

Nicolson, Harold, *Peacemaking 1919* (London: Methuen, 1964)

Owen, Frank, *Tempestuous Journey, Lloyd George His Life and Times* (London: Hutchinson, 1954)

Palmer, Alan, *Kemal Ataturk* (London: Cardinal, 1991)

Palmer, Alan, *The Decline and Fall of the Ottoman Empire* (London: John Murray, 1992)

Parekh, Bhikhu, *Gandhi's Political Philosophy – A Critical Examination* (London: The MacMillan Press, 1989)

Payne, Robert, *The Life and Death of Mahatma Gandhi* (New York: Smithmark, 1995)

Pettifer, James, *The Greeks – The Land and the People Since the War* (London: Viking, 1993)

Ponting, Clive, *Churchill* (London: Consumer Books Ltd, 1994)

Pugh, Martin, *Lloyd George* (London: Longman, 1998)

Sacks, David, *Encyclopaedia of the Ancient Greek World* (London: Constable, 1995)

Seaman, L. C. B., *Post Victorian Britain* (London: Methuen, 1967)

Sharp, Gere, *Gandhi as a Political Strategist* (Boston: Extending Horizon, 1979)

Sharp, Alan, *The Versailles Settlement: Peacemaking in Paris, 1919* (London: MacMillan, 1994)

Smith, Michael Llewellyn, *Ionian Vision: Greece in Asia Minor 1919–1922* (London: Allen Lane, 1973)

Sontag, R. J., *Broken World 1919–1939* (London: Harper Torchbooks, 1971)

Sonyel, Prof. Salahi R., *Turkish Diplomacy, 1918–1923, Mustapha Kemal and the Turkish National Movement* (London: Sage, 1975)

Sonyel, Prof. Salahi R, *Ataturk: The Grand Turk* (London: Cyprus Turkish Association, 2002)

Sonyel, Prof. Salahi R., *The Turco-Greek Conflict* (London: Cyprus Turkish Association, 2001)

Taylor, A. J. P., *English History 1914–1945* (Harmondsworth: Penguin, 1975)

Taylor, A. J. P., *The Struggle for Mastery in Europe 1848–1918* (Oxford: Clarendon Press, 1965)

Toynbee, Arnold J., *The Western Question in Greece and Turkey* (London: Constable, 1922)

Walder, David, *The Chanak Affair* (London: Hutchinson, 1969)

Williams, Jeffery, *Byng of Vimy, General and Governor General* (Barnsley: Leo Cooper, 1983)

Wolpert, Stanley, *Gandhi's Passion – The Life and Legacy of Mahatma Gandhi* (Oxford: Oxford University Press, 2001)

Woodhouse, C. M., *Modern Greece, A Short History* (London: Faber and Faber, 1991)

Zeigler, Philip, *Mountbatten* (London: Guild Publishing, 1985)

Zurcher, Erik J., *Turkey, A Modern History* (New York: I B Tauris & Co Ltd, 1993)

Canadian High Commission, London

Several important books are contained in the library at the Canadian High Commission, London. I am very grateful to the High Commission for granting me access.

William Lyon Mackenzie King, A Political Biography, 1874–1923 (University of Toronto Press, 1958)

Documents on Canadian External Relations, Vol. 3: 1919–1925, edited by Lovell Clark

Mackenzie King of Canada, A Biography (Toronto: OUP, 1949)

Canada's Department of External Affairs, The Early Years, 1909-1946 (John Hilliker, Montreal & Kingston, McGill-Queens University Press, 1990)

University of Manitoba, Chapter II, Section 2, 'Peace Settlement with Turkey' pp. 69-111 (Ottawa: Department of Foreign Affairs, 1970)

National Archives of Canada
The WLM Diaries; Transcripts.

National Archives of Australia
Canberra Document Series No. CP. 78/32, decoded copies of telegrams exchanged between the Governor General and the Secretary of State in connection with the 'Chanak Incident' with Turkey.

Canberra, Series No. A981, Near East Cables (1922) Copies of Cable to Lloyds George from WM Hughes protesting action being undertaken by HBMG against Kemal Ataturk.

Imperial War Museum, Department of Documents
The IWM contains in its archives a considerable amount of primary information in the form of letter, diaries and unpublished memoirs and autobiographies.

Bunter, T. W. 87/22/1

Carus Wilson, Lt M.

Shuttleworth, D. I., Colonel Commandant, Report on activities at Chanak, 1922, 66/130/1

Wood, Major-Gen G. N., Memoir, 'A Subaltern in South Russia, 1919-1920', 78/31/1

Miscellaneous 85 – Greco-Turkish War Intelligence Reports, 1922

Miscellaneous 97, Item 1473 – Anonymous account of the burning of Smyrna, September 1922

Cyprus Turkish Association, London

Guildhall Library, London
Official Report, Fifth Series, Parliamentary Debates Commons, General Index 1922, Volume 158

The National Archives, Kew
The National Archives at Kew in London contain a considerable amount of primary information relating to the events recounted in this book. The most significant of these are as follows:

CAB 21/184 – Turkey – Peace Negotiations

CAB/21/202 – Treaty of Peace with Turkey

CAB/21/203 – Preliminary Peace Conference. Future of Turkey

CAB/21/241 – Turco-Greek Situation

CAB/21/242 – Relations with Dominions

CAB/21/295 – Inter-Imperial Relations

CAB/21/311 – Britain and the Dominions, Mutual Support in time of War. Dominion Neutrality

CAB/21/315 – Imperial Defence

CAB/29 – The Peace Conference and Other International Conferences

Miscellaneous Documents

The following documents were sourced from a variety of archives, primarily from websites found in the World Wide Web.

Treaty of Sevres, The Treaties of Peace, 1919-1923, Vol. III, Carnegie Endowment for International Peace, New York, 1924, www.lib.byu.edu

Treaty of St Lausanne, Hellenic Resources Network.

The McMahon-Hussein Correspondence, 14 July 1915–10 March 1916, www. access.com.

The Sykes-Picot Agreement, 15&16 May 1916, www.lib.byu.edu

The Treaty of London, 26 April 1915 (Extracts) www.lib.byu.edu

Prime Minister Lloyd George on the British War Aims, 5 January 1918, www. lib.byu.edu

President Woodrow Wilson's Fourteen Points, Delivered in Joint Session of Congress, 8 January, 1918, www.lib.byu.edu

Anglo-French Joint Statement of Aims in Syria and Mesopotamia, 8 November 1918, www.lib.byu.edu

Treaty of Alliance between Germany and Turkey, 2 August 1914, www.yale.edu www.britannica.com

www.canschool.org

Alavi, Hamza, *Ironies of History: Contradictions of the Khilifat Movement*, www.ourworld.compuserve.com/homepages/sangat/khiltt.htm

INDEX

Adrianople 6, 10, 158

Aleppo, Battle of 8, 33

Alexander, King of Greece 51, 95

Alexandretta 45

Amasya, Declaration at 67–70

Amritsar, massacre at 129–130, 135, 138

ANZACS, The 173

Armenia, and Armenians 32, 35, 54–55, 64, 72, 75, 83, 87, 106, 108, 113, 116, 120, 206, 221–223

Asquith, Herbert 58, 193–194

Ataturk, Mustapha, Kemal 2, 3, 13–14, 16, 25–26, 30–32, 35, 37, 39, 45, 65–78, 81–85, 90–91, 93–94, 96–97, 99–101, 104–106, 108, 111, 113–116, 118–119, 123, 128, 138, 146, 154, 158–162, 164–166, 183, 203, 206, 208, 210, 219–221, 232

Australia, and contribution to First World War 29–30, 171–173

Austria-Hungary, and annexation of Bosnia 13

Balfour, Arthur 46–47, 59, 69, 79, 81, 198, 233

Balfour Declaration 81, 233

Bengal, and partition of 200

Blair, Tony 3, 4

Boers, war against and Imperial contribution 171

Bombay Chronicle, The 130–131, 192

Bombay, Khilifat Committee in 128, 135, 141–142

Bonar Law, Andrew 191, 194, 198, 207–208, 231

Bos, Subhas Chandra 142

Bouillon Franklin, French emissary to Nationalists 167

Bush, President George W 2–3

Byng, General, Governor-General of Canada 176–179, 225–227

Cabinet, Imperial War, formation of 174

Calthorpe, Admiral 39, 41–42, 57, 62, 67, 69–71, 74, 78

Caliphate, abolition of 134, 220

Canada, Dominion of, contribution to First World War 171–172, 175

Carlton Club, and vote to dissolve coalition 197–198

Caucuses, and fighting in 10–12, 25, 27, 31, 33–35, 220

Chanak, 6, 44, 74, 146–155, 159–160, 162–163, 165, 167, 169–170, 185, 193–194, 200, 202, 225, 229, 231

Chauri Chaura, massacres in 142

Churchill, Winston Spencer 19, 21–23, 28, 45, 49, 75–76, 89–90, 93, 103, 131–132, 138–139, 146, 149–150, 152, 154–155, 157–158, 160–161, 164–166, 169–171, 176, 178–179, 195–196, 199, 224, 227–229

Cilicia, French evacuate 83

Clemenceau, President George, 42, 56, 61, 80–81

Committee of Union and Progress, the 14, 73

Index

Constantine, King of Greece 27, 50–51, 95, 97, 102, 110, 138

Conscription crisis, Canadian 172, 175, 179

Constantinople 7, 13–14, 19–20, 23–25, 29, 31, 37, 39–41, 43–45, 49, 51, 55, 58–59, 61, 66, 67, 68–77, 81–82, 84–87, 89–91, 99, 102, 109–111, 119, 125–127, 131–134, 145–149, 151–156, 158–167, 169, 192–194, 202–204, 216–217, 220

Curzon, Lord Nathanial 69, 71, 76–77, 79, 92, 96, 98, 102–103, 108–110, 132–134, 146, 149, 152–154, 156, 158, 164–166, 168–170, 190, 193, 195–197, 200–202, 205–211, 214, 217, 225, 228–229

Cyprus, British assume administration of 12

Cyrenaica, See Libya

Daily Mail, the 44, 113–114, 119, 121, 191–193, 197

Dardanelles 6, 20–24, 27–28, 30, 41, 43, 86, 90, 125, 146, 149, 156, 159, 173, 183, 215

De Robeck, Admiral 22

Dyer, General 129, 135, 137

Egypt, British annexation of 88

Erzurum, Conference at 69

Evans, Sir Laming Worthington 104, 148, 161, 162–163

Fourteen Points, The 40, 46, 52

French Canadians, and public opposition to war in Canada 179

Gallipoli 6, 7, 27, 29–31, 35, 44, 50, 86–87, 145–147, 160, 162, 169, 173

Gandhi, Mahatma 128–131, 135–138, 140–144, 224

Gault, Hamilton, Canadian entrepreneur 172

George, David Lloyd, British Prime Minister 1–5, 40, 42–43, 46, 48–49, 56, 58–59, 61, 72–73, 77–78, 80, 84, 90–92, 94–95, 98–101, 104, 108, 110–111, 114, 123, 125–127, 139, 143, 145–146, 148–150, 154, 157, 160, 161, 164–165, 170, 174–175, 180–183, 186–200, 218, 227

George V, King 141, 181, 201, 206

Germany 5, 13, 17, 20–23, 25, 28–29, 37, 39, 47–48, 189, 192, 211, 213, 226, 228–232

Government of India Act 224

Governor–General, and role of in Dominions 226

Greece, and occupation of Smyrna 61–63

Halibut Treaty, and arguments over signing of with US 225

Harington, General Charles 123, 145, 152–153, 155–156, 159, 161–170, 204, 217–218

Hartal, call for in response to visit to India of Prince of Wales 141

Hitler, Adolf 223–224, 227, 231

Horton, George, US Consul in Smyrna, and reports from 54–55, 63, 107, 115–116, 120–122

Hughes, William, Prime Minister of Australia and reaction to telegram 174–176, 181–183

Imperial Conferences 226

India, and sympathy with Turkish Nationalists 128, 133–135, 138, 192

Indian National Congress 124

Inonu, Battles of 97, 101

Inonu, Ismit 97, 101, 103, 111, 166–168, 206–210, 214, 217–218, 221

Ionia 53

Ireland, and civil war in 188, 198

Iron Duke, HMS 117–118, 122, 166–167

Isaacs, Rufus, Lord Reading 139, 143, 189

Isonzo, Battles of the, in Italy 48

Izmir, see Smyrna

Jellicoe, Admiral, Governor-General of New Zealand 180

Jihad, and call for in 1914 24–26,

Kemal, Mustapha, see Ataturk

Khan, Aga, and fears for future of the Empire 127, 130, 133, 138

Khilifat Movement, 130, 132, 138

King, William Lyon Mackenzie, Canadian Premier 175–177, 179, 181, 183–184, 225–228

Kosovo, Turkish victory at 7

Kurds 208, 232

Kut 36–37, 138, 155

Lapointe, Ernest, Canadian Minister of Marine, 178

Lausanne, and Treaty of 200–203, 205–206, 210, 215, 217–219, 223, 225, 228–229, 231

Libya, Italians occupy 15

Light Infantry, Princess Patricia's Canadian 172

Locarno, Treaty of 226, 231

London, Treaty of 47–48

MacDonald, Ramsay, British Prime Minister 230
Mehmet V, Sultan 15, 25
Mehmet VI Sultan 39, 202
Meighan, Arthur, Canadian PM 172, 177
Mesopotamia 8, 33, 35–36, 43, 78–81, 83, 87, 125–126, 132, 138, 155, 207, 232
Metaxas, General, 50, 61, 96, 102, 110, 222
Montagu, Lord, Secretary of State for India 125–127, 130, 133, 138, 141, 189–190
Montagu-Chelmsford Reforms 136, 189,
Mudania, Conference at 153, 160, 165–166, 168–169, 195, 206, 219
Mudros, Conference at 40, 65, 73, 86
Murad I, Sultan 6
Murad II, Sultan 7
Mussolini, Benito 205, 207, 223–224
Nations, League of 73, 86–87, 132, 183, 208, 212, 216, 221, 223–224, 226, 232
Nehru, Jawaharlal 138, 224
Neutral Zone, the 86–87, 91, 111, 146–151, 155–157, 159, 161–162, 166, 169, 202
New Zealand, and contribution to war effort 171–172
New Zealand, and response to telegram 180
Non-Cooperation, and movement for Indian independence 131, 136–139, 143
Osman, and foundation of Ottoman Empire 6, 11
Paris Note 159–160, 162, 167
Poincare, President 109, 153–154, 158, 201, 205
Pontic Greeks 108
Populations, exchanges of 16, 222
Pozieres, Australian casualties at 173
Quit India Campaign, the 224
Reading, Lord, Viceroy of India, see Isaacs Rufus
Reparations 189, 210, 213, 229–231
Royal Newfoundland Regiment, and casualties among 173
Ruhr, French occupation of 230–231
Rumbold, Sir Horace 59, 89, 96, 102 106, 108, 110, 146, 152, 156, 159, 163, 165–169, 201, 203–206, 208–211, 214, 229

Russia, Soviet, and aid to Nationalist Turks 94, 100
Sakarya, Battle of 104–106, 112
Samsun, Mustapha lands at 66
Senussi, tribesmen 26
Serbia 6, 7, 10, 12, 25, 33, 51, 149, 151
Sevres, Treaty of 2, 86, 88, 90, 93, 96, 98, 139, 183, 202, 215, 219, 223, 231
Shuttleworth, Colonel DI 147–151, 158–160
Simon Commission, and investigation into Indian reform 224
Sivas, Congress and conference at 71–72
Smuts, General Jan, 180
Smyrna 2, 10, 17, 24, 47, 50, 52–57, 60–67, 74–78, 87, 91–92, 99, 103–105, 107, 109, 113–123, 127, 145, 148–149, 162, 166, 199, 222
Somme, Battle of 58, 173
Sonnino, Sydney, Italian Foreign Minister 47–48
Souchon, Admiral 24
Straits, and Convention 11, 215
Suez Canal 24, 26–28, 38
Suez Crisis 4, 232
Suleiman, Sultan 8
Sultanate, abolition of 134, 220
Syria 2, 3, 8, 11, 14, 39, 43, 45, 78–83, 87, 99, 125, 211
Sykes-Picot, and agreement to divide Middle East 78
Telegraph, the Daily 56
Thrace, Eastern 15, 57, 86, 91–92, 109, 159, 161, 165, 167–170, 222
Thrace, Western 15, 49, 216
Townsend, General 36, 138
Tripolitania, See Libya
Vaheddin, see Mehmet VI
Venizelos, Eleutherios 1, 2, 48–53, 55–64, 72, 76–78, 90–91, 94–96, 103–104, 123, 168, 205, 217, 221
Versailles, Treaty of, and contrast with Lausanne 231
Vittorio Veneto, Battle of 48
Wales, Prince of and visit to India 141–142
Washington Naval Conference 225
Westminster, Statute of 226
Wilson, US President Woodrow 40, 46, 52–53, 56–57, 59–61, 73, 223
Ypres, and Canadian casualties at 172–173